Psychoeducational Interventions
in the Schools
(PGPS-150)

Pergamon Titles of Related Interest

Cartledge/Milburn TEACHING SOCIAL SKILLS TO CHILDREN:
Innovative Approaches, Second Edition
Conoley/Conoley SCHOOL CONSULTATION:
A Guide to Practice and Training
Goldstein/Hersen HANDBOOK OF PSYCHOLOGICAL
ASSESSMENT
Morris/Blatt SPECIAL EDUCATION:
Research and Trends
Plas SYSTEMS PSYCHOLOGY IN THE SCHOOLS
Pryzwansky/Wendt PSYCHOLOGY AS A PROFESSION:
Foundations of Practice
Wielkiewicz BEHAVIOR MANAGEMENT IN THE SCHOOLS:
Principles and Procedures

Related Journals

(Free sample copies available upon request)

JOURNAL OF SCHOOL PSYCHOLOGY
ANALYSIS AND INTERVENTION IN DEVELOPMENTAL DISABILITIES
APPLIED RESEARCH IN MENTAL RETARDATION
JOURNAL OF CHILD PSYCHOLOGY AND PSYCHIATRY AND ALLIED
DISCIPLINES

To the many individuals, groups, and organizations worldwide that have participated with me in the design, implementation, and evaluation of psychoeducational interventions.

CAM

To Charlene, for your love, understanding, inspiration, and support, not only on this project, but in all my endeavors: This one's for you!

JEZ

Contents

Preface

Our professional experiences, those of colleagues, former students, and other school-based special services providers have revealed a trend that, no doubt, will become more apparent during the remainder of the century. This trend reflects the reality that practitioners who are employed in schools and related educational settings—school psychologists, counselors, social workers, consulting teachers—are increasingly expected to provide worthwhile psychoeducational interventions to all students, both with and without handicaps. Further, it has become clear to us that there is indeed a professional desire to expend increased effort developing and implementing effective and efficient interventions, and to devote less time to functions, such as multidisciplinary assessments for special education classification and decision-making purposes. Correspondingly, and not surprisingly, there has been considerable demand among practitioners to learn about psychoeducational interventions intended to enhance children's and adolescents' competence in a variety of areas. Academic achievement, cognitive development, affective functioning, socialization, physical fitness, and vocational preparation are areas in which school professionals and applied educational researchers have indicated need for clear and concise information for both the practice and the focusing of empirical investigations of practical applications.

Numerous volumes covering various interventions are currently available. However, much of this literature is largely theoretical in nature, oriented toward adults, focused on a limited range of specific techniques, and not directed toward school practitioners. Therefore, we have conceptualized, organized, and edited this book in direct response to the aforementioned professional desire, demand, and need for information relative to psychoeducational interventions in schools and related educational settings. We intend that, through careful reading of this volume, you—whether you are the busy school-based practitioner, or the "real world" focused, applied educational researcher, or the intent graduate student—will learn much about state-of-the-art, school-based psychoeducational interventions.

We believe, first of all, that you will appreciate as a given that the area of school-based psychoeducatioal intervention can be viewed as a distinct, important, even fundamental component of any school system (chapter 1). Also, we expect that you will come to value consultation as a much-needed, contemporary service; it may very well be an overarching means for providing effective and efficient direct services (chapter 2). Likewise, we will be pleased if you become familiar with the range of empirically validated psychoeducational interventions discussed in the book by authors whom we have selected for their considerable knowledge and practical experiences (chapters 3 to 11). Given the vast number of potential intervention techniques that could be covered, no attempt was made to be all-inclusive. Rather, the intent was to provide a useful sourcebook on a variety of procedures oriented to the realities of daily practice. Each chapter contains a concise yet thorough presentation of the topic, along with key sources of additional information that will assist you in developing worthwhile interventions.

In accomplishing the tasks of conceptualizing, organizing, and editing this book, we are grateful to a number of persons. First, and most importantly, we acknowledge each of the authors for their diligence, perseverance, and timeliness in completing chapter drafts, as well as their professional adherence to our requests for chapter revision. We also wish to thank Dr. Charlene R. Ponti and Barbara Wehmann—both experienced and highly competent school practitioners—for their constructive, careful reviews of many of the chapters.

One of us (CAM) is appreciative of the experiences in which he has participated with others in various areas of psychoeducational intervention: as a teacher of emotionally disturbed adolescents, a school psychologist, an applied researcher, and as a consultant to practitioners and administrators in the United States, Canada, and Western Europe. These numerous students and professionals have taught him much about life and learning. The other (JEZ) acknowledges the many students, teachers, administrators, and colleagues with whom he has been associated as a school psychologist and applied researcher, and those with whom he has participated in the development of various psychoeducational interventions. In addition, his colleagues in the School Psychology Program at the University of Cincinnati deserve special recognition for the intellectually stimulating, challenging, and supportive environment that they create. He is most grateful and appreciative of the opportunity to learn, collaborate, and grow with them.

1 Framework for School-Based Psychoeducational Interventions

CHARLES A. MAHER and JOSEPH E. ZINS

One distinguishing characteristic of a high-quality school is the extent to which worthwhile programs and services are available to both the normal and exceptional range of student populations (Boyer, 1983). In this sense, worthwhile programs and services are ones that are targeted to important student needs; that are efficient and practical in implementation; and that effectively enhance student performance (Goodlad, 1984; Maher & Bennett, 1984). Naturally, the major function of school education is to offer teacher-directed classroom instructional programs in such academic areas as reading, mathematics, and language arts, as well as in vocational preparation and health and physical education offerings. High-quality schools are those in which competent teachers provide worthwhile classroom instructional programs and services to students.

Recently, it has become apparent that most high-quality schools also include another kind of program and service component, which is of benefit to students and is intended to complement classroom instruction. This emerging area, *school-based psychoeducational intervention*, is reflected in the programs, services, methods, and activities provided by professionals and paraprofessionals in such areas as: study-skills development, social problem solving, substance-abuse prevention, and social-skills training. As with any new area of service delivery, it is important for direct services practitioners, as well as for those who support services delivery (such as administrators) to have a clear conception of its major elements and dimensions. Equipped with such understanding, school professionals will be able to provide needed programs in school-based psychoeducational interventions more effectively and efficiently, and to decide what gaps exist in the delivery of the service. Toward this end, therefore, we describe a broad-based, yet purposeful framework for school-based psychoeducational interventions, with special emphasis on its major definitional elements and constituent dimensions. As an orientation, we discuss how the chapters of the book reflect this framework.

1

PSYCHOEDUCATIONAL INTERVENTION DEFINITION

A psychoeducational intervention addresses both the psychological and educational needs of one or more students. It complements or supplements classroom academic and vocational instruction, but is not intended to supplant it. A school-based psychoeducational intervention can be provided by any of a range of school professionals, including classroom teachers. More typically, however, it is developed and carried out through the collaborative efforts of a number of persons, such as teachers, parents, school psychologists, counselors, social workers, nurses, or paraprofessionals.

Intervention provided in a school or related educational setting can be recognized, and evaluated as to its worth, by reliance on the following definitional elements: (a) implements organized learning experiences targeted to clearly determined psychological and educational needs of one student or groups of students; (b) is provided by a qualified professional, or by a paraprofessional who is closely supervised by a professional; (c) occurs over a definite period of time, typically within the course of a school day or year; (d) is implemented in the form of a particular program, service, method, or set of activities, and designed to achieve one or more important student goals derived from student needs; (e) is intended to complement or supplement classroom instruction; (f) is expected to increase the possibility of enhancing the school performance of one or more students in areas of cognitive development, affective functioning, academic achievement, socialization, physical fitness, vocational development; and (g) can be used in the school with other students.

The focus is on interventions targeted to students. However, in most instances it is necessary to involve teachers, parents, and/or community professionals in such efforts, as well as to take an ecological perspective regarding problem causes and solutions. Collaboration between special services providers and these other constituents may increase the probability of intervention implementation, and thus enhance the prospect of beneficial outcomes for students. In addition, it may be particularly important for generalization and maintenance of change. An ecological perspective indicates that consideration is given to a broad array of possible contributing factors for problems of students and for solutions to these problems (e.g., instructional styles, classroom arrangement, family) rather than focusing primarily on internal student characteristics (e.g., ability, effort). All of these factors should be considered during psychoeducational intervention development and implementation in order to increase effectiveness.

PSYCHOEDUCATIONAL INTERVENTION DIMENSIONS

Table 1.1 is a two-dimensional matrix that portrays three fundamental, interrelated constituents of what will be referred to as *school-based psychoeducational intervention*, or as *psychoeducational intervention*. The intervention domain constitutes the vertical dimension of the matrix, denoting six important aspects or goals of student performance. Each domain can be described further in terms of knowledge, skills, and attitudes considered important for students to possess as a result of their school education: (a) cognitive development includes thinking, reasoning, problem solving, and decision making; (b) affective functioning includes temperament, degree of self-image, self-control, and enthusiasm; (c) socialization includes friendship, interactions with peers, teachers, parents, and others; (d) academic achievement includes reading, language arts, mathematics, social studies, and biological and physical sciences; (e) physical fitness includes writing, walking, running, endurance, coordination, and nutrition; and (f) vocational preparation includes career awareness and goals, specific job skills, and vocational opportunities.

TABLE 1.1 Framework for School-Based Psyhchoeducational Interventions

	Intervention Mode		
Intervention Domain	One-to-one	Group	Consultation
Cognitive development	1	2	3
Affective functioning	4	5	6
Socialization	7	8	9
Academic achievement	10	11	12
Physical fitness	13	14	15
Vocational preparation	16	17	18

The horizontal dimension of the Table 1.1 matrix depicts three intervention modes, ways in which intervention may occur in a school or in a related educational setting: (a) one-to-one mode denotes direct service to a student by a practitioner, (b) group mode denotes direct service to two or more students by a practitioner, and (c) consultation mode denotes indirect service to one or more students through a practitioner serving as a consultant to a teacher or parent.

The intersection of the vertical and horizontal dimensions of the matrix forms 18 cells. These cells represent the third constituent dimension, the *intervention content*. As used herein, each cell represents particular psychoeducational programs, services, methods, and activities intended to enhance student performance in a particular psychoeducational intervention domain, for particular populations of students. In some instances, a particular program or intervention may be targeted to goals in more than one domain and, hence, would pertain in part to more than one matrix cell.

An important feature of this third dimension is that it emphasizes to the practitioner the individual, specific nature of psychoeducational interventions.

CHAPTER FORMAT AND CONTENT

The subsequent chapters in this book provide detailed information about school-based psychoeducational interventions. Each chapter begins with an introduction to familiarize the reader with the content under discussion. This is followed by a review of the major issues and ideas discussed in the relevant literature. The major emphasis, however, is on guidelines for planning, implementing, and evaluating the specific intervention.

The remaining chapters each include psychoeducational intervention content that applies to one or more intervention domains and takes one or more forms (modes) of intervention (Table 1.1). Although many of the psychoeducational interventions discussed in the book can be used in a manner that has a problem-prevention focus, chapters 2 through 4, in particular, advocate building on student strengths to prevent problems. In contrast, chapters 5 through 11 address those psychoeducational interventions primarily targeted to remediation of existing problems.

In presenting an overview of the chapters of the book, we note the specific cells in the matrix that reflect principally a particular psychoeducational intervention. However, we acknowledge that with most chapters there are a number of other cells that could also reflect that intervention, depending upon how it is implemented in a specific situation.

Chapter 2, by Michael Curtis, Joseph Zins, and Janet Graden, contains information regarding a consultative-services delivery system that can provide the basis for discussion of these various psychoeducational interventions. Prereferral intervention relies heavily upon consultation services prior to referral for psychoeducational assessment. It involves a reallocation of available resources in order to prevent the onset of problems, particularly the need for special education placement (Cells, 3, 6, 9, 12, 15, 18).

The development of behaviors that encourage students to achieve healthy, well-adjusted lifestyles with which to meet the demands of daily life is the focus of chapters 3 and 4. In chapter 3, Ellis Gesten, Roger Weissberg, Patricia Amish, and Janet Smith discuss school-based, social problem-solving (SPS) training that attempts to prevent student problems by building interpersonal competence (Cells 5, 6, 8, 9). The authors critically review several recent efforts to enhance student relationships and adjustment through implementation of SPS training in the school curriculum. They cite research evidence that demonstrates that cognitive and behavioral SPS skills can be taught in this context. The Life Skills Training (LST) Program, a prevention-oriented intervention approach, is described by Gilbert Botvin and Linda Dusenbury in chapter 4. Initially, the program was a response to the problem of adolescent smoking, but it has expanded to include alcohol and marijuana use (Cells 8, 9, 14, 15). The authors describe the LST program, provide a summary of research on its efficacy, and include detailed guidelines regarding program operation.

Many children and adolescents experience difficulty related to academic performance. Professionals who work with students often must deal with such problems, since these skills are important prerequisites to later success in school and in life (Cells 10, 11, 12). Study skills (e.g., learning to organize materials, prepare for and successfully take exams; classroom notetaking) are the subject of chapter 5, by Pamela Wise, Judy L. Genshaft, and Mary Byrley. They discuss specific strategies for improving study skills and also include a self-management dimension to increase the likelihood of effective application of these skills. In chapter 6, Janice Miller and David Peterson describe peer and cross-age tutoring as a means of improving academic achievement. They also present specific techniques to train students to work cooperatively with one another to promote the development of academic skills, and discuss the use of peer-mediated interventions for the practice of social and problem-solving skills as well as academic instruction and practice.

Providing children and adolescents with counsel and advice on academic, vocational, personal, and social matters has a long history in schools and is the subject of chapter 7 by Charles Maher and Judith Springer (Cells 4, 5, 7, 8, 16, 17). Included are practical guidelines for assessing the need for counseling, for linking these needs to appropriate interventions, and suggestions for implementing and evaluating counseling programs in schools. There is particular emphasis on the importance of matching student needs to appropriate interventions, and on the desirability of collaboration among students, teachers, and parents in counseling programs.

School personnel constantly face major problems in dealing with discipline issues. Despite the widespread occurrence of such behaviors, educators are frequently at a loss with regard to specific actions to take. Howard Knoff, in chapter 8, presents a comprehensive conceptual framework that emphasizes systematic problem-solving and a preventive emphasis in services delivery (Cells 5, 6, 8, 9). He also reviews a broad range of discipline-related intervention approaches that are appropriate for use in schools and related educational settings.

Next, Stephen Elliott, Frank Gresham, and Robert Heffer emphasize in chapter 9, the importance of learning appropriate social skills in order to maximize adjustment in school (Cells 7, 8, 9). They suggest use of a multimethod approach to assessment and treatment, combining the manipulation of antecedents or consequences with modeling/coaching procedures. In addition, they note that social validity of intervention goals, procedures, and effects is critical to maintenance and generalization effects.

In the past two decades there have been rapid advances in behavioral and cognitive-behavioral intervention strategies for development of a wide range of appropriate skills necessary for adjustment. Chapter 10, by F. Charles Mace, D. Kirby Brown, and Barbara West, includes a discussion of interventions for teaching students behavioral self-management skills that will enable them to increase their interpersonal and behavioral effectiveness (Cells 3, 6, 9, 12, 15, 18). In particular, the chapter examines self-monitoring, self-evaluation, self-reinforcement, and self-instruction as approaches to self-management. These skills can be utilized in conjunction with a number of the other interventions discussed throughout the book.

In chapter 11, Jonathan Sandoval addresses the difficult issue of intervention in crisis situations (Cells 1, 2, 3, 4, 5, 6). Crises can occur at any time in schools, and intervening in these situations requires special skills. Sandoval's techniques are designed to assist students to reach a "state of stability", so that other interventions may then be attempted. He addresses various types of crisis situations, that have unique features requiring different types of responses. He concludes by emphasizing the importance of preventing crisis situations.

REFERENCES

Boyer, E. L. (1983). *High school: A report on secondary education in America*. New York. Harper & Row.

Goodlad, J. (1984) *A place called school: Prospects for the future*. New York: McGraw-Hill.

Maher, C. A., & Bennett, R. E. (1984). *Planning and evaluating special education services*. Englewood Cliffs, NJ: Prentice-Hall.

2 Prereferral Intervention Programs: Enhancing Student Performance in Regular Education Settings

MICHAEL J. CURTIS, JOSEPH E. ZINS, and JANET L. GRADEN[1]

Over the past few years, criticism has continued to mount regarding the drawbacks of current approaches to services delivery for students with special needs. The needs of many students who experience behavioral and/or learning problems are often believed to exceed the knowledge and skills of the regular classroom teacher. Consequently, such students are frequently referred for psychoeducational assessment, for possible placement in special education classes. In other words, services for students who are perceived as having special needs are often thought to be only available in special education classes, if they exist at all. The results of this services delivery system are (a) an extensive, time-consuming psychoeducational assessment process, oriented toward decision-making, that leads to placement rather than to intervention; (b) overidentification of students for special education, and thereby exhaustion of resources intended to serve the handicapped; and (c) the absence of effective intervention services for many children who experience difficulties in regular education settings.

One approach to services delivery that is responsive to the inadequacies of the current system is *prereferral intervention*. Prereferral intervention refers to the systematic provision and documentation of interventions within the regular classroom setting prior to referral for special education evaluation and decision-making (Graden, Casey, & Christenson, 1985). Prereferral intervention is characterized by the provision of consultative assistance to the teacher in an attempt to intervene effectively in the regular classroom environment where the problems of students are first noticed. This approach emphasizes a major shift in the functions of special services personnel from assessment and placement activities to the development, implementation, and evaluation of interventions in the regular classroom.

---

[1] Appreciation is extended to Francis E. Lentz, Jr. for his helpful comments on an earlier draft of this chapter.

Prereferral intervention has the potential to improve services delivery and to benefit students in several significant ways. First, attention to the needs of students is immediate. Time and resources that under the current system are usually invested in the assessment process are instead used to develop effective interventions. Second, assessment activities are focused on intervention rather than identification and placement decision-making. Thus, in those cases in which prereferral interventions do not enable students to succeed in the regular classroom, the functional assessment activities carried out during the prereferral process are likely to prove highly valuable in subsequent decision-making as well as in individualized education program (IEP) development. Third, the systematic approach to documentation and evaluation of interventions that are implemented can enhance the likelihood of meaningful changes for the students served. And fourth, the intended reduction in the numbers of students inappropriately placed in special education would increase its availability for those who really need more intensive interventions.

Prereferral intervention is most appropriate for students with mild behavior and/or learning problems, who with assistance can function effectively in regular classrooms. It is not intended to divert or even delay services for those handicapped students who can best be served through special education.

This chapter provides a review of prereferral intervention programs as a means of services delivery. It begins by examining research demonstrating the limitations of current practices, and proposes an alternative emphasis on systems and ecological perspectives. Next, is a discussion of the foundation of prereferral intervention in consultation theory and practice, and of the skills necessary to intervene effectively prior to referral. Specific prereferral approaches are described, and there is an examination of program implementation strategies. The conclusion is a discussion of ethical, evaluation, and accountability issues.

FOUNDATIONS OF PREREFFERAL INTERVENTION

Rationale for Alternative Services Delivery Systems

Review of current practices

Recent research on special education practices had highlighted problems at each phase of the services delivery system, including referral, assessment, decisionmaking, placement, and special class services. In the years since implementation of PL 94–142, (Education of all Handicapped Children Act) special educators have sought to identify and to provide services to a wide range of handicapped students, which has resulted in overidentification of students as mildly handicapped (e.g., learning disabled, mentally retarded, and behaviorally disordered). One contributing factor to this overidentification has been a reliance on the initial teacher decision to refer a student as an indicator that there is a problem *with* or *in* the student (Gerber & Semmel, 1984; Pugach, 1985), In fact, once a student is referred, data collected nationally indicate that 92% are tested, and once tested, 73% are declared eligible for special education services (Algozzine, Christenson, & Ysseldyke, 1982). Problems in the referral process are compounded by inadequate assessment strategies and inconsistent decision-making frameworks (Ysseldyke et al., 1983). As a result, alternative services delivery approaches are needed to provide effective data-based services. Examples include alternative frameworks for referral (e.g., prereferral intervention and consultation to the referring teacher), alternative methods of assessment, (e.g., direct assessment of students' skills, assessment of the learning environment, and curriculum-based assessment), and alternative procedures for making decisions regarding service eligibility and for providing services based on need rather than on categorical labels.

Systems and Ecological Perspectives

To shift the focus from referral for testing and placement to referral for consultative assistance implies a shift in the underlying conceptualization of students' problems. Frequently, a referral for testing is based on a notion of internal causes of the problems that students display in the classroom. Research has demonstrated that teachers overwhelmingly attribute student problems to either internal student or home factors, neither of which are under the control of the teacher (Medway, 1979). In contrast, a prereferral, consultative approach assumes that a wide range of factors may affect student performance, many of which can be altered. These include the classroom environment, instructional strategies, curriculum, and student opportunities to learn. Further, it implies that student problems often result from the interaction of the student and the classroom environment. Thus, interventions may focus on identifying and altering critical features of this interaction, to help the student succeed in the regular classroom.

Foundation in Consultation

Prereferral intervention programs are founded on the consultation model for services delivery, both in the process for delivering services and in data supporting the efficacy of these programs (cf. Gutkin & Curtis, 1982). Consultation involves the provision of indirect services to the student through direct services to the classroom teacher and/or parents. It emphasizes the use of special services personnel as supportive resources for those with primary responsibility for students (e.g., teachers) and reduces the emphasis on diagnostic and placement functions.

Although there are different theoretical models of school-based consultation, Curtis and Meyers (1985) offer a "systems model of consultation" that integrates the elements common to other approaches within a systems/ecological framework. They define consultation as:

A collaborative problem solving process in which two or more persons [consultant(s) and consultee(s)] engage in efforts to benefit one or more other persons [client(s)] for whom they bear some level of responsibility, within a context of reciprocal interactions. (p. 80)

This definition suggests a number of major assumptions that underlly effective consultation. The following discussion of these assumptions is based on Curtis and Meyers (1985).

Collaborative relationship

Perhaps the most fundamental assumption underlying consultation is the necessity of a genuinely collaborative relationship between the consultant and consultee for successful problem solving. This model assumes that the knowledge and skills of both participants are essential to the development and implementation of effective interventions. The meaningful involvement of the consultee in every phase of the process and the right to accept or reject potential strategies, are both critical in establishing a sense of "ownership" of the ideas generated. Without that commitment, there is little likelihood that strategies will be implemented effectively.

Indirect service

Another role of the consultant is to provide services indirectly, by assisting the person who has primary responsibility for direct services to the student. In this sense, consultation differs from services, such as counseling, provided directly to the student. However, the indirect nature of consultation should be viewed as complementary to direct services. In some cases, it is highly appropriate for the services provider to consult with the classroom teacher as well as to work directly with the student.

Work-related focus

Consultation always focuses on work-related concerns, and it is clearly differentiated from therapy that focuses on the feelings and concerns of the person receiving assistance. Although it is appropriate and necessary to attend to the work-related feelings of the consultee, the primary focus of the interaction is the student-related problem under discussion.

Goals of consultation

Consultation has two goals. The first is to intervene effectively with the referred problem. The second is to improve the knowledge and skills of the consultee, and thereby to improve the consultee's ability to deal with similar problems in the future.

Affective/cognitive components

Consultation is conceptualized as involving both an affective and a cognitive component. The *affective* component refers to the interpersonal aspects of the consultant-consultee relationship, and is characterized by how the consultant views the consultee. The *cognitive* component refers to the consultant's approach to problem solving from a theoretical perspective, and is characterized by how the consultant views the problem. Regardless of the approach, problem solving follows a sequence of phases (described later), including problem clarification, strategy generation, implementation, and evaluation.

A more comprehensive discussion of these assumptions is provided by Curtis and Meyers (1985) and Gutkin and Curtis (1982). These authors also examine other issues, such as the voluntary and confidential nature of the consultative relationship, the use of confrontation, client responsibility, and the foundation in systems theory.

Requisite Skills

Implementation of a consultative services delivery model such as prereferral intervention requires four areas of expertise.

Problem solving

This skill area relates primarily to the cognitive component of consultation. It is essential that those who use a consultation approach demonstrate expertise in problem solving, because consultation, by definition, is a problem-solving process. Consequently, consultants must be able to identify, clarify, analyze, and evaluate problems.

Communication and human relations

This area relates primarily to the affective component of consultation and pertains to the interpersonal interaction between consultant and consultee. The consultant must demonstrate both knowledge and skills regarding effective communication and the development and maintenance of positive working relationships. Skills such as listening and questioning —

combined with the conveyance of empathy, genuineness, and nonpossessive warmth—are essential to the interpersonal process, as is consideration of the student's socio-cultural context.

Content expertise

This domain requires a strong foundation of knowledge and skills specific to the problem(s) under discussion. In prereferral intervention, expertise is required especially in the development of effective classroom intervention strategies. For example, knowledge of children's learning, behavior management strategies, and instructional methods is essential.

Systems analysis and change strategies

The consultant needs to understand the organizational context within which services are provided, as well as the ecology in which interventions are developed. System variables are major determinants of the types and numbers of referrals made by teachers. Furthermore, organizational information is vital in clarifying the diverse factors that contribute to student-related problems, and consequently, in developing effective interventions within that context.

GUIDELINES FOR PLANNING AND EVALUATION
Phases and Activities of Prereferral Intervention

The primary intent of prereferral intervention is to provide opportunities for more students to be successful while remaining within regular classrooms. It is designed to assist teachers, both in providing alternative instructional and behavioral strategies and in enhancing student competence. Prereferral intervention can also focus on existing personnel and resources to provide needed assistance to more students and teachers by using these professionals in a consultative capacity. Furthermore, with an emphasis on a systems perspective of student problems, instead of viewing problems as being solely internal to the student, a prereferral intervention approach seeks to broaden the range of interventions considered. Rather than assume that the problem exists within the student because of a handicap, it assumes that the problem may be a result of the interaction of the student with the classroom environment. Interventions are implemented to alter the ecology of the situation. Thus, the system of services delivery within a school is altered, and the focus of problem solving is shifted from the individual student to include the contexts in which they function.

Prereferral intervention is based on the use of consultative problem solving to design, implement, and evaluate interventions. When a teacher is concerned about a student's classroom performance, a prereferral approach attempts systematically to develop and implement interventions in the regular classroom in order to assist the student. Classroom teachers may choose to implement classroom-based prereferral interventions either on their own, before any referral is initiated, or more commonly, with assistance provided through consultation. Prereferral intervention assistance can be provided in a variety of ways, as discussed.

Phases of the prereferral intervention process are listed in Table 2. 1 and are described briefly here. The first phase is the *request for assistance*, which needs to be clearly differentiated from a formal referral for psychoeducational evaluation. This is to clarify the notion that at this stage the student is not suspected of being handicapped, but that a problem that needs attention has been noted in the classroom. Parents should be informed of this concern and of the request for assistance. During this process and throughout the prereferral intervention, parents frequently are active collaborators with classroom teachers regarding classroom-based, and possibly home-based interventions (see Zins, Graden, & Ponti, in press). Moreover, either teachers or parents may initiate a request for prereferral assistance.

TABLE 2.1 Phases of the Prereferral Intervention Process

- Request for assistance
- Problem identification/clarification
- Problem analysis/classroom environment analysis
- Development of intervention plan
- Implementation of intervention plan
- Evaluation of intervention-plan effectiveness
- Determination of intervention effectiveness and decision regarding subsequent action

In the next phase, *problem identification/clarification*, the concern is specified in objective, measurable, and behaviorally specific terms. One way to describe the student's classroom-based problem is in terms of the discrepancy between current performance level and the teacher's expectation of adequate performance. Once this discrepancy is specified, an intervention is developed to help the student succeed in the classroom.

During *problem analysis*, classroom-environment variables that may affect the student's performance are analyzed. This analysis is conducted through consultative interviews and includes a focus on factors such as the curriculum, task format, situational context and demands, causes and consequences of behavior; the student's current skill or performance level, instructional factors, and the student's opportunity to respond or spend time on tasks. As necessary, the teacher may undertake other methods of analyzing the problem, including gathering data or observing the occurrence of certain behaviors and the environmental context in which they occur. Ysseldyke and Christenson (1986) and Fuchs and Fuchs (1986) provide useful strategies for observing relevant classroom environmental variables.

Once critical variables affecting the problem have been analyzed, the next phase is *development of the intervention plan*. The planned intervention includes what specifically is to be done (e.g., social skills training, tutoring), by whom (e.g., teacher, peer tutor, parent), location (e.g., classroom, home), duration and frequency (e.g., 50 minutes each day, four days per week), and evaluation methods (e.g., weekly goal-attainment measures). The teacher and the consultant develop the intervention plan collaboratively, with the teacher retaining the final choice regarding intervention decisions. Next, *implementation of the intervention plan* occurs, with the consultant serving in a supportive role and following up regularly to assist the teacher in monitoring the intervention and in making any necessary modifications.

Following implementation of the intervention for a specified period of time, is the *evaluation of intervention-plan effectiveness* according to the criteria identified in the plan. Specific and measurable criteria should be established to evaluate effectiveness. Once data are gathered, the *determination of intervention effectiveness* leads to a *decision regarding subsequent action* to be taken. A continuum of possible decisions includes phasing out a successful intervention, modifying the intervention plan, developing a new plan, or referring for more in-depth and formalized evaluation to aid in further decisions.

Approaches to Prereferral Intervention

There are many ways to operationalize a prereferral intervention program. The most common methods include (a) a consultation approach in which one or more special services personnel provide prereferral assistance to teachers (e.g., Ponti, Zins, & Graden, 1986; Ritter, 1978) and (b) a team approach such as Teacher Assistance Teams (Chalfant, Pysh, & Moultrie, 1979), Intervention Assistance Teams (Ohio Department of Education, 1985), or Teacher Resource Teams (Maher, in press). In reality, it would be both likely and appropriate for multiple methods to be utilized simultaneously. For example, within any given setting, the effectiveness of a prereferral intervention program would be enhanced by the availability of both consultative assistance through individual special services personnel, as well as coordinated intervention assistance through a team. It should be noted that the effectiveness of a team is usually dependent on the use of an individual consultant (e.g., school psychologist, speech and language therapist, special education teacher) assigned to assist with interventions as indicated by the nature of the concern (e.g., Graden, Casey, & Christenson, 1985). All methods emphasize the consultant role for special services personnel. Each of these approaches has engendered positive outcomes, and there are at present no studies to support the differential effectiveness of any one approach.

Overall, consultation services delivery in general and prereferral intervention approaches in particular have shown a number of positive results for students, teachers, and school systems. Consistent findings demonstrate that prereferral, consultative approaches (a) increase the number of total students served through consultation, (b) decrease the number of students tested for special education eligibility and subsequently placed in special education, (c) are favored by classroom teachers, and (d) can result in improvements and changes in terms of attitudes, practices, procedures, and resources. Gutkin and Curtis (1982) provided a comprehensive review of research demonstrating the benefits of consultation.

Target populations

Prereferral intervention approaches have been implemented at both elementary and secondary levels, and are most appropriate for students experiencing mild learning or behavior problems in the classroom. However, there has been increasing support for serving even more severely handicapped individuals in more natural environments. Consequently, the concept of allowing students every opportunity to succeed in the regular classroom, before other alternatives are considered, should be applied in most cases.

Methods and procedures

The stages of the prereferral intervention process were described previously. In addition, the process by which a prereferral intervention program, as a services delivery system, is introduced into the school or the district is important. Introducing a new services delivery approach involves changing beliefs, attitudes, practices, and skills of organizational members. The process of introducing prereferral consultation services into schools is described later.

Roles, responsibilities and relationships

Within the prereferral intervention system, there is a need to coordinate the services provided by special services personnel, as well as to involve regular education teachers and parents in intervention development and implementation. Coordination among special services staff members may be needed, since there is potential overlap in the types of problems with which they deal. For example, both speech and language therapists and special education teachers may have expertise in academic problems.

Counselors and school psychologists may have expertise regarding behavioral/emotional concerns. Hence, conflicts among these professionals can develop if there is not clear agreement regarding respective roles and provision of services.

Clearly, regular education teachers are to be involved in prereferral interventions. Unfortunately, though, there is often a lack of specification of parental roles and responsibilities. Most discussion of prereferral intervention focus on teachers and virtually ignore parents, despite the potential contribution the latter can make, such as providing information regarding a child's behavior at home or reinforcing the child for engaging in behaviors (e.g., studying) that will complement the school's efforts (cf. Zins et al., in press).

Resolving practical issues

A number of practical considerations regarding program operation and maintenance are important to success. For example, procedures should be established to enable teachers and parents to access the prereferral intervention process with minimal difficulty. Meeting times and locations can also be problematic because classroom teachers usually have little time during the school day for consultation. Meeting before or after school may be the easiest means to avoid schedule conflicts, but such times may be unacceptable to some school personnel. One alternative is to arrange for a substitute teacher or aide to fill in, on a rotational basis, for classroom teachers participating in individual prereferral meetings.

If a team approach to prereferral intervention is to be implemented, a determination needs to be made regarding persons who can be prereferral team members. Options include special services personnel representing different disciplines, regular classroom teachers from different grade levels, and the building principal. There is no single team composition appropriate for all situations. Different members may be more helpful in dealing with different problems. Prereferral consultants or team members might be selected because of their content expertise related to the case at hand, or based on their problem solving, communication, or group process skills. Another issue is that of incentives for participation in the prereferral process. Recognition for service on assistance teams might range from additional salary to release-time from lunchroom or playground duties.

Written records must be maintained regarding interventions that are implemented. In the event that a psychoeducational evaluation is necessary at a later time, records will then contain data about intervention effectiveness.

IMPLEMENTATION OF PREREFERRAL
INTERVENTION PROGRAMS

Two levels of skills and effort are needed with regard to implementing prereferral intervention programs. First are those directed toward individual practitioners and their management of individual cases. Specific skills necessary for these activities were discussed earlier. Second is implementation of a new system of services delivery, which is discussed next. While these areas are presented separately in this chapter, it is clear that these skills are interdependent and essential to successful program provision.

Organizational Assessment

Prior to the introduction of any program into a school organization, it is important to determine the school's need and readiness for change. Unless an organization is willing to accommodate change, the probability of implementing successfully even the most effective program will be diminished greatly (Maher & Illback, 1985).

There are numerous methods to ascertain a school's current functioning and its perceived need and readiness for change (e.g., Katz & Kahn, 1978; Maher & Bennett, 1984). The specific approach utilized depends in part on whether the practitioner is new to the system or has been associated with it in the past. However, even when individuals have worked within the system, they should examine the school in terms of its existence within a larger organizational context and its need and readiness for instituting a prereferral program.

All services provided within a school, even at an individual practitioner level, occur within a larger organizational context. Too often, however, this larger context is ignored or its importance minimized by harried practitioners facing overwhelming demands for direct services, such as teaching, counseling, or assessment of individual students. As a result, many potentially effective programs are unsuccessful because they did not deal with relevant organizational considerations.

In assessing organizational need for change, the practitioner first must become familiar with the organization, including its history, current status, and future directions. Reviews of organizational records, policies, procedural manuals, self-studies, and accreditation reports, as well as newspaper articles, real estate information, and voter support, may provide important information about the organization and the larger community in which it exists. In addition, interviews with a sample of organization and community members can be conducted to obtain their perspectives, and questionnaires can be distributed and observations undertaken. The goal of these activities is to determine the effectiveness of the current services delivery system and the perceptions of needed changes. Of specific interest would be such issues as the support that is provided for students and teachers in the regular education setting, and special education identification and placement procedures.

To determine perceived readiness for change, it is necessary to know who is initiating consideration of the prereferral intervention program. Is the impetus arising from the school administration, teachers, parents, or special services providers? Sanction and support from those who may be affected by the program is necessary. For example, if special services providers are instituting the idea, they will have to "sell" the school on the potential benefits of the program. In all cases, the attitudes of administrators, teachers, special services personnel, and parents need to be considered, because they are important constituencies who must lend their support in order for the alternative services program to succeed.

In addition to determining the need and readiness for change, the assessment process should encompass other areas of organizational functioning. For example, formal and informal leaders, lines of communication, staff morale and cohesiveness, administrative leadership style, and school climate should be considered. Another area of potential importance is parental and community support for the school, both past and future.

Program Implementation

Implementation is a multifaceted process, involving organizational- and building-level activities that are initiated in response to student needs and organizational assessment data. At the *organizational* level, the following accomplishments are considered essential for successful program implementation:

1. Approval and sanction for the prereferral program must be obtained from the administration. Specific steps to secure approval will depend primarily upon local decision-making procedures. Further, a thorough explanation of the prereferral program must be presented to administrators, who need to be informed of program-implementation activities as these occur. Also, any administration concerns about the program must be addressed as they arise.

2. Active involvement and support of administrators in actual program planning and implementation is critical. Administrative support includes making available the human, technological, financial, and physical resources necessary to undertake the program, as identified in the needs assessment.

3. Organizational philosophy, policies, and services must be structured to encourage the development and application of the prereferral system (Maher, Illback, & Zins, 1984). The school's philosophy, for example, may emphasize the importance and desirability of meeting to the maximum degree possible the individual needs of all students within the regular

classroom. Policies may be written that, for example, stipulate that at least three specific interventions must be attempted and documented before a student is referred for psychoeducational evaluation. Services available from the organization might include prereferral consultation and intervention, as well as other services. In addition, there will likely be a need for adaptation of various facets of the organization or the prereferral program once it becomes operational, in order to accommodate unanticipated problems.

4. Decisions must be made regarding the type of program to implement (e.g., team-/versus primary-consultant approach) as well as the extent of implementation (e.g., as a pilot project or district wide).

At the *building level*, the following activities will facilitate program implementation:

1. Including staff in program planning and implementation is crucial to securing their commitment and involvement in the change process, and to ensure the practicality of the program. Staff input about the program design is essential, because there may be otherwise unanticipated problems that could undermine an entire approach.

2. A primary means to introduce staff to the plan is an in-service session that describes program goals and objectives and includes a thorough description of the operation of the system (Zins & Curtis, 1984). Demonstration of a team meeting may also be helpful. Relatedly, efforts can be directed to change teacher perceptions to include consultation as one of the roles and functions of special services staff. In addition, presentations can be made to other consumer groups such as the PTA/PTO, school board, and community professionals; written descriptions can be disseminated through school newsletters and in publications routinely distributed to teachers and parents. Orientation sessions for new staff could likewise include clear and concise explanations of the prereferral system. Positive expectations about the program can be developed through these activities.

3. In most instances, special services staff will need to receive training in the specific skills (e.g., consultation) needed to carry out prereferral intervention activities. Failure to ensure staff preparation is often a primary contributing factor of unsuccessful programs. Assisting these persons in preparing for program implementation can enhance their expectations of the program's efficacy.

4. Incentives for participation may be needed to encourage staff involvement. Recognition would be one type of encouragement, as would release from other responsibilities. Simply adding the responsibilities of participation in the prereferral intervention process to existing staff duties would serve as a disincentive for many personnel.

5. The implementation process must continue over time, because full adoption of the prereferral approach is likely to take several years. During this time, it is not uncommon for teachers to have concerns or miscon-

ceptions about the process. These are often best dealt with on an individual basis. When special services staff interact with teachers, they should be sensitive to possible concerns that may exist.

Barriers to Implementation

Resistance to organizational change is a natural reaction and therefore should be anticipated by those initiating a prereferral program. Change takes time and, even though it may result in long-term positive outcomes, on a more immediate basis it is usually associated with increased levels of stress and tension. As a result, change is often not immediately reinforcing and resistance may develop. Data from the organizational assessment may be useful in the identification of potential barriers and sources of resistance. This information can also be used to address problematic areas before they become significant difficulties. Several examples of specific barriers to prereferral programs follow.

At an organizational level, a primary barrier is lack of administrative support. For example, if the school principal neither encourages use of the prereferral system nor provides the mechanisms necessary for successful operation, chances for success are diminished. As noted earlier, administrative support includes more than verbal agreement; it must be demonstrated in action. Also at this level, new programs are often introduced into schools without the input and involvement of the staff who will be most affected. This frequently results in the demise of the programs (Sarason, 1982). By involving teachers and parents, their concerns and misconceptions can be dealt with directly, and they will have more commitment to ensuring that the program succeeds.

Individual teachers may resist carrying out interventions developed during consultation, for several reasons: for example, previous failure to establish a collaborative relationship between regular education and special services staff, blocking effective communication and cooperation. Further, teachers are usually responsible for carrying out the major portion of prereferral interventions. As a result, additional time and effort demands may be placed upon them, adding to the many responsibilities they already hold. Also, some teachers do not possess the necessary technical skills for carrying out prereferral interventions. Finally, there may be a perception that some interventions (e.g., curricular modifications) are not sanctioned by the administration; and some approaches may not be acceptable to those who must implement them (cf. Witt & Elliott, 1985).

Certain misunderstandings about the purposes and objectives of special education can lead to resistance. Since the introduction of PL 94–142 (Education of all Handicapped Children Act of 1975), special services providers have been encouraging teachers and parents to refer students for special education services by informing them that these students needed specialized assistance not available in regular classrooms. As a result, a certain mystique has developed about special education, and many now view placement in these programs as the means for solving student problems. Moreover, special education teachers may feel that their job security is threatened by a prereferral program, since such a program's ultimate goal is to maintain more students in the regular classroom, with potentially fewer students in special classrooms. In actuality, special education teachers, because they are required to serve as consultants to classroom teachers, may have additional demands for service delivery placed upon them.

Finally, the staff members required to provide prereferral consultation and intervention may not have the necessary training for an expanded role, and therefore may be understandably resistant to providing these services. Alternatively, such staff may engage in ineffective consultation and problem solving.

Legal and Ethical Considerations

Prereferral interventions must be delivered in a manner that is consistent with federal and state regulations as well as ethical guidelines. A common concern in this regard is that the system may be used to delay or deny services to handicapped students who should be placed in special education. However, the purpose of the system is to expand opportunities for students rather than to narrow them, and to provide opportunities to succeed in the least restrictive environment.

Parents must be made aware of prereferral interventions involving their child. For that reason, the prereferral phases begin by establishing communication with parents regarding the school's concern, and by securing parental approval for the prereferral process. Understandably, practitioners may desire written permission from parents before they implement specific interventions in the classroom, although a requirement to obtain written permission must result from a district policy decision. In making such decisions, though, it is important to ensure that parental and student rights are recognized, and to avoid adding layers of unnecessary bureaucracy that inhibit meaningful participation in the process. Also, parents and, when possible, students should be involved in identifying target behaviors for intervention, as well as in specific intervention procedures.

Issues of confidentiality also need to be dealt with explicitly, and there should be a clear understanding between consultants and consultees regarding the limits of confidentiality. School psychologists and school counselors may have some legal protection regarding confidentiality, but other special services personnel probably do not. Further, consultants need to clarify who their client is (i.e., student/family or school).

An additional consideration is that the efficacy of prereferral intervention systems, both short- and long-term, needs further empirical verification. Presently data exist that provide preliminary support (e.g., Graden, Casey, & Bonstrom, 1985; Ponti et al., 1986), but additional documentation through well-controlled studies is needed to provide a better understanding of important process variables.

Evaluation and Accountability issues

Evaluative data should be obtained to determine both if the prereferral program was implemented as planned and whether intended outcomes were attained. Thus, a focus on both systems-level and individual-level variables is needed. Relevant program evaluation issues are discussed in the following section, and a more detailed presentation is contained in Maher and Bennett (1984).

In order to ascertain effectiveness at the system level, attainment of program goals are examined. These should be clearly specified beforehand and might include such goals as increasing the number of requests for consultative services, decreasing the number of students tested and placed, and increasing the percentage of time spent in consultation by special services staff. Personnel, administrative, and other costs associated with the program also should be investigated to determine if increases/decreases occurred as anticipated. Consumer satisfaction can be examined through such methods as usage patterns, questionnaires, and interviews. Using this multifaceted approach, both the process and the outcomes of the prereferral intervention system can be evaluated, and needed changes or future directions identified.

Of greatest importance is the determination of improvement in the educational and behavioral performance of individual students. This can be ascertained by investigating whether specific interventions were successful. In order to obtain the information necessary to determine intervention effectiveness, a data-based approach to intervention development must be used. For example, both single-subject and multiple-baseline designs may be appropriate to ascertain the effects of various interventions in areas such as student behavior or academic achievement.

Data obtained regarding system effectiveness and individual intervention effectiveness may be used in several ways. These include improving actual intervention services to students and as a means of providing information about the program to decision-makers. Such data can be used to improve and expand available services (see Zins, 1981).

CONCLUSIONS AND FUTURE DIRECTIONS

The activities discussed above relate to the implementation of a prereferral intervention program in schools. This approach is intended primarily to enhance instructional options for students who experience mild learning and/or behavioral problems in regular education settings. Special services are provided through consultative assistance to school personnel and parents, with the following goals: (a) expanding mainstream instructional options and related student learning outcomes; (b) decreasing placements in special education programs; and (c) increasing consultative interactions among special services and regular education staffs.

There is increasing empirical support for prereferral intervention, particularly in the consultation literature. However, there remains a critical need for additional research that examines various intended and unintended outcomes. Such research is especially needed with regard to the application of consultation services on a systemic basis.

In spite of the need for additional research, numerous states are already encouraging, or even requiring, the establishment of prereferral intervention systems. Moreover, it is likely that interest in this area will increase—as the search for more efficient and effective services delivery systems continues, funding for special education decreases, and limitations of current approaches attract more attention.

It is of particular concern that many districts are "jumping on the bandwagon" before they are prepared adequately to implement the approach. Despite the centrality of consultation to the prereferral intervention process, few special services personnel have received formal, supervised training in the area. Without the requisite knowledge and skills, there is great risk that attempts to implement the new system will not be successful. Likewise, many personnel do not have up-to-date knowledge and skills regarding recent developments in instructional and behavioral interventions because the emphasis in recent years has been on diagnosis and labeling. At the same time, many special services providers who may wish to encourage and to assist their districts in establishing prereferral systems may not be adequately prepared to undertake such organizational change, due to their own lack of training in systems-level intervention. Unfortunately, many training institutions have been slow to provide the relevant knowledge and skills. As a result, professional organizations may have to assume major responsibility for professional development opportunities.

Prereferral intervention programs are one means to improve educational services delivery. In combination with other alternative approaches (e.g. curriculum-based measurement, prevention programs, and alternative instructional and service arrangements for special education), prereferral intervention has the potential to improve significantly the instructional options available to all students.

ANNOTATED BIBLIOGRAPHY

Curtis, M. J., & Meyers, J. (1985). Best practices in school-based consultation. In A. Thomas & J. Grimes (Eds.), *Best practices in school psychology* (pp. 79–94). Washington, DC: National Association of School Psychologists.

Describes a model for consultation that integrates elements common to the three major approaches to school-based practice (i.e., behavioral, mental health, and organizational). The model emphasizes a systems/ecological perspective to problem solving. Also examines best practices in consultation in terms of the integration of consultation with direct services, the implementation of a consultation model, and the process of consultation.

Graden, J. L., Casey, A., & Christenson, S. L. (1985). Implementing a prereferral intervention system: Part I. The model. *Exceptional Children, 51*, 377–384.

Discusses problems in current assessment, decision making and special education service delivery practices, as well as the responsiveness of prereferral intervention approaches to those concerns. Explains prereferral intervention systems in terms of six stages, and describes specific activities associated with each stage. Notes the foundation of prereferral approaches in a consultation model of services delivery, and also discusses the central features of a consultation model.

Gutkin, T.B., & Curtis, M. J. (1982). School-based consultation: Theory and techniques. In C. R. Reynolds & T. B. Gutkin (Eds.), *The handbook of school psychology* (pp. 796–829). New York: Wiley.

Presents a state-of-the-art review of the theory and practice of school-based consultation. Examines the historical roots of consultation and the core characteristics of school-based consultation models. Explains in detail the problem solving, behavioral, and mental health models. Also discusses the "technology of communication" and issues relative to the implementation of school-based consultation services.

Zins, J.E., & Curtis, M. J. (1984). Building consultation into the educational services delivery system. In C. A. Maher, R. J. Illback, & J. E. Zins (Eds.), *Organizational psychology in the schools: A handbook for professionals* (pp. 213–243). Springfield, IL: Charles C Thomas.

Discusses issues and strategies for the implementation of a consultative model for services delivery in the schools. Reviews research supportive of consultative services, and examines numerous factors to be considered in connection with this research. Covers prerequisite skills and contextual variables, bases of interpersonal influence, program planning and evaluation, changing role expectations, accountability, value dilemmas, barriers to implementation, and marketing services.

REFERENCES

Algozzine, B., Christenson, S., & Ysseldyke, J. E. (1982). Probabilities associated with the referral to placement process. *Teacher Education and Special Education, 5*, 19–23.

Chalfant, J. C., Pysh, M. V., & Moultrie, R. (1979). Teacher assistance teams: A model for within building problem solving. *Learning Disabilities Quarterly, 2*, 85–96.

Curtis, M. J., & Meyers, J. (1985). Best practices in school-based consultation. In A. Thomas & J. Grimes (Eds.), *Best practices in school psychology* (pp. 79–94). Washington, DC: National Association of School Psychologists.

Fuchs, L. S., & Fuchs, D. (1986). Linking assessment to instructional interventions: An overview. *School Psychology Review, 15*(3), 318–323.

Gerber, M. M., & Semmel, M. I. (1984). Teacher as imperfect test: Reconceptualizing the referral process. *Educational Psychologist, 19*, 137–148.

Graden, J. L., Casey, A., & Bonstrom, O. (1985). Implementing a prereferral intervention system: Part II. The data. *Exceptional Children, 51*, 487–496.

Graden, J. L., Casey, A., & Christenson, S. L. (1985). Implementing a prereferral intervention system: Part I. The model. *Exceptional Children, 51*, 377–384.

Gutkin, T. B., & Curtis, M. J. (1982). School-based consultation: Theory and techniques. In C. R. Reynolds & T. B. Gutkin (Eds.), *The handbook of school psychology* (pp. 796–829). New York: Wiley.

Katz, D., & Kahn, R. L. (1978). *The social psychology of organizations*. New York: Wiley.

Maher, C. A. (in press). Providing prereferral support services to regular classroom teachers: The teacher resource team. *Education and Treatment of Children*.

Maher, C. A., & Bennett, R. E. (1984). *Planning and evaluating special education services*. Englewood Cliffs, NJ: Prentice-Hall.

Maher, C. A., & Illback, R. J. (1985). Implementing school psychological service programs: Description and application of the DURABLE approach. *Journal of School Psychology, 23*, 81–89.

Maher, C. A., Illback, R. J., & Zins, J. E. (1984). Applying organizational psychology in the schools: Perspective and framework. In C. A. Maher, R. J. Illback, & J. E. Zins (Eds.), *Organizational psychology in the schools* (pp. 5–20). Springfield, IL: Charles C. Thomas.

Medway, F. J. (1979). Causal attributions for school-related problems: Teacher perceptions and teacher feedback. *Journal of Educational Psychology, 71*, 809–818.

Ohio Department of Education. (1985) *Intervention assistance teams*. Columbus, OH: Author.

Ponti, C. R., Zins, J. E., & Graden, J. L. (1986, August). *Implementing a prereferral consultation and intervention program: Organizational considerations*. Paper presented at the annual meeting of the American Psychological Association, Washington, DC.

Pugach, M. C. (1985). The limitations of special education policy: The role of classroom teachers in determining who is handicapped. *The Journal of Special Education, 19*, 123–137.

Ritter, D. (1978). Effects of a school consultation program upon referral patterns of teachers. *Psychology in the Schools, 15*, 239–242.

Sarason, S. (1982). *The culture of the school and the problem of change* (2nd ed.). Boston: Allyn & Bacon.

Witt, J. C., & Elliott, S. N. (1985). Acceptability of classroom intervention strategies. In T. R. Kratochwill (Ed.), *Advances in school psychology* (Vol. 5, pp. 251–288). Hillsdale, NJ: Erlbaum.

Ysseldyke, J. E., & Christenson, S. (1986). *The Instructional Environment Scale*. Austin, TX: Pro-Ed.

Ysseldyke, J. E., Thurlow, M., Graden, J., Wesson, C., Algozzine, B., & Deno, S. (1983). Generalizations from five years of research on assessment and decision making: The University of Minnesota Institute. *Exceptional Education Quarterly, 4*, 75–93.

Zins, J. E. (1981). Using data-based evaluation in developing school consultation services. In M. J. Curtis & J. E. Zins (Eds.), *The theory and practice of school consultation* (pp. 261–268). Springfield, IL: Charles C Thomas.

Zins, J. E., & Curtis, M. J. (1984). Building consultation into the educational services delivery system. In C. A. Maher, R. J. Illback, & J. E. Zins (Eds.), *Organizational psychology in the schools: A handbook for professionals* (pp. 213–243). Springfield, IL: Charles C Thomas.

Zins, J. E., Graden, J. L., & Ponti, C. R. (in press). Prereferral intervention to improve special services delivery. *Special Services in the Schools*.

3 Social Problem-Solving Training: A Skills-Based Approach to Prevention and Treatment

ELLIS L. GESTEN, ROGER P. WEISSBERG, PATRICIA L. AMISH, and JANET K. SMITH

One of the most significant indicators of a child's overall adjustment is the ability to develop and enjoy satisfying peer relationships. In recent years the peer environment has become even more salient as family ties appear to be weakening and increasing numbers of children enter pre-school/child-care settings at younger ages. As agents of socialization, peers function in the positive sense by teaching children how to cope with aggression, in learning about sex, developing moral standards, and in finding emotional security (Hartup, 1983). However, an inability to under-stand and to negotiate successfully the complexity of an expanding social world frequently leads to confusion and rejection. Repeated failures over time in this arena may result in social isolation, aggression, and/or school failure, as a child participates in fewer and fewer positive interactions. Longitudinal follow-up studies indicate that unpopular, socially deficient children have higher rates of delinquency (Roff, Sells, & Golden, 1972), and more frequent contact with mental health professionals (Cowen, Pederson, Babigian, Izzo, & Trost, 1973) than their better-liked peers.

In this chapter we review recent efforts to enhance children's rela-tionships and adjustment status via curriculum-based social prob-lem-solving (SPS) training models. Six recently published reviews describe more than 50 child-focused SPS interventions (Durlak, 1983; Kirschenbaum & Ordman, 1984; Pellegrini & Urbain, 1985; Rubin & Krasnor, 1986; Spivack & Shure, 1982; Urbain & Kendall, 1980), several of which represent programmatic efforts with curriculum materials available for direct application and adaptation by teachers and special services staff.

At the outset it may be useful to differentiate among three terms—social competence, social skills, and social problem-solving—often used inter-changeably in the literature, and with special significance for this volume,

26

appearing as they do in the titles of two chapters. *Social competence*, the most general or overarching term, represents a summary judgment of performance across a range of interpersonal situations. For the most part, there is a lack of consensus regarding which specific social behaviors constitute successful performance in social situations (Hops, 1983). Accordingly, we rely instead upon the impact of such behaviors on key informants—parents, teachers, or peers—as reflected in their subjective ratings of the target child. The other chapters on life skills and social skills share a focus with our own on the promotion of social competence.

Social skills, by contrast, refers to the highly specific patterns of learned, observable behavior, both verbal and nonverbal, through which we influence others and attempt to meet our needs. Microskills include relatively simple behaviors, such as making appropriate eye contact or smiling in context; whereas more complex skills include those behaviors required to join a group, pay a compliment, or carry on a conversation. As noted in chapter 9, these and related skills derive their importance from such key social outcomes as peer popularity and school adjustment, and are therefore included in social-skills interventions. Complex behavioral sequences associated with group entry or friendship making (Ladd & Asher, 1985) have been taught successfully via a variety of behavioral coaching programs (Bierman & Furman, 1984). Although social skills programs differ in the content of selected target behaviors, these programs share (a) a common focus on situation-specific response repertoires, and (b) an extensive reliance upon teaching principles derived from social learning theory.

Social problem-solving is a component of social competence, and represents a cluster of interrelated skills used to resolve conflicts that require either initiation of action or reaction to the responses of others. The earliest programmatic work in this area by Spivack and Shure (1974) emphasized the importance of covert cognitive skill processes, such as alternative-solution generation and consequential thinking, assumed to influence overt social behavior. Thus, by teaching *thinking* skills, Spivack and Shure's interpersonal cognitive problem-solving (ICPS) program was designed to facilitate generalization of newly acquired skills across situations, thereby reducing the need for multiple training trials and costly monitoring of environmental contingencies (Kendall & Braswell, 1985). More recent SPS interventions, particularly those with older elementary school-age (Gesten et al., 1982; Weissberg, Gesten, Carnrike et al., 1981) and emotionally or behaviorally disordered children (Amish, Gesten, Smith, Clark, & Archer, 1986), have broadened this cognitive base to incorporate both affective and behavioral skill-training components.

Social problem-solving interventions typically utilize a systematic three-to seven-step framework to guide children's (a) conceptualization of conflict situations, (b) solution planning, and (c) behavioral implementation of selected strategies. Examples of conflicts include reacting to a bully's threats, entering an ongoing interaction, making friends, being falsely accused of misbehavior, wanting to spend time with someone, suspecting a classmate of stealing, and being teased. Differences in problem structure and frequency notwithstanding, children's ability to resolve conflicts appropriately and successfully helps them to shape their feelings about themselves and the school experience, as well as to enhance the quality of their peer relationships. Exactly which SPS component skills are taught and in what sequence depends to an extent upon the age of the children (Kendall & Fischler, 1984; Spivack, Platt, & Shure 1976) and the biases of the investigator. Though the exact steps emphasized may vary, virtually all successful programs are derived from the early theoretical work of D'Zurilla and Goldfried (1971) to apply then-current models of behavior modification to problems of everyday life. Typical steps include feelings identification, problem and goal identification, various impulse-control strategies, brainstorming or alternative-solution generation, consequential thinking, solution selection, means-ends thinking (i.e., step-by-step solution planning), and overcoming obstacles.

The potential value of school-based SPS training derives from several sources. First, SPS skills may be taught by teachers and thus mass-targeted to larger numbers of children than are accommodated in more conventional treatments. Second, SPS programs represent a cost-effective supplement, or perhaps alternative, to other behavior management and discipline systems. Children are taught proactively how to resolve conflicts more independently, while teachers and students share a common language and framework for discussing problems as they occur on an individual, small group, or classroom basis. In this manner, social-competence promotion becomes a formal part of the school curriculum rather than an abstract goal or value. Finally, SPS training serves as a useful bridge between the predominant academic concerns of teachers and the mental health focus of many special services staff. School psychologists, social workers, counselors, and others function in this model as trainers and consultants, who introduce mental health concepts and skills to teachers within a familiar educational rather than therapeutic context. In our experience, such ongoing collaboration is often desired but rarely achieved.

REVIEW OF THE LITERATURE

The proliferation of problem-solving interventions required selectivity in considering studies to include in this brief review. Accordingly, we have chosen to feature preventive- and treatment-oriented research of a programmatic, ongoing nature. Virtually all studies described utilized a control group and examined the effects of training on SPS-skill acquisition as well as on adjustment, or peer relations. In most cases curriculum and related assessment measures are available directly from the authors. The interested reader is referred to more comprehensive reviews by Durlak (1983) and Pellegrini and Urbain (1985), each of which includes tables detailing program structure and outcomes of individual studies.

Prevention Studies

George Spivack and Myrna Shure's long-standing collaboration at Hahnemann University in Philadelphia represents the earliest as well as the most comprehensive and frequently referenced ICPS research program. Working with disadvantaged inner-city black children, their research team demonstrated consistent linkages between generation of alternative solutions and adjustment in three- to six-year-olds, and between step-by-step planning and adjustment in adolescents (Spivack, Platt, & Shure, 1976). Based on these findings, Spivack and Shure developed a 46-lesson curriculum, to be implemented by teachers and targeted to preschoolers who were divided by behavior ratings into aggressive, inhibited, and well-adjusted groups. Over a 3-month period, 20-minute sessions were conducted with groups of from six to nine children (Spivack & Shure, 1974). Discussion, puppet play, some role play, and games were used to teach prerequisite language skills (e.g., "why–because," "if–then"), feelings identification, alternative-solution generation, and the anticipation of consequences. Trained youngsters improved significantly on ICPS skills and adjustment ratings as compared to a no-treatment control group. Evidence for the causal or mediational impact of ICPS skills on adjustment was suggested by correlated gains in children's problem-solving performance and teacher-rated adjustment. The linkage between ICPS skills and IQ in this and other studies has been consistently either absent or minimal. Follow-up studies have demonstrated the benefits of a second year of training, the effectiveness of mothers as trainers of their children, and, more recently, the applicability of their work to fifth graders (Shure, 1984; Spivack & Shure, 1985).

Spivack and Shure's intervention efforts have had an enormously positive impact on the field, but they have attracted criticism as well. Their acknowledged contributions include: (a) establishment of a place in the school curriculum for social competence promotion, (b) development and dissemination of detailed practical training manuals and materials, (c) cost-effective benefits to thousands of children and, finally, (d) the many extensions and alternative models this work has spawned. Critics of Spivack and Shure, and of related SPS interventions, cite: (a) the absence of attention-placebo control groups in many studies, (b) the heavy reliance on potentially biased teacher behavior ratings, (c) the use of training packages that include an amalgamation of procedures (e.g., modeling or role playing) that make it difficult to identify the most active elements (Gresham, 1985) and, (d) the fact that not all replications have been successful (Durlak, 1983).

Four published studies that used Shure and Spivack's curriculum, or one modeled closely on their work, will be reviewed briefly. Vaughn and Ridley (1983) added both a contact control group and an affective-training component. They demonstrated significant improvement with middle-class preschoolers on blind-observer-rated peer interactions. Using an intervention based upon Spivack and Shure's, Mannarino, Christy, Durlak, and Magnussen (1982) used undergraduates to train 32 first- through third-graders who were at risk for the development of emotional problems. Positive changes were obtained on behavior ratings made by the classroom teacher and, most importantly, on sociometric status. Using the Spivack and Shure curriculum with low-income rural preschoolers, Feis and Simons (1985) reported gains in problem-solving and adjustment, as well as an interaction between the two. While these results are qualified by methodological shortcomings (i.e., Mannarino et al., 1982, did not assess SPS outcome; Feis and Simons, 1985, used only one teacher in their third and most promising outcome study), they are still encouraging.

The fourth study of this group is a replication failure (Sharp, 1981) that is often cited and difficult to interpret. On one hand, noteworthy efforts were made to eliminate earlier methodological problems. Nursery school teachers were not used as trainers, thus removing an important source of bias from their ratings. Further, an attention-control group was added, and blind observers made pre-post ratings of children's free-play interactions. Unfortunately, this design also eliminated the ongoing in vivo use of problem-solving discussion by the classroom teacher to help youngsters work through spontaneous real-life problems in a structured manner. Spivack and Shure have insisted that this supplementary activity, built into the original program, is essential. In light of these program modifications, the presence of alternative thinking, but not adjustment gains, at post-testing and follow-up testing (Rickel, Eshelman, & Loigman, 1983), may be attributed either to the absence of dialoguing or to the use of more rigorous methodological controls.

Whereas early attempts to teach problem-solving skills to older children demonstrated weak and unstable adjustment gains (Allen, Chinsky, Larcen, Lochman, & Selinger, 1976; McClure, Chinsky, & Larcen, 1978), recent efforts have yielded more positive outcomes. One of the most comprehensive and promising of these interventions is the product of a seven-year research program, directed by Elias and his associates, known as the Improving Social Awareness – Social Problem-Solving Project (ISA–SPS) (Elias, Clabby, Corr, Ubriaco, & Schuyler, 1982). In its current form, the scripted curriculum consists of 16 readiness, 24 instructional, and 12 formal application-phase lessons. Forty-minute lessons are taught twice weekly by teachers to their fifth-grade classes. Activities include discussion, skill demonstrations, and role play.

Early results of the ISA–SPS project indicated that children acquired alternative thinking and related skills, and that their adjustment was enhanced (Elias et al., 1982). At follow-up, ISA–SPS training was also related to reductions in the severity of experienced middle-school stressors (Elias et al., 1986). Sophisticated analyses revealed that although the absence of these social competence-related skills is associated with higher stress levels, their presence alone does not guarantee positive outcomes. Some children with good ISA–SPS skills, but lacking in other strengths (such as social support) also encounter significant stress. Thus, although social problem-solving plays an important mediating role in the transition to middle school, other personal and environmental factors, not surprisingly, also contribute to adjustment.

An SPS research program directed by Gesten and Weissberg began with a pilot project to teach conflict-resolution skills to second and third graders using teacher trainers in two middle-income neighborhood schools. This project led to implementation of a modified program in three successive years (Gesten et al., 1982; Weissberg, Gesten, Carnrike et al., 1981; Weissberg, Gesten, Rapkin, Cowen, & McKim, 1981), two follow-up studies (Gesten et al., 1982; Liebenstein, 1981), and a program for kindergarteners (Winer, Hilpert, Gesten, Cowen, & Shubin, 1982). Overall results indicate that children acquired SPS skills and successfully applied them behaviorally to a simulated peer-problem situation outside the classroom. Adjustment gains not apparent during the first pilot program appeared at one-year follow-ups and in each subsequent implementation. Results from one-, two-, and three-year follow-up investigations reveal that some, but not all, program benefits are retained even in the absence of booster sessions (Liebenstein, 1981). Moreover, pre- to post-program SPS-skill acquisition was correlated significantly with pre- to follow-up improvements in 5 of 13 blind teacher and peer-adjustment ratings. These and other recently reported linkages between problem solving and adjustment status, combined with the use of independent raters, supports the applicability of Spivack and Shure's general approach to older children.

The strengths of the preventive program developed by Gesten and Weissberg rest upon its integration of affective, cognitive, and behavioral dimensions of problem solving. The 34-lesson curriculum presently in use (Weissberg, Gesten, Liebenstein, Doherty-Schmid, & Hutton, 1980) emphasizes component SPS skills included in Table 3.1. Thus far, this curriculum has been used in over 30 school districts to train approximately 200 teachers and 10,000–12,000 children in second through fifth grades.

TABLE 3.1 Components of Gesten and Weissberg's Preventive Curriculum

Component Skill	Social Problem-Solving Step
Feelings identification	Look for signs of upset feelings.
Problem identification	Know exactly what the problem is.
Goal identification	Decide on your goal.
Impulse control	Stop and think before you act.
Alternative-solution generation	Think of as many solutions as you can.
Consequential thinking	Think ahead to what will probably happen next after each solution.
Solution selection	When you think you have a really good solution, try it!
Overcoming obstacles; recycling	If your first solution doesn't work, try again!

Treatment Studies

Whereas the previously described interventions were targeted to both normal and at-risk youngsters and would therefore be classified as either primary or secondary prevention, several published and in-progress interventions have been designed for use with clinical groups of maladjusted or seriously disturbed children. Elias (1983) used a program that combined videotaped depiction of children's responses to problem situations and follow-up discussion with emotionally disturbed adolescent boys in residential treatment. Results included reductions in teacher-rated emotional and behavioral self-control, as well as increased peer-rated popularity compared with controls. Michelson et al. (1982) reported mixed findings for their intervention with outpatient boys that compared social skills, social problem solving, and non-directive training. Although the first two groups improved initially on a variety of measures, including peer sociometric ratings, only the social-skills group maintained those gains at one-year follow-up. Lochman, Burch, Curry, and Lampron (1984) used a 12-session problem-solving intervention with aggressive 9 to 12-year-old boys in an elementary school setting. Despite limited improvement in SPS skills, boys who were taught to use social problem solving as an anger-coping device reduced their observer-rated disruption and aggressive classroom behavior, and exhibited decreased aggression at home.

Several investigators have used the Weissberg et al. (1980) curriculum or adaptations based upon that model. Yu, Harris, Solovitz, and Franklin (1986) had staff psychologists teach the 34 lessons to 7- to 12-year-old boys in outpatient therapy groups, many of whom had conduct disorders. Compared to a traditional psychotherapy-treatment group, SPS-trained youngsters generated more problem solutions and exhibited greater reductions in externalizing symptomatology. Ollendick has developed a large-scale intervention for predelinquent school-age children designed to compare a group receiving a modified version of Gesten and Weissberg's program with one relying more exclusively upon behavioral strategies, and with an attention-placebo control group. Preliminary results indicate that for this sample the cognitive SPS strategies were more effective for withdrawn children, whereas social-skills training approaches worked best with aggressive children (Ollendick & Winett, 1985). Gesten and his associates have developed a new SPS curriculum, which was taught to two samples of 7 to 13-year-olds in special education classes for seriously emotionally disturbed children. This program makes extensive use of behavioral technologies, videotape feedback, and self-control training, among other approaches. Preliminary results are encouraging and should be available soon (Amish et al., 1986).

GUIDELINES FOR PLANNING AND EVALUATING SPS INTERVENTIONS

Professionals interested in establishing a school-based social problem-solving program face a host of decisions and few available guidelines. For example, review articles that catalogue pilot and replicated programs frequently fail to provide the comparative analyses needed to match specific curricula and assessment devices to various subject populations and resource circumstances. The following is a survey of selected implementation issues and some guidelines for their resolution.

To Whom Should Social Problem Solving Be Taught

The attractiveness of the SPS competence-promotion model derives in part from its broad applicability. Whereas our initial work was of a primary-preventive nature, problem-solving programs have been designed for groups of children all along the prevention–treatment continuum. SPS concepts have been taught successfully to a broad range of age groups, including young children, adolescents, and adults. One important advantage associated with earlier training as opposed to later training—in addition to the greater malleability associated with youth—is that young children spend all or most of the school day with the same teacher. This arrangement makes it structurally easier to access target groups, provides opportunities for practice, reinforcement and generalization, and allows teachers more flexibility in scheduling lessons. Middle-school interventions are made logistically more difficult by the number of different teachers and class periods in a typical day. To combat this problem, our beginning efforts at this level have utilized social studies teachers as trainers. In other settings, a program may fit better in another context (e.g., health classes).

Problem-solving interventions may be implemented preventively to all children at given ages or grade levels, or to selected emotionally and/or behaviorally disturbed groups. Classroom-based preventive SPS programs have demonstrated positive short- and intermediate-term outcomes and provide more cost-effective intervention to larger numbers of children than would be reached by other means. Perhaps even more urgently needed are SPS applications to the many seriously emotionally disturbed children who receive special education services under the mandate of Public Law 94–142 and related statues. Illustratively, during the 1980–1981 school year, approximately 350,000 children, less than one third of all potentially eligible children, received some type of help (Knitzer, 1982). Even when placed in specially designed programs, such children rarely receive any form of structured skill-oriented intervention required to facilitate their reintegration into mainstream classes. Thus, despite a more favorable student/teacher ratio, opportunities for academic enrichment, and the occasional utilization of a behavior-management system, we find that direct assistance both with the behavioral deficits and with the excesses for which children were initially referred is sadly lacking. Special education teachers, typically sensitive to this deficiency but at a loss as to how to proceed, are generally very receptive to problem-solving interventions.

Special-needs children who are mainstreamed may also be appropriate candidates for SPS training. Between 5% and 25% of young children experience significant difficulties with interpersonal relationships (Asher & Renshaw, 1981), and from 6% to 11% of children in the third to sixth grades have no friends in their class (Ladd & Asher, 1985). Especially at risk are children whose low sociometric status category reflects peer rejection as opposed to neglect. Such active rejection is more often associated with children's aggression and impulsivity than with patterns of social withdrawal or isolation (Coie, 1985). Vaughn, Ridley, and Bullock (1984) used teacher ratings to identify aggressive preschoolers for an SPS program that also taught perspective taking and empathy. Significant problem-solving gains were reported postprogram and at three-month follow-up as compared with a contact control group. Nonetheless, the failure to include a measure of adjustment represents a significant shortcoming of this study.

Program Design and Structure

Curriculum

Although several training programs have been published and marketed, curricula are more typically available directly from the author of published intervention studies. In most cases, manuals are highly detailed, providing such information as a rationale for each lesson, a set of objectives, teaching procedures, and, in some cases, supplementary activities and/or homework assignments. In general, few additional materials are required, and those that are needed are inexpensive and usually available locally. Thus far, no single investigator has developed a comprehensive set of SPS curriculum materials for children at successive age/development levels. Persons who are setting up such a program must therefore identify relevant options available for the specific grade levels of interest.

Given the qualifications raised earlier. Shure and Spivack's (1974a, 1974b) preschool, kindergarten, and first-grade curricula remain the best validated choices for the youngest age group. Increased reliance on improvised role-play and behavioral rehearsal would likely further strengthen program benefits. However, curriculum possibilities for children in grades two through four or five are much greater. Frequently used classroom curricula include those of Weissberg et al. (1980), and of Shure and Spivack (1982), both discussed earlier. Positive results also have been found with Project Aware (Elardo & Cooper, 1977), which combines social role-taking with SPS training.

At least two well-designed curricula embed social problem-solving components in a highly structured behavioral package emphasizing multiple social skills. The 17-module Michelson, Sugai, Wood, and Kazdin (1983) classroom curriculum is based upon an earlier intervention with socially maladjusted outpatient boys. Whereas most SPS programs teach a generic or structural approach to conflict resolution that uses specific problems as illustrations or for practice, lessons in this program are each built explicitly around specific interpersonal behaviors or conflict situations. Kendall and Braswell's (1985) 12-session cognitive-behavioral therapy model for impulsive children combines problem-solving and self-instructional training using both individual and group formats.

The previously described three-stage, 52-lesson Improving Social Awareness–Social Problem Solving curriculum (Elias et al., 1986) holds much promise for use with fifth through seventh graders. Designed in part to moderate the effects of stress, this curriculum goes further than most to promote systematically the generalization of acquired SPS skills. Toward this end, application-oriented exercises make use of such activities as composition writing and television viewing.

Critical Skills

The choice of a curriculum largely determines which specific SPS skills will be emphasized in a training program. Nonetheless, knowledge of the mediating role that component problem-solving skills play in children's adjustment at different ages is useful to help structure program emphases and target particular behaviors for reinforcement. Research evidence suggests that the ability to generate multiple solutions, regardless of quality, is most closely related to adjustment in inner-city preschool and primary-grade samples. Teaching such brainstorming skills seems intuitively quite simple. In practice it can be difficult for trainers to become aware of and to control the subtle, and not so subtle ways in which particular responses are encouraged or discouraged. Converging findings from several recent correlational studies indicate that the quality of solutions, that is, their assertiveness and effectiveness, rather than the quantity of solutions alone is most predictive of healthy adjustment with older, middle-income groups (Asarnow & Callan, 1985; Gesten et al., 1982; Hopper & Kirschenbaum, 1985; Richard & Dodge, 1982). Strategically, this finding suggests that SPS training with 7- to 12-year-olds should place greater emphasis on teaching the consequences associated with each solution choice, along with coaching and role plays that permit the practice of selected adaptive strategies.

Adolescents seem to require less training in solution generation or consequential thinking than in the means-ends thinking that is required to overcome obstacles and to implement successfully the chosen solutions. One of the best ways to teach this skill is through modeling and role plays. Unfortunately, such procedures are sometimes uncomfortable for adolescents who possess normative levels of self-consciousness. In this respect, commercially produced videotapes depicting children in conflict situations (e.g., the *Inside/Out* [Agency for Instructional Television, 1975] and *On the Level* [Agency for Instructional Television, 1980] series) may serve as useful icebreakers.

Group versus Individual Instruction

Problem-solving training can be conducted using class, small group, and individual approaches. The highly interactive nature of the skills being taught, combined with a need for practice, makes some type of group format perhaps best suited ecologically to SPS program goals. However, assuming six to eight children per group, personnel and time constraints may make the costs prohibitive, except when implemented in the context of an existing developmental guidance program. This is particularly the case for prevention programs targeted to large numbers of children. Fortunately, classroom training with some opportunity for small-group demonstrations and independent work has been found to be sufficient to produce problem-solving skill and adjustment gains.

Working comfortably and effectively with severely emotionally disturbed (SED) youngsters, on the other hand, requires smaller groups (i.e., ideally not more than five to six children) and more intensive supervision. For example, in our program targeted toward children whose problems had caused them to be excluded from regular public schools, each teacher was assisted by a full-time classroom aide who was part of the ongoing SED program, and by an undergraduate or graduate student assistant for approximately half the lessons. During all role plays, children in the "audience" were given cue cards to focus their attention on discrete aspects of the performance (e.g., "How did Mary show her feelings?"). By making their feedback a central feature of the exercise and by giving points for on-task behavior, involvement was kept high and disruptiveness minimized.

The problem-solving model can also be used to structure individual counseling sessions in school or in outpatient settings. In our experience working in a private-practice model, this has typically begun with semi-structured assessment of SPS-skill strengths and deficits in children who experience difficulties with peers. After discussing both hypothetical and real problem situations with appropriate probes (e.g., "How else could you have tried to solve that problem?"), formal and informal lessons have been used that are modifications of the Weissberg et al. (1980) curriculum. Though they are not empirically evaluated, we believe that these exercises have been well received and that they have contributed to significant treatment benefits. School psychologists and other special services team members may use the SPS approach individually with children identified by teachers as needing extra training experiences, as well as to support ongoing counseling with others.

Dialoguing

Since the goals and related competence-building programs are to effect a significant and durable change in the quality of children's peer relationships, it seems intuitively reasonable to suspect that formal 20 to 30-minute lessons, whether involving as few as 12 or as many as 50 sessions, may not be enough. Children in fact benefit when teachers use the SPS approach to resolve conflicts that occur daily both inside and outside the classroom (Spivack & Shure, 1985). Thus, teachers are encouraged to talk children through the SPS steps whenever possible instead of simply suggesting an alternative solution or resorting to a more exclusively punishment-oriented strategy. This approach can be used with individuals, dyads, small groups, or even the entire class, and may initially require prompting to remind children what comes next (e.g., "How did you/he feel about____?"; "What solution did you try?"; "What happened next?"; "What else might you try?"). This process encourages children to approach conflicts constructively, and to assume greater responsibility for their own behavior. For example, they may be required to generate (and at times either to role play or actually to implement) other, more adaptive solutions to their problems. Such practice is facilitated by the availability of a common, shared language with which to discuss problem situations. In the absence of this supportive structure, teachers often express discomfort about dealing with students' distress, wanting to avoid the role of therapist, but lacking a viable alternative.

Spivack and Shure (1985) refer to this process as *dialoguing* and Elias et al. (1982) call it *life-space intervention*, but both agree that such practice is essential if effective problem solving is to become part of children's everyday behavioral repertoire. We believe that heightened emphasis on dialoguing contributed to increasingly positive program outcomes after our first pilot effort. An acknowledged failure to incorporate dialoguing or other such devices may, moreover, account for the earlier mentioned failure to replicate Shure and Spivack's findings (Sharp, 1981).

Assessment Issues and Strategies

Problem-Solving Skills

Many problem-solving measures have been reported in the literature, each with its own unique profile, none of which is suited ideally for either researchers or practitioners (Butler & Meichenbaum, 1981; Kendall, Pellegrini, & Urbain, 1981). Program-outcome differences across investigators may actually be accounted for in part by unintentional diversity among the underlying constructs being examined, as well as by the often less-than-satisfactory psychometric properties of these scales (Gesten & Weissberg, 1979). Such measurement issues are especially salient when .working with younger children, whose responses are by nature less reliable and for whom language and attentional issues present unique format problems.

While the search for psychometrically sound, comprehensive SPS measures continues, several useful, easily administered tests exist, especially for persons interested in measuring *cognitive*, or problem-solving thinking skills. Shure and Spivack's (1974b) Preschool Interpersonal Problem-Solving (PIPS) Test assesses children's ability to generate solutions to a series of hypothetical peer and authority problems. Comparable measures are also available from these investigators to measure consequential and means-ends thinking. Weissberg, Gesten, Rapkin et al., (1981) developed the Open-Middle Interview to assess alternative-solution generation and qualitative indices of solution effectiveness. Test–retest reliability was low to moderate (r = approximately .60), but was consistent with a variety of measures of children's affective functioning. Like the PIPS, this instrument must be administered during an individual interview, and it requires approximately 15 minutes to complete. At least one measure for second through sixth graders, the Purdue Elementary Problem-Solving Inventory (PEPSI), can be group administered (Feldhusen, Houtz, & Ringenbach, 1972).

Persons working with middle-school students or with older adolescents with better developed language skills have a wider range of instruments to chose from, and many of these instruments are group administered. Illustratively, Elias has developed a group version of and complete scoring guide to his sophisticated Social Problem Situation Analysis Measure (SPSAM) that assesses multiple dimensions of problem-solving cognition in third through seventh graders (Elias, Rothbaum, & Gara, 1986).

Cognitive or hypothetical-reflective measures of SPS skills (Krasnor &

Rubin, 1981), although they provide useful information about children's understanding of social situations, are of limited value in predicting performance in real-life situations. As with moral reasoning and moral behavior, the relationship between SPS cognition and behavior is weak, dependent largely upon characteristics and constraints of the situation, as well as on motivational variables (Smith-Tuten, Gesten, Amish, Clark, & Archer, 1986). Investigators have recently developed simulated problem-assessment formats that avoid the low base-rate and cost factors associated with direct observation of children's social behavior. In one paradigm the subject is required to borrow a felt-tip marker from a peer confederate instructed to be noncompliant (Gesten et al., 1982), in another the subject is asked to make friends with a new student in the school (Smith-Tuten et al., 1986). Though logistically more complex to administer than cognitive scales, the use of such behavioral assessment in outcome studies based upon a small random sample (e.g., 5 to 6 children from a class of 25 to 30) may help to assure that behavioral implementation of newly acquired skills actually took place.

Adjustment

A variety of psychometrically sound child-behavior rating scales are available for use by teachers. Many of these scales tap the range of internalizing and externalizing behaviors affected by SPS interventions. It is suggested that children's personal and social competence as well as their pathology be measured, because these dimensions of behavior are relatively independent at the level of some individual scale factors. The Devereux Elementary School Behavior-Rating Scale (Spivack & Swift, 1967) is one among many commonly used measures of pathology. The Health Resources Inventory (Gesten, 1976) has been used to assess children's strengths or adaptive abilities. Interestingly, normal and at-risk children in several social-skills projects have made significant teacher-rated competence gains even though there were no significant improvements in problem behaviors (Kirschenbaum, 1979).

More critical perhaps than the choice of specific scales are decisions regarding who should serve as raters and when the ratings are to be completed. To reduce rater bias, teachers involved in program implementation may serve as one, but not the only source of such information. The use of additional raters, blind to children's intervention status but who nonetheless know them well, is strongly urged. Furthermore, adjustment ratings ideally should not be collected until trained youngsters have one to two months' experience using newly acquired SPS skills. This time is required for skills to affect adjustment and/or for changes in observed behavior to affect the student's reputation.

Other socially valid measures of program benefit are those that reflect peer acceptance. As is the case for other types of social-skills training, social problem-solving programs have yielded inconsistent effects in this arena. We have found a roster-rating approach, in which all children in a class receive scores (for example on likability), to be preferable and less reactive than sociometric procedures in which children nominate their peers for a limited number of positive and negative roles. Our most positive sociometric gains did not appear until six to eight months postprogram, after children were dispersed to multiple classes in the next grade level (Gesten et al., 1982). We recommend that future program evaluations require children to rate their peers on a few key behavioral dimensions, because such gains may occur before changes in peer acceptance take place.

Teacher Selection and Training

Based on our experience, we suggest that initial introduction of SPS programming be on a small scale. It may be preferable to work with two to four volunteer teachers in a single school and with an involved, supportive principal than with "draftee" teachers. It is essential, moreover, that teachers receive some form of support and consultation so that they can share their successes and obtain help with inevitable program difficulties. When special-services staff serve both as primary trainer and follow-up consultants, this ongoing process is facilitated.

After an introductory two- to three-hour workshop, during which the curriculum is reviewed and program procedures discussed, ongoing meetings (typically 45 to 75 minutes) should take place initially at least twice a week. Since most curricula require that two lessons be taught each week, allowing more time to elapse between meetings leads to an overwhelming agenda and may significantly diminish program impact. Arranging for teachers to receive compensation in the form of in-service credit or compensatory time has helped to ease the time burden and has served to underscore the importance of such meetings.

Training sessions should be structured to allow for the give-and-take required to ensure that teacher input is encouraged. Illustratively, one teacher shared with the group her solution to problems her inner-city class was having memorizing the SPS steps. Youngsters wrote and recorded rap tapes (following the currently popular music format) that described problem situations and incorporated the SPS steps in the lyrics. This sort of improvisation is common and over the years has led to modification in our own curricula. Most importantly, this practice reflects that teachers acquire a high degree of involvement and program ownership that contributes to positive outcomes. Much of each week's training is spent reviewing prior lessons and planning and/or role playing upcoming class exercises. Observation of actual lessons by trainers and fellow teachers has generated exciting and productive discussions about children and teaching strategies, and has also helped to ensure the fidelity of implementation across classrooms. Moreover, videotapes of lessons taught by teacher trainers from both current and prior years have proved enormously useful. Videotape feedback has also been incorporated successfully into role playing lessons with emotionally handicapped children in order to provide the micro-skill training they require.

CONCLUSIONS

Social problem-solving training is an important, structured approach to social-competence promotion in children and adolescents. Research results have demonstrated that cognitive and behavioral SPS skills can be taught in classroom and small-group contexts. Accompanying adjustment gains have been generally, but not always, reported. Future efforts will benefit from the development of psychometrically sound assessment devices, the use of multiple outcome criteria, longer term follow-up studies, and systematic attention to implementation issues and differences that may in fact account for some inconsistent findings in the literature.

Several effective field-tested curricula are available for use by school-based practitioners. Needed still are sequential, age-linked materials that would integrate SPS training into the broader school experience across multiple years.

ANNOTATED BIBLIOGRAPHY

Kendall, P. C., & Braswell, L. (1985). *Cognitive-behavioral therapy for impulsive children.* New York: Guilford Press.
  Provides a comprehensive overview of this successful intervention that combines problem-solving and self-control training. Presents research findings along with detailed lesson plans and practical information regarding assessment measures.
Ladd, G. W., & Mize, J. (1983). A cognitive-social learning model of social skill training. *Psychological Review, 90,* 127–157.
  Explores the purposes, methods, major findings, and future directions of social-skill training from a cognitive-social learning approach to viewing behavior change. Considers what technologies seem to work, with whom, and why.
Spivack, G., & Shure, M. B. (1985). ICPS and beyond: Centripetal and centrifugal forces. *American Journal of Community Psychology, 13,* 226–253.
  Perhaps the best overview of Spivack and Shure's seminal contribution to children's mental health. Conceptual, research, and anecdotal information are presented, along with a comprehensive bibliography and a list of training materials.
Strain, P. S., Guralnick, M. J., & Walker, H. M. (Eds.). (1986). *Children's social behavior: Development, assessment, and modification.* New York: Academic Press.
  Examines the manner in which children's social behavior is acquired, as well as assessment and intervention approaches. Considers various sociometric assessment strategies, reviews social skills and social problem-solving interventions, as well as strategies to maximize the generalization of newly acquired skills.
Pellegrini, D. S., & Urbain, E. S. (1985). An evaluation of interpersonal cognitive problemsolving training with children. *Journal of Child Psychology and Psychiatry, 26,* 17–41.

Provides the most recent comprehensive review of ICPS and SPS interventions with children. Examines primary, secondary, and tertiary prevention programs. Compares program structure and outcomes directly in a series of detailed tables.

REFERENCES

Asavanow, J. R., & Callan, J. W. (1985). Boys with peer adjustment problems: Social cognitive processes. *Journal of Consulting and Clinical Psychology 53*, 80–87.

Agency for Instructional Television. (1975). *Inside/Out: A guide for teachers*. Bloomington, IN: Author.

Agency for Instructional Television. (1980). *On The Level: A guide for teachers*. Bloomington, IN: Author.

Allen, G. J., Chinsky, J. M., Lavcen, S. W., Lochman, J. E., & Selinger, H. V. (1976), *Community psychology and the schools: A behaviorally oriented multilevel preventive approach*. Hillsdale, NJ: Erlbaum.

Amish, P., Gesten, E. L., Smith, J., Clark, H. B., & Archer, C. (1986). *Social problem-solving skill training with emotionally/behaviorally disturbed children*. Unpublished master's thesis, University of South Florida, Tampa, FL.

Asher, S. R., & Renshaw, P. D. (1981). Children without friends: Social knowledge and social skill training. In S. R. Asher & J. M. Gottman (Eds.), *The development of children's friendships* (pp. 273–296). New York: Cambridge University Press.

Bierman, K. L., & Furman, W. (1984). The effects of social skills training and peer involvement on the social adjustment of preadolescents. *Child Development, 55*, 151–162.

Butler, L., & Meichenbaum, D. (1981). The assessment of interpersonal problem-solving skills. In P. C. Kendall & S. D. Hollon (Eds.), *Assessment strategies for cognitive-behavioral interventions* (pp. 197–225). New York: Academic Press.

Coie, J. D. (1985). Fitting social skills intervention to the target group. In B. H. Schneider, K. H. Rubin, & J. E. Ledingham (Eds.), *Children's peer relations: Issues in assessment and intervention* (pp. 141–156). New York: Springer-Verlag.

Cowen, E. L., Pederson, A., Babigian, H., Izzo, L. D., & Trost, M. A. (1973). Long-term follow-up of early detected vulnerable children. *Journal of Consulting and Clinical Psychology, 41*, 438–446.

Durlak, J. A. (1983). Social problem-solving as a primary prevention strategy. In R. D. Felner, L. A. Jason, J. N. Moritsugu, & S. S. Farber (Eds.), *Preventive psychology* (pp. 31–48). Elmsford, NY: Pergamon Press.

D' Zurilla, T. J., & Goldfried, M. R. (1971). Problem solving and behaviour modification. *Journal of Abnormal Psychology, 78*, 107–126.

Elardo, P. J., & Cooper, M. (1977). *AWARE—Activities for social development*. Menlo Park, CA: Addison-Wesley.

Elias, M. J. (1983). Improving coping skills of emotionally disturbed boys through television-based social problem solving. *American Journal of Orthopsychiatry, 53*, 61–72.

Elias, M. J., Clabby, J., Corr, D., Ubriaco, M., & Schuyler, T. (1982). *The improving social awareness–social problem-solving project: A case study in school-based action research* (Action Research Workshop Report No. 4). New York: William T. Grant Foundation.

Elias, M. J., Gara, M., Ubriaco, M., Rothbaum, P. A., Clabby, J. F., & Schuyler, T. (1986). Impact of a preventive social problem solving intervention on children's coping with middle-school stressors. *American Journal of Community Psychology, 14*, 259–275.

Elias, M. J., Rothbaum, P. A., & Gara, M. (1986). *Development of a group administered assessment of social problem solving in children*. Unpublished manuscript, Rutgers University, New Brunswick, NJ:

Feis, C. L., & Simons, C. (1985). Training preschool children in interpersonal cognitive problem-solving skills: A replication. *Prevention in Human Services, 4*, 59–70.

Feldhusen, J. F., Houtz, J. C., & Ringenback, S. (1972). The Purdue Elementary Problem-Solving Inventory. *Psychological Reports, 31*, 891–901.

Gesten, E. L. (1976). A Health Resources Inventory: The development of a measure of the personal and social competence of primary-grade children. *Journal of Consulting and Clinical Psychology, 44*, 775–786.

Gesten, E. L., Rains, M. H., Rapkin, B. D., Weissberg, R. P., Flores de Apodaca, R., Cowen, E. L., & Bowen, R. (1982). Training children in social problem-solving competencies: A first and second look. *American Journal of Community Psychology, 10,* 95–115.

Gesten, E. L., & Weissberg, R. P. (1979, September). *Social problem-solving training and prevention: Some good news and some bad news.* Paper presented at the annual meeting of the American Psychological Association, New York, NY.

Gresham, F. M. (1985). Utility of cognitive-behavioral procedures for social skills training with children: A critical review. *Journal of Abnormal Child Psychology, 13,* 411–423.

Hartup, W. W. (1983). Peer relations. In E. M. Hetherington (Ed.), *Handbook of child psychology: Socialization, personality, and social development* (Vol. 4, pp. 103–196). New York: Wiley.

Hopper, R. B., & Kirschenbaum, D. S. (1985). Social problem solving and social competence in preadolescents: Is inconsistency the hobgoblin of little minds? *Cognitive Therapy and Research, 9,* 685–701.

Hops, H. (1983). Children's social competence and skill: Current research practices and future directions. *Behavior Therapy, 14,* 3–18.

Kendall, P. C., & Braswell, L. (1985). Cognitive-behavioral self-control therapy for children: A component analysis. *Journal of Consulting and Clinical Psychology, 50,* 672–689.

Kendall, P. C., & Braswell, L. (1986). *Cognitive-behavioral therapy for impulsive children.* New York: Guildford Press.

Kendall, P. C., & Fischler, G. L. (1984). Behavioral and adjustment correlates of problem solving: Validational analyses of interpersonal cognitive problem-solving measures. *Child Development, 55,* 879–892.

Kendall, P. C., Pellegrini, D. S., & Urbain, E. S. (1981). Approaches to assessment for cognitive-behavioral interventions with children. In P. C. Kendall & S. D. Hollon (Eds.), *Assessment strategies for cognitive-behavioral interventions* (pp. 227–285). New York: Academic Press.

Kirschenbaum, D. S. (1979). Social competence intervention and evaluation in the inner city: Cincinnati's social skill development program. *Journal of Consulting and Clinical Psychology, 47,* 778–780.

Kirschenbaum, D. S., & Ordman, A. M. (1984). Preventive interventions for children: Cognitive behavioral perspectives. In A. W. Meyers & W. E. Craighead (Eds.), *Cognitive behavior therapy for children* (pp. 377–409). New York: Plenum Press.

Knitzer, J. (1982). *Unclaimed children: The failure of public responsibility to children and adolescents in need of mental health services.* Washington, DC: Children's Defense Fund.

Krasnor, L. R., & Rubin, K. H. (1981). The assessment of social problem solving skills in young children. In T. V. Merluzzi, C. R. Glass, & M. Genest (Eds.), *Cognitive assessment* (pp. 452–478). New York: Guilford Press.

Ladd, G. L., & Asher, S. R. (1985). Social skills training and children's peer relations: Current issues in research and practice. In L. L. Abate & M. Milan (Eds.), *Handbook of social skill training.* New York: Wiley.

Liebenstein, N. (1981). *Social problem-solving skill building in elementary school classrooms: A follow-up evaluation.* Unpublished doctoral dissertation, University of Rochester, Rochester, NY.

Lochman, J. E., Burch, P. R., Curry, J. F., & Lampron, L. B. (1984). Treatment and generalization effects of cognitive-behavioral and goal-setting interventions with aggressive boys. *Journal of Consulting and Clinical Psychology, 52,* 915–916.

Mannarino, A. P., Christy, M., Durlak, J. A., & Magnussen, M. G. (1982). Evaluation of social competence training in the schools. *Journal of School Psychology, 20,* 11–19.

McClure, L. F., Chinsky, J. M., & Larcen, S. W. (1978). Enhancing: social problem-solving performance in an elementary school setting, *Journal of Educational Psychology, 70,* 504–513.

Michelson, L., Mannarino, A. P., Marchione, K., Stern, M., Figaruao, J., & Beck, S. (1982). *A comparative outcome study of behavioral social skills training, cognitive problem-solving and Rogerian control treatment for psychiatric outpatient in children.* Unpublished manuscript, University of Pittsburgh, Pittsburgh, PA.

Michelson, L., Sugai, D., Wood., R., & Kazdin, A. (1983). *Social skill assessment and training with children.* New York: Plenum.

Ollendick, T. H., & Winett, R. A. (1985). Behavioral-preventive interventions with children: Current status, conceptual issues, and future directions. In P. H. Bornstein & A. E. Kazdin (Eds.), *Handbook of clinical behavior therapy with children* (pp. 805–832). Homewood, IL: Dorsey.

Pellegrini, D. S., & Urbain, E. S. (1985). An evaluation of interpersonal cognitive problem solving training with children. *Journal of Child Psychology and Psychiatry, 26,* 17–41.

Richard, B. A. & Dogde, K. A. (1982), Social maladjustment and problem solving in school-age children. *Journal of Consulting and Clinical Psychology, 50,* 226–233.

Rickel, A. U., Eshelman, A. K., & Loigman, G. A. (1983). Social problem-solving: A follow-up study of cognitive and behavioral effects. *Journal of Abnormal Child Psychology, 11,* 15–28.

Roff, M., Sells, B., & Golden, M. M. (1972). *Social adjustment and personality development in children.* Minneapolis, MN: University of Minnesota Press.

Rubin, K. H., & Krasnor, L. R. (1986). Social cognitive and social behavioral perspectives in problem solving. In M. Perlmutter (Ed.), *The Minnesota symposia on child psychology: Cognitive perspectives on children's social and behavioral development (Vol. 18, pp. 1–68).* Hillsdale, NJ: Erlbaum.

Sharp, K. E. (1981). Impact of interpersonal problem-solving training on preschoolers' social competency. *Journal of Applied Developmental Psychology, 2,* 129–143.

Shure, M. B. (1984, August). Social competence through problem-solving in inner-city fifth graders: Is it too late? In J. R. Asarnow (Chair), *Social skills in preadolescents: Assessment and training.* Symposium conducted at the meeting of the American Psychological Association, Toronto.

Shure, M. B., & Spivack, G. (1974a). *Interpersonal cognitive problem-solving (ICPS): A mental health program for kindergarten and first-grade children: Training script.* Philadelphia: Hahnemann University, Department of Mental Health Sciences.

Shure, M. B., & Spivack, G. (1974b). *Preschool Interpersonal Problem Solving (PIPS) Test: Manual.* Philadelphia: Hahnemann Community Mental Health/Mental Retardation Center.

Shure, M. B., & Spivack, G. (1982). *Interpersonal cognitive problem (ICPS): A training program for the intermediate elementary grades.* Philadelphia: Hahnemann University, Department of Mental Health Sciences.

Smith-Tuten, J. K., Gesten, E. L., Amish, P., Clark, H. B., & Archer, C. (1986). *A comparison of social problem-solving assessment formats.* Unpublished master's thesis, University of South Florida, Tampa, FL.

Spivack, G., Platt, J. J., & Shure, M. B. (1976). *The problem-solving approach to adjustment.* San Francisco: Jossey-Bass.

Spivack, G., & Shure, M.B. (1974). *Social adjustment of young children: A cognitive approach to solving real-life problems.* San Francisco: Jossey-Bass.

Spivack, G., & Shure, M. B. (1982). The cognition of social adjustment: Interpersonal cognitive problem-solving thinking. In B. B. Lahey & A. E. Kazdin (Eds.), *Advances in child clinical psychology* (Vol. 5, pp. 323–372). New York: Plenum Press.

Spivack, G., & Shure, M. B. (1985). ICPS and beyond: Centripetal and centrifugal forces. *American Journal of Community Psychology, 13,* 226–243.

Spivack, G., & Swift, M. (1967). *Devereux Elementary School Behavior Rating Scale Manual.* Devons, PA: The Devereux Foundation.

Urbain, E. S., & Kendall, P. C. (1980). Review of social–cognitive problem-solving interventions with children. *Psychological Bulletin, 8,* 109–143.

Vaughn, S. R., & Ridley, C. A. (1983). A preschool interpersonal problem-solving program: Does it affect behavior in the classroom? *Child Study Journal, 13,* 1–11.

Vaughn, S. R., Ridley, C. A., & Bullock, B. (1984). Interpersonal problem-solving training with aggressive young children. *Journal of Applied Developmental Psychology, 5,* 213–223.

Weissberg, R. P., Gesten, E. L., Carnrike, C. L., Toro, P. A., Rapkin, B.D., Davidson, E., & Cowen, E. L. (1981). Social problem-solving skills training: A competence-building intervention with second to fourth grade children. *American Journal of Community Psychology, 9,* 411–423.

Weissberg, R. P., Gesten, E. L., Leibenstein, N. L., Doherty-Schmid, K., & Hutton, H. (1980). *The Rochester social problem-solving (SPS) program: A training manual for teachers of 2nd-4th grade children.* Rochester, NY: University of Rochester.

Weissberg, R. P., Gesten, E. L., Rapkin, B. D., Cowen, E. L., & McKim, B. J. (1981). Evaluation of a social problem-solving training program for suburban and inner-city third grade children. *Journal of Consulting and Clinical Psychology, 49,* 251–261.

Winer, J., Hilpert, P., Gesten, E., Cowen, E., & Shubin, W. (1982). The evaluation of a kindergarten social problem-solving program. *Journal of Primary Prevention, 2,* 205–216.

Yu, P., Harris, G. E., Solovitz, B. L., & Franklin, J. L. (1986). A social problem-solving intervention for children at high risk for later psychopathology. *Journal of Clinical Child Psychology, 15,* 30–40.

4 Life Skills Training: A Psychoeducational Approach to Substance-Abuse Prevention

GILBERT J. BOTVIN and LINDA DUSENBURY

A variety of psychoeducational interventions have been developed and implemented in school settings over the past decade. These include interventions designed to address the development of social skills, self-control, problem solving, and study skills. Some of these interventions have been designed to treat or ameliorate existing conditions, but others can be conceptualized more appropriately as prevention efforts.

The kind of psychoeducational intervention that will serve as the central focus for this chapter is the latter—a primary-prevention approach that is proactive and is targeted at all of the students on a particular grade level. The Life Skills Training (LST) Program is a comprehensive psychoeducational intervention that is designed to prevent tobacco, alcohol, and drug abuse (Botvin, 1983). It is comprehensive both in the sense that it is designed to teach a broad range of personal and social skills and in the sense that it has the potential to prevent the development of several problems, conditions, and diseases. For example, this type of intervention strategy may be applicable for the prevention of psychological disorders, teenage pregnancy, truancy, and delinquency. In this chapter we provide the background and rationale for the LST program, describe the intervention strategy, summarize the results of evaluation research, and provide general guidelines for planning, implementation, and evaluation.

LITERATURE REVIEW

Traditional Approaches to Substance-Abuse Prevention

In an effort to decrease substance abuse among teenagers, many schools have provided students with tobacco-, alcohol-, and drug-education classes designed to increase awareness of the adverse health, social, and legal consequences of using these substances. The implicit assumption of this approach to substance-abuse prevention is that individuals begin smoking, drinking, or using drugs because they are not sufficiently aware of the inherent dangers, and that if the students are properly informed about these dangers, they will make a logical and rational decision not to use these substances (Goodstadt, 1978).

Frequently embedded within such programs are fear-arousal messages intended to scare students into not engaging in these behaviors. For example, in an effort to deter cigarette smoking, many smoking-prevention programs involve showing students pictures of cancerous lungs or filmed interviews with smokers who are dying of cancer. Despite the intuitive appeal of informational or fear-arousal approaches, the existing research evidence indicates that they are not effective (Berberian, Gross, Lovejoy & Paparella, 1976; Braucht, Follingstad, Brakarsh & Berry, 1973; Goodstadt, 1974; Schaps, Bartolo, Moskowitz, Palley & Churgin, 1981; Thompson, 1978). Thus, while health information may be necessary to promote health behavior, it does not appear to be sufficient in itself.

Causes of Adolescent Substance Abuse

The development of effective preventive interventions would seem logically to necessitate an understanding of the causes of a given behavior, condition, or disorder. In the case of substance abuse, it is now apparent that informational approaches that rely primarily on the provision of factual information are based on a rather limited conceptualization of the etiologic factors and of the underlying process. The causes of cigarette smoking, for example, appear to be much more complex than was previously thought, and require more sophisticated preventive interventions (Botvin, 1982).

Available evidence indicates that substance use generally begins during adolescence (Millman & Botvin, 1983) and is the result of a complex mixture of social, intrapersonal, and developmental factors (Blum & Richards, 1979; Braucht et al., 1973; Jessor, 1976; Wechsler, 1976). Social factors such as the modeling of cigarette smoking by influential high-status role models (e.g., peers, older siblings, parents, media figures) and the perception that the use of psychoactive substances such as tobacco, alcohol, or marijuana is highly normative (i.e., that "everybody's doing it") promote substance use among adolescents. Together, these influences help foster the image that substance use is not only socially acceptable, but that it may even be an important ingredient in becoming popular, attractive to the opposite sex, cool, sophisticated, macho, manly, tough, intelligent, and mature.

Intrapersonal factors appear to determine susceptibility or vulnerability to pro-substance-use social influences. These include cognitive, attitudinal, and personality factors. Cognitive factors relate to accurate and relevant knowledge of the pros and cons of substance use. All things being equal, individuals who are aware of the negative consequences of substance use that are salient to them will be less likely to smoke, drink, or use drugs.

Similarly, attitudes toward both substance users and substance use play a role in determining whether individuals will become substance users themselves.

A variety of personality variables have been found to be associated with substance use and abuse. These include low self-esteem, low self-satisfaction, low self-confidence, greater need for social approval, a low sense of personal control, high anxiety, low assertiveness, rebelliousness, greater impulsivity, and an impatience to assume adult roles or to appear grown-up. In addition, users differ from nonusers along several behavioral dimensions. This suggests a difference with respect to orientation, values, and aspirations. For example, substance users tend to get lower grades in school, to not participate in organized extracurricular activities such as sports or clubs, and to be more likely than nonusers to engage in antisocial behaviors such as lying, stealing, and cheating (Demone, 1973; R. Jessor, Collins & S. L. Jessor, 1972; Wechsler & Thum, 1973).

LIFE SKILLS TRAINING

Rationale and Conceptual Framework

Recognition of the array of different factors that promote substance abuse, and the utilization of more comprehensive conceptual models of substance-use initiation are important—not only to provide the basis for formulating theories concerning the etiology of substance abuse, but also for the development of more effective prevention strategies. In our own work, we have used social learning theory (Bandura, 1977) and problem-behavior theory (R. Jessor & L. Jessor, 1977) to order the available data concerning the factors associated with tobacco, alcohol, and drug abuse into a coherent conceptual framework. From the perspective of these two theories, substance use is conceptualized as being socially learned, purposive, and functional, and is viewed as the consequence of the complex interplay of personal and social-environmental factors. Moreover, two alternative conceptual models of the initiation of adolescent substance use can be derived from an examination of existing etiologic data.

One way of interpreting these etiologic data is through the use of what may be referred to as a *coping model*. This model suggests that some individuals may begin smoking, drinking, or using drugs as a means of coping with expected failure, or as an alternative way of achieving some specific desired goal. For example, adolescents who are not doing well academically may begin using drugs as an alternative means of achieving popularity, social status, or self-esteem. The use of tobacco, alcohol, and drugs may also be the result of an effort to cope with anxiety, particularly with anxiety induced by social situations. From this perspective, there is an internal or intrapersonal motivation to engage in substance use. These individuals would be likely to seek out other individuals who smoke, drink, or use drugs, and to enter high-risk situations with the actual intent of engaging in substance use (Friedman, Lichtenstein, & Biglan, 1985).

The other model suggested by the existing etiologic data is a *social-influence model*. From the perspective of this model, there is an external or interpersonal motivation to engage in substance use. Tobacco, alcohol, and drug use result from a social-influence process involving repeated exposure to high-status role models who engage in these behaviors (e.g., older siblings, influential adults, peers, or celebrities). A second type of social influence comes from the persuasive appeals made by advertisers, particularly with respect to tobacco and alcoholic beverages.

Social psychological research has established that individuals have differential responsiveness to social influence, mediated by personality characteristics. For example, there is evidence to indicate that the individuals most likely to succumb to these influences are those having low self-esteem, low self-confidence, low personal autonomy, high anxiety, and a low sense of personal control (Bandura, 1969; Rotter, 1972). Individuals with frequent exposure to high-status, substance-using role models (high social risk) and a greater susceptibility to social influence, resulting from various personal characteristics (such as vulnerability to social influence), would be the most likely to begin smoking, drinking, or using drugs.

These conceptualizations of substance-use initiation have the following implications for the development of effective substance-abuse prevention programs. First, prevention programs should be designed to decrease students' motivations for engaging in any of these behaviors. Second, prevention programs should, if possible, decrease exposure to high-status substance-using role models. Third, prevention programs should attempt to increase students' ability to respond to direct social influences to smoke, drink, or use drugs. Finally, prevention programs should decrease general susceptibility to social influence.

Students who are motivated to begin using tobacco, alcohol, or drugs as a means of coping could be helped by teaching them more adaptive coping skills. Teaching to students the specific skills with which they can resist direct social influences to engage in substance use might involve helping students develop specific tactics for dealing with these influences. For example, students can be taught skills for refusing offers to smoke, drink, or use drugs as well as techniques for critically evaluating the persuasive appeals advertisers utilize to sell tobacco products and alcoholic beverages. Although it may not be possible to decrease student exposure to substance-using models, it might be possible to decrease their general susceptibility to social influences by increasing self-esteem, self-confidence, sense of personal autonomy, sense of personal control, and providing students with techniques for coping effectively with anxiety. These goals might be accomplished through a program oriented toward the development of personal and social competence.

Thus, the theoretical rationale for the prevention strategy incorporated into the Life Skills Training Program is as follows. General personal and social skills are taught in an effort to decrease both motivations to smoke, drink, or use drugs, as well as to decrease vulnerability to negative social influence. In addition, pressure-resistance or assertive skills are taught in order to provide students with the skills necessary to say no when confronted directly by situations in which they are presented with an offer to smoke, drink, use drugs, or in which they otherwise experience peer pressure. Students are taught to identify and to avoid high-risk situations in which they are likely to experience peer pressure. Finally, the program contains problem-specific material (i.e., material directly related to the problem of substance abuse). Included is basic information concerning the adverse consequences of tobacco, alcohol, and marijuana use; information and activities designed to correct misperceptions about substance-use norms; knowledge related to the social liabilities resulting from substance use (e.g., smoker's breath, nicotine stains on teeth and fingers) and the decreasing social acceptability of substance use (i.e., it is no longer cool or macho).

Program Description

The Life Skills Training Program is a psychoeducational program designed to facilitate the development of the skills necessary for coping effectively with social influences to smoke, drink, or use drugs, within a larger and more general intervention design to enhance generic personal and social skills. Consequently, the Life Skills Training Program can be conceptualized as having three major components: (a) a personal-skills training component; (b) a social-skills training component; and (c) a problem-specific component that tailors the program to substance abuse. Table 4.1 provides an overview of the Life Skills Training Program in terms of the topic areas covered and the recommended number of class sessions per topic.

The *problem-specific component* is composed of six sessions. Three of these sessions contain material on short- and long-term negative consequences of tobacco, alcohol, and marijuana use; current prevalence rates, norms, and the decreasing social acceptability of engaging in these behaviors; and the stages of tobacco, alcohol, and marijuana use leading from initial experimentation to regular (compulsive) patterns of use. A fourth session is designed to illustrate and to dramatize immediate physiological effects of cigarette smoking, using biofeedback-type apparatus. A fifth session examines the techniques used by advertisers to sell tobacco products and alcoholic beverages. The sixth session teaches pressure-resistance tactics and refusal skills that are designed for the student to utilize in saying no to substance-use offers and in resisting peer pressure.

TABLE 4.1 Life Skills Training Program Description

Number of sessions	Topic	Description
4	Substance use: myths and realities	Common attitudes and beliefs about tobacco, alcohol, and marijuana use; current prevalence rates of adults and teenagers; the social acceptability of using these substances; the process of becoming a regular (habitual) user, and the difficulty of breaking these habits; and the immediate physiological effects of smoking.
2	Decision-making and independent thinking	Routine decision making; a general decision-making strategy; social influences affecting decisions; recognizing persuasive tactics; and the importance of independent thinking.
2	Media influences and advertising techniques	Media influences on behavior; advertising techniques and the manipulation of consumer behavior; formulating counter-arguments and other cognitive strategies for resisting advertising pressure; cigarette and alcohol advertising as case studies in the use of these techniques.
2	Self-image and self-improvement	Discussion of self-image and how it is formed; the relationship between self-image and behavior; the importance of a positive self-image, alternative methods of improving one's self and self-image.
2	Coping with anxiety	Discussion of common anxiety-inducing situations; demonstration and practice of cognitive-behavioral techniques for coping with anxiety; instruction on the application of these techniques as active coping strategies in everyday situations.
2	Communication skills	Verbal and nonverbal communication; techniques for avoiding misunderstandings; basic conversational skills; giving and receiving compliments; making introductions.
1	Social skills (a)	Overcoming shyness; initiating social contacts, giving and receiving compliments; basic conversational skills.
1	Social skills (b)	Boy-girl relationships, the nature of interpersonal attraction, conversing with the opposite sex; asking someone out for a date.
2	Assertiveness	Situations calling for assertiveness; reasons for not being assertive; verbal and nonverbal assertiveness skills; resisting peer pressures to smoke, drink, or use marijuana.

The *personal-skills training component* focuses on the development of personal skills. Included in this component is material designed to improve decision-making and critical thinking, self-change and self-improvement techniques, skills for resisting persuasive advertising appeals, and techniques for coping effectively with anxiety. In addition to one class session dealing with principles of self-change and self-reinforcement, students participate in a self-improvement project. The self-improvement project provides an opportunity for students to work on a program designed to improve a specific skill or personal behavior. Students are asked to select an overall self-improvement goal. The goal must be realistic, measurable, and achievable during the available time. Students are assisted in dividing their overall self-improvement goal into a series of weekly subgoals by using the general principle of successive approximation. This approach provides them with the opportunity to shape their own behavior gradually and to obtain fairly immediate feedback concerning their progress.

The third major component, consisting of five sessions, focuses on *social-skills training*. Two sessions are devoted to communication skills, in which both verbal and nonverbal communication are discussed, along with the causes of misunderstandings, and guidelines for avoiding them. The next two sessions deal with general social skills. These sessions contain material concerning overcoming shyness and initiating social contacts, complimenting, and basic conversational skills. Material related to boy–girl social interactions is also included (e.g., learning to relax and converse with the opposite sex, asking someone out for a date, etc.). The final unit in this component deals with assertiveness. Students are taught general, verbal, and non-verbal assertiveness skills relating to requests, refusals, and the honest and open expression of feelings.

Methods and Teaching Techniques

A mixture of standard teaching techniques and methods derived from cognitive–behavior modification approaches are utilized to implement the Life Skills Training Program. Some of the material in the program lends itself to lecturing and to small-group discussion. However, due to the emphasis on skill development, much of the program involves the utilization of cognitive–behavior modification techniques. As part of the self-improvement project, students learn basic principles of self-change, including goal setting, successive approximation, and reinforcement. Students learn to monitor their self-statements, replacing negative self-statements with positive ones—a technique referred to in its most general form as cognitive restructuring.

In order to help students cope more effectively with anxiety, they are introduced to several cognitive–behavioral self-management techniques. These include relaxation training, mental rehearsal, diaphragmatic breathing, and the use of guided imagery. Students are also taught a variety of social skills relating to general social interactions, such as learning how to initiate brief social exchanges, basic conversational skills, complimenting, and skills related to social interactions between boys and girls (e.g., asking someone out for a date).

Finally, in teaching general assertiveness skills, students learn to attend to both verbal and nonverbal dimensions of assertive responses (i.e., not just what to say but how to say it). These and related skills are taught using a combination of techniques that include instruction, modeling and demonstration, rehearsal and practice, feedback and reinforcement (particularly social reinforcement in the form of praise), and extended practice through behavioral homework assignments.

Through the Life Skills Training Program, students learn a wide range of personal and social skills to facilitate the development of general competence, thereby reducing potential motivation for engaging in substance use and abuse. In addition to general life skills, the students are taught the application of specific skills to situations in which they might experience some degree of social pressure to smoke, drink, or use marijuana. For example, in addition to teaching students general assertiveness skills (i.e., the use of *no* statements, requests, and the assertive expression of rights), students are taught how to use these techniques to resist direct interpersonal pressure to smoke, drink, or use marijuana. They are taught how to identify high-risk situations, how to avoid these situations beforehand and, if offered a cigarette, how to say no in the most effective way possible. Recognizing that these situations are indeed difficult to handle, students are taught to develop a repertoire of responses (referred to as *action plans*). By helping them to formulate these action plans ahead of time and to practice basic refusal skills, students' confidence in their ability to handle these situations effectively (self-efficacy) is enhanced, thereby increasing the likelihood that they will utilize these skills.

Evaluation Studies

Over the past five years, we have conducted a series of evaluation studies with the Life Skills Training Program. The initial pilot research with this program (Botvin, Eng, & Williams, 1980) tested its short-term effectiveness for prevention of the onset of cigarette smoking when implemented by outside health professionals. This study was conducted with 8th, 9th, and 10th graders ($N = 281$) from two different schools in suburban New York City. One school participated in the Life Skills Training Program, while the other served as a control. Cigarette smoking was assessed using a monthly measure ("Have you smoked any cigarettes in the past month?"), a weekly measure ("Have you smoked any cigarettes in the past week?"), and a daily measure ("Have you smoked any cigarettes in the past day?").

The Life Skills Training Program produced a 75% reduction in new cigarette smoking over the 3 months between the pretest and the posttest. A follow-up study indicated that there still were 67% fewer new smokers among the students who had participated in the program compared with the control group 3 months after the completion of the program (Botvin & Eng, 1980).

The second study tested the effectiveness of the Life Skills Training Program when implemented by older (11th and 12th grade) peer leaders (Botvin & Eng, 1982). The program was conducted with 7th graders ($N = 426$) from two public junior high schools in the suburbs of metropolitan New York. Schools were randomly assigned to experimental and control conditions. Furthermore, saliva samples were collected prior to administration of the self-report questionnaire in a variant of the "bogus pipeline" procedure used by Evans and his co-workers (Evans et al., 1977) in order to insure high-quality self-reports and to provide an objective measure of smoking status (the level of saliva thiocyanate, SCN). Once again, the results indicated that there were significantly fewer new smokers in the experimental group (8%) than in the control group (19%). These self-report results were corroborated by the results of the SCN analysis that showed a significant increase in SCN levels (indicating increased smoking) among the students in the control group and that showed no significant increase among the students in the experimental group.

One year later these students were assessed again and the two groups compared. Although there were still differences between the experimental (24%) and control groups (32%) with respect to all new smoking, these differences were no longer significant. However, when more regular cigarette smoking was examined (using the weekly measure), significant differences were evident between the experimental group (11%) and the control group (25%). This study demonstrated a 58% reduction in new smoking at the initial posttest, and a 56% reduction in regular smoking at the one-year follow-up.

The third study was designed to provide a real-world test of this type of smoking-prevention strategy when it is implemented by regular teachers under conditions typical of most classrooms (Botvin, Renick, & Baker, 1983). Seventh-grade students drawn from seven schools in the suburbs of New York ($N = 902$) were randomly assigned to three conditions: (a) a treatment condition that involved conducting the prevention program once a week for 15 weeks, (b) a treatment condition that involved conducting the program several times a week for about 5 weeks, and (c) a control condition. Two schools were assigned to each treatment condition and three schools were assigned to the control condition. As in the previous study, saliva samples were collected. In addition, some students in Condition 2 received 10 booster sessions during the eighth grade that were designed to reinforce the material covered previously in the seventh grade.

Comparison of the combined experimental group and the control group revealed significant differences in the proportion of new smokers (6% and 13%), respectively. No significant differences between the two scheduling formats were apparent at the initial posttest. However, at the one-year follow-up, it became clear that the more intensive approach was more effective on all measures (monthly, weekly, and daily) of smoking status. Furthermore, respective comparison of the measurements of the combined experimental group with those of the control group indicate, for the combined experimental group, significantly fewer new smokers on the monthly recall measure (15% vs. 22%), the weekly measure (8% vs. 15%), and the daily measure (6% vs. 11).

Finally, the results indicated that providing students with additional booster sessions can help to maximize the effectiveness of the prevention program. Thus, for example, while the best non-booster group had an onset rate for regular smoking of 5% (compared with a 15% rate for the controls), the booster group had an onset rate of only 2%. Therefore, based on the most inclusive measure of new smoking (monthly smoking), the prevention program resulted in a 50% reduction in new cigarette smoking at the end of the first year, and in a 55% reduction at the end of the second year for the intensive-format condition. Furthermore, new regular smoking was reduced by 87% at the end of the second year for the students who participated in the additional booster sessions.

Research has also been conducted to test the impact of the Life Skills Training Program on alcohol and marijuana use (G. J. Botvin, Baker, Renick, Filazzola, & E. M. Botvin, 1984). The study involved approximately 1,200 seventh-grade students from 10 suburban New York junior high schools. The students in these schools were from predominantly white middle-class families. Two schools were assigned to each of the following five experimental conditions: (a) teacher-led prevention curriculum, (b) peer-led prevention curriculum, (c) teacher-led prevention curriculum plus booster sessions, (d) peer-led prevention curriculum plus booster sessions, and (e) control.

Results of this study indicate that the prevention program had a significant impact on tobacco, alcohol, and marijuana use (Botvin et al., 1984). The students in the peer-led condition reported drinking significantly less alcohol per occasion than students in either the control condition or the teacher-led condition. Perhaps most dramatic was the impact of the prevention program on marijuana use. Not only were there significantly fewer students reporting marijuana use with respect to both the monthly and the weekly recall measures, but the magnitude of these differences was also quite substantial. Comparing the proportion of students reporting marijuana use in the peer-led condition with those students in the control condition, the prevention program reduced total marijuana use by 71% and regular (weekly or daily) marijuana use by 83%.

In summary, the evaluation studies conducted thus far have documented the effectiveness of the Life Skills Training Program with respect to cigarette smoking, alcohol drinking, and marijuana use. These studies have also found that this intervention program has a positive impact on health knowledge and attitudes, assertiveness, self-mastery and personal control, self-confidence, self-satisfaction, and social anxiety. Anecdotal evidence suggests that this type of program may even help some students improve their academic performance. In sum, the Life Skills Training Program is a promising new approach that may be applicable to a wide range of health-comprising behaviors, and therefore might reasonably be used as the core of any junior high school health education curriculum.

GUIDELINES FOR PLANNING, IMPLEMENTATION AND EVALUATION

Target Population

The Life Skills Training approach to substance-abuse prevention has been designed for use with junior high school students, and has been found to be effective when implemented with students from grade 7 to Grade 10. However, it appears to be most effective when implementation of the program begins in the seventh grade. The research that we have conducted underscores the importance of implementing this type of psychoeducational program throughout at least the junior high school period. Booster sessions have been developed for grades 8 and 9. These sessions not only help to sustain positive program effects, but may also actually enhance such effects.

Although it has been argued that it is advisable to identify students at risk for becoming substance abusers on the basis of a set of specific criteria, the Life Skills Training Program has been designed as a program that is appropriate for all students at a particular grade level. Based on the research we have conducted thus far, a logical intervention model would be one that involves conducting the Life Skills Training Program initially with seventh graders and conducting additional booster sessions in Grades 8 and 9.

Curriculum Materials

The materials necessary for conducting the Life Skills Training Program include a teacher's manual and student guide, along with a 15-minute relaxation tape for the unit denoted to coping with anxiety. Together they form a program that is completely self-contained; no additional materials are needed to conduct the program effectively. Although teachers involved in the evaluation studies were provided with a one-day orientation workshop, sufficient detail is provided in the *Life Skills Training Teacher's Manual* (Botvin, 1983) for the average teacher to conduct the Life Skills Training Program without special training.

Scheduling Considerations

The seventh grade level of the Life Skills Training Program consists of nine topic areas designed to be covered in approximately 18 class periods. The program should be taught in sequence. The lesson plans in the *Teacher's Manual* contains a major goal, several measurable student objectives, program content, and classroom activities for each session. The program can be integrated into any subject area, although health education and science are probably the most appropriate. Two programming options are available. The program can be taught at a rate of one class period per week. Alternatively, it can be programmed as a curriculum module or minicourse, so that the entire program is conducted on consecutive class days. In evaluation studies conducted thus far, both scheduling formats have been found to be effective. However the evidence from one study suggests that the more intensive module or minicourse format may produce somewhat better results (Botvin et al., 1983).

Administrative Clearance/School Recruitment

For any program to be successful, the approval and, most importantly, the support by a broad range of individuals associated with the school is necessary. Because there is a wide degree of variability from one school district to another, it is difficult to lay out a specific prescription for obtaining administrative clearance (see Maher & Bennett, 1984; or Maher, Illback, & Zins, 1984, for detailed discussions of these issues). In our own work, we have found it necessary to obtain permission and to secure support on a variety of levels.

As outsiders to the system, we have found it more expeditious to begin on the district level and to work our way down through the system, meeting next with principals and assistant principals, department heads, and eventually classroom teachers. It is essential that individuals on all levels be supportive of new psychoeducational programs. Without such support the routine obstacles that are encountered in an attempt to implement any new program may become insurmountable, or, at best difficult. Worthwhile programs may never get started, or once underway may languish and eventually be discontinued without sufficient support for institutionalizing them.

Clearly, a valuable asset for any educational program is the support of parents. It is helpful to send a letter from the district superintendent or principal to parents, informing them about the new intervention program. Most schools do not routinely obtain parental approval for programs such as LST if it is incorporated into the existing curriculum. It is then treated like any other subject area or academic subject. However, if the data being collected identify students either directly (by name) or indirectly (through the use of ID codes), some form of parental consent should be obtained.

Many researchers who test smoking-prevention programs, for example, have utilized a passive-consent procedure. Unlike traditional consent procedures that require parents to sign a consent form indicating approval of their child's participation, the passive approach sends a notification form home to parents that requires action only if parents do not wish their child to participate. This is clearly a weaker procedure than those normally followed for obtaining informed consent. However, several researchers have argued that meaningful research cannot be conducted in this area if standard active-consent procedures are required (Severson & Ary, 1983).

First, the practical matter of having enough signed consents returned within a reasonable period of time is often a virtually insurmountable problem, particularly with high-risk populations. Second, a disproportionate percentage of the students who fail to return signed consents are those students who are the most likely to smoke, drink, or use drugs—thus introducing a sampling bias into the study and thereby compromising the validity of the study. Still, although the risks to students participating in this type of program are generally viewed as minimal and the potential benefits are seen as substantial, these issues should be given careful consideration.

In recruiting schools for our own research, we have used several different strategies. One that we have found to be particularly effective when selecting from a relatively large pool of schools involves the following. First, a cover letter that describes briefly the nature of the program and the likely benefits for participating students is sent to the superintendents of the target schools. Enclosed with that letter is a flyer describing the intervention program, its background and its rationale. Schools are informed that only a limited number of schools can be selected for inclusion in the new project, and the letter includes a response date by which schools must indicate their interest in being considered for inclusion in the project.

In our experience, we have found that most schools will be very quick to respond to this kind of letter. They will not only indicate their interest, but frequently they may also even try to sell their school or school district as one that would be ideal for such a project. This, of course, sets up quite a different psychology than that of most projects conducted by outside researchers, in which the researchers are typically in the position of trying to persuade schools to participate.

After such an initial contact, and with the blessing of the school superintendent, arrangements are made for meetings with principals, department heads, and teachers. A critical factor that should be emphasized here is that it is essential for teachers not to feel that a particular program is being mandated by the administration. Even in situations in which the administration is extremely enthusiastic about a program, it is still necessary to recruit actively those teachers or other individuals who would be potential providers. Even programs acknowledged by teachers to be intrinsically meritorious can sometimes be sabotaged or at least not given the necessary support if teachers feel that they are being pressured into conducting the program by the administration and that they have not been able to choose to become involved on their own volition.

Leader Selection and Training

The Life Skills Training Program, according to the results of our evaluation studies, can be implemented effectively by outside health professionals, older peer leaders, and regular classroom teachers. Although it is certainly desirable to have individuals with previous experience in teaching the kind of personal and social skills included in the LST program (e.g., health teachers, counselors), it is not necessary. We have found that good teachers can implement this type of program by simply following the detailed lesson plans in the *Life Skills Training: Teacher's Manual* (Botvin, 1983).

Two types of peer leaders have been used to implement substance-abuse prevention programs—same-age peer leaders and older peer leaders. Moreover, peer leaders have had different degrees of responsibility. In some instances, peer leaders may have primary responsibility for program implementation. In others they may have more limited responsibility, such as assisting teachers in leading small-group discussion, demonstrating skills, or organizing role plays.

Based on our experience, we would recommend the following selection criteria. First, participation should be voluntary. Individuals should become involved in implementing a psychoeducational program such as LST because they want to, and not as a result of an administrative mandate. Second, individuals should be good role models. In the case of a substance-abuse prevention program, this is particularly important for peer leaders. They should be able to serve as reasonably good models with respect to the personal and social skills being taught, and also with respect to substance-use behavior. However, it is also important that students selected to be peer leaders have credibility with the target group and do not appeal primarily to honor students or to student council members. Third, once selected, teachers or peer leaders should be willing to make a commitment to implement the entire program in a manner consistent with the curriculum guide. Fourth, to the extent possible, leaders should have skills or experience related to those necessary for conducting this type of psychoeducational program (e.g., class-management skills, teaching experience in conducting role plays or leading small-group discussion, etc.). Teachers are recruited through orientation meetings with individuals who are identified by principals and department heads as likely to fit the above criteria; a similar procedure is used for recruiting peer leaders.

Since the Life Skills Training Program involves the teaching of personal and social skills with little emphasis on factual information or on the kind of fear-arousal messages found in traditional tobacco-, alcohol-, and drug-education programs, a training workshop is generally advisable. The type of training workshop necessary depends largely on the background and experience of the leaders. In general, we have found that a one-day workshop is sufficient for most teachers. The workshop is designed to provide program leaders with a general orientation toward both the problem of substance abuse and the LST approach. The course of the workshop is devoted to the background and rationale for the LST approach, the content and activity of the program, and guidelines for implementation.

More specifically, the training workshop is designed to:

- provide participants with an understanding of substance abuse, its significance, its contributing factors, and its onset and developmental course
- provide participants with an understanding of the background and rationale for the LST approach
- provide a complete description of the program and of the curriculum materials necessary to implement the program successfully
- provide guidelines for scheduling and implementation
- familiarize participants with the content and activities of the program
- provide experience in participation in and/or teaching selected program activities (e.g., the classroom biofeedback experiments, the acquisition of skills for resisting peer pressure to smoke, drink, or use drugs)
- generate a sense of enthusiasm and commitment among individuals who will be involved in program implementation.

In the peer-leader programs that we have conducted, peer leaders have had the entire responsibility for program implementation. Consequently, in addition to an orientation workshop, weekly training sessions lasting approximately one hour were held with peer leaders. These sessions were conducted by our staff members to provide a detailed review of the upcoming session and to provide peer leaders with feedback from the previous session.

Ongoing Support and Consultation

Another factor relating to successful implementation concerns the availability of ongoing consultation. Providers, particularly in the early stages of adoption, need to feel that their efforts will be supported and that they can discuss potential problems with someone who has previous experience implementing this type of program. Periodic monitoring can be very helpful for determining the extent to which the program is being implemented properly. This also provides an opportunity for feedback, both to permit any necessary fine tuning and to provide reinforcement.

Evaluation Guidelines

Although evaluation research has already indicated that this type of primary prevention strategy is effective under well-controlled research conditions, it is important when conducting intervention of this kind to include an evaluation component in order to determine whether the program is being effectively implemented. Evaluation can proceed on a variety of levels. Minimally, process evaluation should be conducted to determine if the program has been implemented successfully and completely. This can be accomplished by making a list of the objectives and activities of each session (taken directly from the *Teacher's Manual*) and using that as a checklist. The checklist can be completed after each session by program providers or by individuals monitoring program implementation.

In addition, we also recommend undertaking some kind of outcome evaluation. An evaluation can be accomplished by pretesting and posttesting participating students with respect to tobacco, alcohol, and marijuana use. Common measures involve assessment of use during the past month, week, or day in terms of frequency and amount. Substance-use status can be accomplished by means of dichotomous (yes/no) items (e.g., "Have you smoked one or more cigarettes in the past month?") or by using a general measure for each substance that incorporates several categories of use into one time (e.g., "How often, if ever, do you generally smoke cigarettes?"). Response categories might range from "never" to "several times a day." Additional information concerning the kinds of measures used as well as on data collection procedures (e.g., the bogus pipeline technique) is contained in several of our research reports (see Botvin et al., 1983, 1984).

Special care should be taken when collecting data from students that concerns illegal behaviors. It is essential that the confidentiality of students is protected by researchers. One way to accomplish this is through the use of anonymous questionnaires. However, in longitudinal research, where it is important to track individual students and to examine changes over time, some means of linking data collected at different time points is necessary. This can be accomplished by the use of unique ID codes matched to students' names on a master list. The master list should always be kept in a secure location (for example, in a locked filing cabinet in a locked room) controlled by the researchers. The original questionnaires and master list should be destroyed as soon as possible after data analyses have been completed.

There are fundamental differences between primary prevention programs and treatment programs that affect how these interventions are evaluated. Treatment programs, at the level of outcome analysis, can be evaluated in terms of reductions in the target behaviors or by the proportion of individuals engaging in the target behavior. However, due to the very nature of preventive interventions, evaluation must be on the bases of reductions in rate of increase of a given target behavior, or on the proportion of individuals manifesting that behavior relative to a comparison group.

Thus, for example, in the case of cigarette smoking, a prevention program would be evaluated in terms of the extent to which it reduced the proportion of individuals becoming experimental or regular smokers relative to the comparison group, rather than in terms of the proportion of individuals who quit. Outcome evaluation would, therefore, need to demonstrate that fewer individuals began to smoke in the intervention group relative to a comparison group (e.g., a nonintervention group or a group receiving a different intervention). Since it would normally be expected that among teenagers there would be an increase in new smokers, drinkers, and marijuana users, even in the group receiving a preventive intervention, meaningful evaluation cannot be accomplished without using a comparison group. Simply looking at whether substance use increased in the intervention group alone would be extremely misleading, since it might lead to the erroneous conclusion that the intervention was not effective when it may actually have produced a 50% or 75% reduction in the smoking-onset rate.

Evaluation of a psychoeducational intervention program such as the Life Skills Training Program might also focus on the extent to which the intervention affected hypothesized mediating variables. This would involve examining program effectiveness with respect to specific knowledge, skills, attitudes, and personality characteristics. Furthermore, other factors should be considered in evaluating the effectiveness of this type of prevention program, including school characteristics, degree of exposure to the intervention, characteristics of the leaders and teachers, and fidelity of program implementation.

SUMMARY, CONCLUSIONS, AND FUTURE DIRECTIONS

Cognitive and fear-arousal approaches to substance-abuse prevention generally have been found to be ineffective. One of the most promising new approaches to substance-abuse prevention among junior high school students is a psychoeducational prevention program called Life Skills Training. This approach is designed to address both the interpersonal and the intrapersonal factors that promote substance-use initiation. Students are taught a wide range of general personal and social skills, as well as specific skills for resisting social pressure to smoke, drink, or use drugs. The LST program has been implemented successfully by outside health professionals, peer leaders, and teachers. Evaluation studies have demonstrated reductions in smoking, excessive drinking, and marijuana use of between 50% and 83% when comparing participating students to those from control schools.

Issues important to the successful implementation of this type of psychoeducational intervention are those of obtaining the permission and support of school officials, notifying parents and securing their support, recruiting teachers or peer leaders, and providing the necessary training and support. Evaluation determines if the intervention is being implemented effectively. However, the evaluation of preventive interventions can be complex. Careful considerations should be given to the choice of measures, to the use of a control or a comparison group, and to issues of consent and confidentiality.

The approach utilized in the LST program is one that might also be applied when intervening in areas such as truancy, delinquency, teenage pregnancy, and mental health promotion. However, this possibility remains to be tested. Additional research is needed to determine the extent to which this intervention is effective with a wide range of students under various implementation conditions. Longer term follow-up is also needed to determine the durability of program effects. In view of the magnitude and scope of the problem of substance abuse, perhaps the most pressing concern now is how programs such as LST can be disseminated most effectively.

ANNOTATED BIBLIOGRAPHY

Botvin, G. J. (1979). *Life skills training: Teacher's manual*. New York: Smithfield Press.
 Contains an introductory section that provides the background and rationale for this program as well as general guidelines for its implementation. Most significantly, the *Teacher's Manual* contains detailed lesson plans for the LST program. Each lesson plan includes an overall goal, behavioral objectives, content material, and classroom activities.
Botvin, G. J. (1984) Prevention of adolescent substance abuse through the development of personal and social competence. In T. Glynn (Ed.), *Preventing adolescent drug abuse: Intervention strategies*. (NIDA Research Monograph Series). Washington, DC: U.S. Government Printing Office.
 Provides background information concerning the initiation and early stages of substance abuse, the determinants of substance use, developmental factors that increase individual risk of becoming a substance user or abuser, and a summary of previous educational approaches to substance-abuse prevention and their effectiveness. Describes the conceptual framework for the Life Skills Training Program, and provides a justification for the teaching of specific skills. Contains a detailed reference list.
Botvin, G. J., & Wills, T. A. (1985). Personal and social skills training: Cognitive- behavioral approaches to substance abuse prevention. In C. S. Bell (Ed.), *Prevention research: Deterring drug abuse among children and adolescents* (NIDA Research Monograph Series). Washington, DC: U.S. Government Printing Office.
 Provides a comprehensive discussion of cognitive-behavioral approaches to substance- abuse prevention. In addition to including material concerning the Life Skills Training Program,

other similar approaches to substance-abuse prevention are discussed in terms of their similarities and differences. Also discusses several important methodological issues as well as potential limitations of the research that has been conducted with these programs.

Glasgow, R. E., & McCaul, K. D. (in press). Life skills training programs for smoking prevention: Critique and directions for future research. In C. Bell & R. Battjes (Eds.), *Prevention research: Deterring drug abuse among children and adolescents* (NIDA Research Monograph). Washington, DC: U.S. Government Printing Office.

Provides a critique of the psychoeducational intervention strategy discussed in this chapter. Outlines the distinguishing features of this type of intervention strategy, discussing potential advantages and disadvantages of this approach. The effectiveness of this type of prevention strategy is compared with that of competing strategies. Also tackles the issue of how and when this psychoeducational program works, and makes suggestions for future research.

Schinke, S. P., & Gilchrist, L. D. (1984) *Life skills counseling with adolescents*. Baltimore: University Park Press.

Written for human services professionals. Details well-tested teaching strategies and proven methods for designing, implementing and evaluating life-skills programs. Describes the life-skills approach as a counseling technique that can be used with adolescents. Focus is on a number of important areas including interpersonal relationships, coping with sexuality, managing stress, promoting health, employment, and building social responsibility. Also included is practical material relating to issues of implementation and evaluation.

REFERENCES

Bandura, A. (1969). *Principals of behavior modification*. New York: Holt, Rinehart & Winston.

Bandura, A. (1977). *Social learning theory*. Englewood Cliffs, NJ: Prentice-Hall.

Berberian, R. M., Gross, C., Lovejoy, J., & Paparella, S. (1976). The effectiveness of drug education programs: A critical review. *Health Education Monographs, 4*(4), 377–398.

Blum, R., & Richards, L. (1979). Youthful drug use. In R. I. Dupont, A. Goldstein, & J. O'Donnel (Eds.), *Handbook on drug abuse* (pp. 257–267). Washington, DC: U.S. Department of Health, Education, and Welfare; and Office of Drug Abuse Policy, National Institute on Drug Abuse.

Botvin, G. J. (1983). *Life skills training: Teacher's manual*. New York: Smithfield Press.

Botvin, G. J., Baker, E., Renick, N., Filazzola, A. D., & Botvin, E. M. (1984). A cognitive-behavioral approach to substance abuse prevention. *Addictive Behaviors, 9*, 137–147.

Botvin, G. J., & Eng. A. (1980). A comprehensive school-based smoking prevention program. *Journal of School Health, 50*, 209–213.

Botvin, G. J., & Eng, A. (1982). The efficacy of a multicomponent approach to the prevention of cigarette smoking. *Preventive Medicine II, 11*(2), 199–211.

Botvin, G. J., Eng, A., & Williams, C. L. (1980). Preventing the onset of cigarette smoking through life skills training. *Preventive Medicine, 9*, 135–143.

Botvin, G. J., Renick, N., & Baker, E. (1983). The effects of scheduling format and booster sessions on a broad-spectrum psychosocial approach to smoking prevention. *Journal of Behavioral Medicine, 6*(4), 359–379.

Braucht, G. N., Follingstad, D., Brakarsh, D., & Berry, K. L. (1973). Drug education: A review of goals, approaches and effectiveness, and a paradigm for evaluation. *Quarterly Journal of Studies on Alcohol, 34*, 1279–1292.

Demone, H. W. (1973). The nonuse and abuse of alcohol by the male adolescent. In M. Chafetz (Ed.), *Proceedings of the second annual alcoholism conference* (pp. 24–32). (Publication No. HSM 73–9083). Washington, DC: Department of Health, Education, and Welfare.

Evans, R. I., Rozelle, R. M., Mittlemark, M. B., Hansen, W. B., Bane, A. L., & Havis, J. (1977). Deterring the onset of smoking in children: Knowledge of immediate physiological effects and coping with peer pressure, media pressure, and parent modeling. *Journal of Applied Social Psychology, 8*, 126–135.

Friedman, L. S., Lichtenstein, E., & Biglan, A. (1985). Smoking onset among teens: An empirical analysis of initial situations. *Addictive Behaviors, 10*(1), 1–14.

Goodstadt, M. S. (1974). Myths and methodology in drug education: A critical review of the research evidence. In M. S. Goodstadt (Ed.), *Research on methods and programs of drug education.* Toronto: Addiction Research Foundation.

Goodstadt, M. S. (1978). Alcohol and drug education. *Health Education Monographs,* 6(3), 263–279.

Jessor, R. (1976). Predicting time of onset of marijuana use: A developmental study of high school youth. In D. J. Lettieri (Ed.), *Predicting adolescent drug abuse: A review of issues, methods and correlates* (DHEW Publication No. ADM 77, Research Issues No. 11). Rockville, MD: National Institute on Drug Abuse.

Jessor, R., Collins, M. I., & Jessor S. L. (1972). On becoming a drinker: Social-psychological aspects of an adolescent transition. *Annals of the New York Academy of Sciences, 197,* 199–213.

Jessor, R., & Jessor, L. (1977). *Problem behavior and prosocial development: A longitudinal study of youth.* New York: Academic Press.

Maher, C. A., & Bennet, R. E. (1984). *Planning and evaluating special education services.* Englewood Cliffs, NJ: Prentice-Hall.

Maher, C. A., Illback, R. J., & Zins, J. E. (Eds.). (1984). *Organizational psychology in the schools: A handbook for professionals.* Springfield, IL: Charles C. Thomas.

Millman, R. B., & Botvin, G. J. (1983). Substance use, abuse, and dependence. In M. D. Levine, W. B. Carey, A. C. Crocker, & R. T. Gross (Eds.), *Developmental-behavioral pediatrics* (pp. 683–708). Philadelphia: Saunders.

Rotter, J. B. (1972). Generalized expectancies for internal versus external control of reinforcement. In J. B. Rotter, J. E. Chance, & E. J. Phares (Eds.), *Applications of a social learning theory of personality* (pp. 260–295). New York: Holt, Rinehart & Winston.

Schaps, E., Bartolo, R. D., Moskowitz, J., Palley, C. S., & Churgin, S. (1981). A review of 127 drug abuse prevention program evaluations. *Journal of Drug Issues,* pp. 17–43.

Severson, H. H., & Ary, D. V. (1983). Sampling bias due to consent procedures with adolescents. *Addictive Behaviors, 8;* 433–437.

Thompson, E. I. (1978). Smoking education programs: 1960–1976. *American Journal of Public Health, 68,* 250–257.

United States Department of Health and Human Services. (1979). *Healthy people: The surgeon general's report on health promotion and disease prevention.* Washington, DC: U.S. Government Printing Office.

Wechsler H. (1976). Alcohol intoxication and drug use among teenagers. *Journal Studies on Alcohol, 37*(11) 1672–1677.

Wechsler, H., & Thum, D. (1973). Alcohol and drug use among teenagers: A questionnaire study. In M. Chafetz (Ed.), *Proceedings of the second annual alcoholism conference* (pp. 33–46). (DHEW Publication No. HSM 73–9083). Washington, DC: U.S. Government Printing Office.

5 Study-Skills Training: A Comprehensive Approach

PAMELA S. WISE, JUDY L. GENSHAFT, and MARY B. BYRLEY

Maximizing students' chances for academic success is a goal of everyone involved in education. A major resource available for this purpose is the use of psychoeducational interventions directed toward the acquisition and use of *study skills*. Study skills are specific techniques that are used to acquire, retain, and demonstrate knowledge. Study skills can also be viewed as ways of problem solving (Marshak & Burkle, 1981). In the process of acquiring study skills, students can become aware of how they learn best and thus can become more responsible for their own learning. Although the study-skills literature clearly points out the need for organizing training, few models have emerged for doing so. Applied research is needed to substantiate the necessity of these skills and to suggest which skills should be taught and by whom.

Academic performance is strongly influenced by students' knowledge of appropriate study-skills techniques (Lingren, 1969; Robyack & Downey, 1979). However, mere exposure to study skills information does not guarantee that this knowledge will be translated either easily or automatically into effective behaviors. For this training to be truly effective, attention must also be given to helping students to remove obstacles to the application of study skills. A well-planned, coordinated approach to study-skills training that includes individualized plans of action that address these obstacles appears highly warranted.

Students strive to meet the expectations of family, peers, and school personnel on a daily basis, in part through the attainment of success in school learning. Although student performance is evaluated in a variety of ways, tests are by far the most frequent form of evaluation, and test or test-like situations are among the most anxiety-inducing in school (Phillips, 1978). The relationship between anxiety and school achievement has been well documented (Hill, 1972; Phillips, 1978; Ruebush, 1963), and the most consistent findings are that low achievement is associated with high anxiety at all academic levels (Gaudry & Spielberger, 1971). This anxiety is the type of obstacle that can be addressed by a more broadly defined approach to study skills training.

A combination of a variety of rewards with an undue emphasis on ability forces many students to struggle to avoid failure rather than to strive for success. The most direct way to avoid school failure is simply not to participate. Academic achievement and autonomy in learning, then, might best be enhanced by applying a combination of study-skills techniques and self-management strategies that reduce anxiety and increase students' personal involvement in the educational process.

The purpose of this chapter is to provide an overview of the study-skills area and to propose the addition of a self-management dimension that increases the likelihood of effective application of these skills. Emphasis is placed on providing a multidisciplinary framework for school personnel that organizes the knowledge needed to build more specific interventions, both remedial and developmental in nature. This chapter may prove most helpful to educators at the secondary level, where coordinated efforts become particularly needed because, starting with the middle school grades, students are expected to handle independently, an ever-increasing quantity of knowledge. However, much of this approach, especially aspects of basic skill development, is also applicable to elementary school students.

REVIEW OF THE LITERATURE

Organization of Study Skills

There has been considerable difficulty in defining exactly what study skills are and which skills to teach. Study skills have been called part of an invisible curriculum (Towle, 1982) because students are expected to acquire these skills and yet rarely are taught them systematically (Marshak & Burkle, 1981). Study skills may well be one of the most neglected areas in the curriculum (Barron, McCoy, P. Cuevas, S. Cuevas, & Rachal, 1983).

The lack of both a viable definition of study skills and the identification of specific skill components has no doubt impeded progress toward the development of logical sequences and methods for teaching these skills. Definitions of study skills have often relied on listing specific skills, such as organizing, processing, and using information gained from reading (Salinger, 1983). Perhaps the best general definition available is that study skills are those skills that have an impact on the development of autonomy in learning (Dean, 1977).

Recent conceptualizations have organized study skills into a variety of components. Barron et. al. (1983), for example, divided study skills into learner-selected objectives, strategies, and habits. Archer and Neubauer (1981) offered a slightly different conception that emphasizes time management, test-taking, classroom behavior, and study/concentration modules. Markel (1981) suggested yet another taxonomy of skills that are specifically tailored to improving test-taking skills of learning-disabled (LD) adolescents. She argued that the component skills in the taxonomy are best taught through a team effort that includes special education consultants, regular education teachers, and supportive personnel. Although Markel focused on test-taking competence, her multicomponent approach is productive in more general applications.

Towle (1982) has identified four steps, each with its own particular strategies for students learning how to study: processing information, learning to organize information, rehearsing information, and recalling and applying information. Two major emphases emerge from all of these approaches. First, there is a common emphasis on teaching specific study and test-taking strategies and techniques. Within this emphasis, Towle's stages are appealing because they incorporate both a process and the component skills required to move through this process. The other approaches contribute to the second emphasis, on self-management skills, which addresses the needs of students to control and regulate themselves within the learning environment. This emphasis includes anxiety management, concentration, scheduling, time management, reward systems, and increasing time on task (see chapter 10 for an in-depth discussion of behavioral self-management).

Several intervention studies have combined anxiety management with some form of study counseling in order to increase test-taking competence (Allen, 1971; Katahn, Strenger, & Cherry, 1966; McManus, 1971; Mitchell & Ng, 1972), but extensive research of component models of study-skills training is lacking. Systematic teaching of study skills requires an organizational framework for these skills. Combining study and test-taking techniques with self-management skills is logical and captures current thinking in the study-skills training area.

Study Skills: Some Suggestions from Research

Teachers, counselors, and other support personnel frequently operate without adequate knowledge of the research literature on study skills and habits (Thompson, 1981). Although there are no simple solutions to study problems, there are some suggestions based on research that might prove helpful.

Early in the history of study skills, emphasis was placed on mastering a particular series of behaviors (Marshak & Burkle, 1981). The Survey, Question, Read, Recite, and Review (SQ3R) method, developed in 1941 by Robinson, is the best known of these approaches. Despite the popularity of the SQ3R method, research on it has been scant and conflicting. Study methods such as SQ3R deserve more focused study by researchers in order to establish their efficacy (Diggs, 1973; Donald, 1967; Gufrola, 1975; Wilmore, 1966; Wooster, 1958).

A more recent trend has been to view study skills as part of a concentration on basic skills. Research has focused on the effectiveness of a variety of specific skills or on a combination of skills. For example, McAndrew (1983) stated that the skills of underlining and notetaking have been found to be the most frequently used. He made suggestions, based on research, that are relevant for teaching underlining techniques to secondary students. First, teachers are encouraged to consider preunderlining reading assignments, because relevant underlining produces better recall than irrelevant underlining, and preunderlined passages produce better recall than student-underlined passages. Specific training in underlining is suggested in circumstances where students themselves have to underline the material to be studied. This training includes assisting students to underline higher level, superordinate sentences rather than subordinate details, because this method of underlining has been found to increase recall of both underlined and nonunderlined material. If students learn to underline only higher level general statements rather than details, they will be underlining less and saving time spent on their reading tasks. Students are instructed to use this saved time for studying the underlined information.

Based upon McAndrew's (1983) review of notetaking research, he suggested the following for instructors:

1. Realize that the external storage function of notes is more important than the act of taking the notes.
2. Use a spaced lecture format to increase effectiveness.
3. Insert questions or verbal and nonverbal cues into lectures to highlight structure.
4. Write material on the blackboard to be sure students will record it.
5. Be aware of the need when using transparencies or slides to compensate for possible information overload.
6. Tell students what type of test to expect.
7. Use handouts, which are especially helpful for poor notetakers.
8. Give handouts with both full notes and space for additional student notes.

Self-management techniques have also received research attention in the study-skills training literature. There are several worthwhile reviews of the current status of anxiety-management interventions, especially test anxiety (e.g., Sarason, 1980). Self-management techniques aimed at increasing the amount of study time have also been a source of positive results, based on the premise that increased study time leads to improved academic performance. Techniques such as self-monitoring and self-recording of study time have been shown to increase study time (Champlin & Karoly, 1975; Miller & Gimpl, 1972; Tichenor, 1977) and so have self-reinforcement techniques, in which rewards are contingent upon a predetermined amount of studying (Greiner & Karoly, 1976; Richards, McReynolds, Holt, & Sexton, 1976). Dean, Malott, and Fulton (1983) reported an increase of one letter-grade when such management procedures as hourly self-recording, student-developed rule statements, and environmental management (establishing surroundings most favorable to studying) were implemented.

These suggestions serve only as examples of how training in study skills can be more closely linked to research. Typically, it is the responsibility of those who develop interventions to derive pertinent guidelines from research. Reviews such as Thompson's (1981), which includes sections on research evidence as well as suggestions for students, may be helpful.

Test-Wiseness and Test-Taking Skills

Acquiring skills to prepare for and to take tests is also crucial to adequate study training. *Test-wiseness* has been defined as "the capacity to utilize the characteristics and formats of the test and/or test-taking situation to receive a high score" (Millman, Bishop, & Ebel, 1965, p. 707). The teaching of skills that increase test-wiseness also improves the validity of test results by minimizing format-related problems in taking tests. Most students need certain skills with which to approach and demonstrate knowledge on tests. Millman et al. (1965) have provided a list of test-wiseness strategies, including time-using strategy, error-avoidance, guessing, deductive reasoning, intent consideration, and cue-using. McPhail (1981) suggested that these principles can be learned either through associative learning or through a problem-solving approach.

Associative learning involves having specific strategies pointed out, practice, and drill. Several researchers have concluded that programmed materials can be used as an effective instructional tool (Moore, Schutz, & Baker, 1966; Slakter, Koehler, & Hampton, 1970). Form Z (Ferrell, 1977) is a self-administered test that can be used as a teaching aid for test-wiseness with high school students. It demonstrates the application of 10 test-wise strategies, half of which pertain to deductive reasoning, and the other half dealing with recognition of cues that may be subsumed within the questions on test items.

The Test-Making Activity (McPhail, 1981) illustrates a problem-solving approach to learning test-wiseness. Secondary students learn inductively about test-wiseness through experiences in test construction. Students are sensitized through this exercise to identify cues in test items.

The SCORER (Schedule your time, use Clue words in the question, Omit difficult questions, Read carefully, Estimate your answers, Review your work) system (Carman & Adams, 1972) combines test-wiseness principles with other test-taking strategies appropriate for both essay and objective tests. SCORER purports to help students organize important test-taking principles in a way that is easily remembered during stressful testing situations. However, SCORER has not been thoroughly researched.

McCabe (1982) describes the Time-Use Chart as a tool that can be used effectively to increase students' awareness of how they spend their time. This grid of the Time-Use Chart displays the days of the week and hourly time slots for each day, where a student's activities can be recorded. McCabe also suggests using the Study-Skills Questionnaire as a basis for group discussion that focuses on study strategies and skills.

Analyzing what students must be able to do in order to recall and to apply knowledge on different test formats provides a framework for teaching the necessary skills. Towle (1982) listed the requirements for responding to multiple-choice, short-answer, essay, oral report, and construction formats for applying knowledge. Essay questions require abilities in (a) outlining main points, (b) writing topic sentences, (c) providing supporting detail such as who, what, when, where, and how, (d) using transition phrases, and (e) writing conclusion or summary sentences. Short-answer responses require students to (a) use all key words from the question in the answer, (b) use strategies to retrieve relevant information, (c) organize answers into facts, concepts, and generalizations, (d) follow directions accurately and, (e) write phrases, sentences, or lists. The multiple-choice format requires that students be able to (a) use cue words in questions, (b) use association, and (c) use visual imagery. Each format poses a particular challenge to students beyond simple mastery and recall of content knowledge.

Performance on tests can also be enhanced by general strategies, such as studying on a regular basis and having a consistent and realistic review schedule. Saleebey (1981) suggests emphasizing key ideas during review and anticipating test questions. Other key instructions include: read directions and questions carefully; survey the entire test and answer easy questions first; write down memory devices; answer every item and give the best answer; and proof-read.

Finally, all students can learn from their performance on tests by evaluating what questions were missed and why they were missed. Tests can yield valuable information about the effectiveness of a student's study regime and about his or her progress in acquiring test-taking skill, as well as about mastery of content knowledge. If students can be encouraged to see the personal value in this performance feedback, they may come to experience tests more as opportunities than as threats.

GUIDELINES FOR PLANNING AND EVALUATION

Identifying and Assessing Student Needs

TABLE 5.1 Outline of a Comprehensive Study-Skills Program

When	Who	What	How	Where
Phase I	Counselors, school psychologists	organize the needs assessment	preparing materials; scheduling time	at school
	Teachers	administer study-skills assessment	group administration	in class
	Students	identify level of study skills	taking assessment measures	in class
Phase II	Administrators	support and promote program; contribute to the design of the program	providing resources, ideas and materials	at school
	Counselors, school psychologists	design the program's developmental component	planning content, methods and materials	at school
	Counselors school psychologists and learning specialists	consult with teachers on specific needs; train staff	developing and delivering staff training sessions; consultation	at school
	Teachers	participate in staff training	attending and being active in training sessions; communicating with specialists	at school
Phase III	Teachers	teach study skills and general self-management	classroom instruction	in class
	Students	learn study skills and general self-management	classroom instruction	in class
	Students	apply study skills and self-management	using what they have learned (practice)	at school and at home
Phase IV	LD & reading specialists; school psychologists, counselors	consult with teachers concerning special needs; organize the remedial component	meeting with teachers; planning for remediation	in school
	Counselors	intervene with students who have difficulty with self-management	individual counseling work	in school
Phase V	School personnel, students, parents	evaluate program	process and outcome evaluations; analysis of relevant data	at school
All phases	Parents	support program; reinforce important skills at home	becoming knowledgeable about the program; encouraging students; providing rewards & recognition	at home

Table 5.1 provides a summary outline of the phases and activities in a study-skills program. Phase I entails the assessment of student needs in the area of study skills and self-management. Phase II is program planning, design, and staff training. The implementation of the developmental and remedial components takes place during Phase III, and remediation occurs in Phase IV. Phase V, the final phase, is program evaluation.

A needs assessment should be conducted to determine the initial level of study and self-management skills present in the student population. All students should participate in the assessment, regardless of their level of academic achievement. This general form of assessment provides an overview of study skills for the entire school, helps to identify particular skills that are not being acquired adequately, and helps to identify students who could benefit from assistance. Specifically, the assessment is intended to identify the individual student's particular learning style, her or his study-skills deficits, and problems with self-management. A variety of assessment instruments, measures, and procedures are available. Several practical ones are described briefly.

Research shows that students' academic achievement, behavior, and attitudes all improve when learning-style preferences are recognized and addressed (Griggs, 1985). The Learning Style Inventory (R. Dunn, K. Dunn, & Price, 1978) is intended for use with students in grades 3 through 12, and takes about 35 minutes to administer. The instrument was normed on 1700 students in grades 3 through 12 who represented a variety of geographic regions. Kirby (1979) has reviewed the reliability and validity of this instrument and found it to be adequate.

Another tool for assessing learning style preference is the Swassing-Barbe Modality Index (Zaner-Bloser, Inc., 1979), which would most often be used with elementary school children, although it can also be used with preschoolers, older children, and adults. This index is individually administered and takes approximately fifteen minutes. Test–retest reliability is reported at $r = .60$ and above. The aim of this instrument is to identify the student's perceptual modality strengths (visual, auditory, or kinesthetic) so that strength-oriented techniques can be used in teaching study techniques.

The Survey of Study Habits and Attitudes (Brown & Holtzman, 1967) was created for students in grades 7 to 12 and in grades 12 to 14. This self-report instrument measures skills presently used by students. The test is divided into two sections: study habits, which include delay-avoidance and work methods; and study attitudes, which cover teacher approval and education acceptance. A score for each section is given, as well as an overall score, which is referred to as the study orientation. Test–retest reliabilities range from $r = .82$ to $r = .92$.

Strengths and deficits in study skills can also be assessed with the Cornell Learning and Study Skills Inventory (CLASS I), which Pauk and Cassel

(1971) designed for use with students in Grades 7 through 13 and in Grades 13 through 16. It covers goal orientation, activity structure, textbook mastery, examination mastery, scholarly skills, lecture mastery, and self-mastery. Test reliability is high ($r = .90$) and validity data are available (Pauk & Cassel, 1971).

Checklists of particular study skills are also useful measurement devices, especially for younger students, or when skills targeted by a particular intervention are not included in other standardized inventories. Checklists can be used easily by teachers, other school personnel, or by students themselves. Rogers (1984), for example, designed a checklist of study skills that assesses his model of "study–reading skills," on which students rated on their degree of skill (absent, low, or high).

As a part of the general needs assessment, information can be gathered about the self-management techniques presently being employed by students. Self-management includes such activities as time scheduling, planning, concentrating, staying focused on the task at hand, and managing anxiety. One way to gather information about this component is through examining the appropriate sections of Brown and Holtzman's (1967) Survey of Study Habits and Attitudes. Checklists may be particularly appropriate for assessing self-management skills, as these skills are not typically inventoried on standardized instruments.

The Test Anxiety Scale (Mandler & Sarason, 1952) can be used to assess this aspect of self-management. This paper-and-pencil test is comprised of 19 agree or disagree items and has reliabilities ranging from $r = .82$ to $r = .91$ (Tryon, 1980).

Anxiety may be manifest in a variety of ways, including physical symptoms (increased heart rate, tense muscles, increased motor activity) and cognitive signs (negative thinking). Anxiety related to academic performance and evaluation is often presented to teachers and parents indirectly in the form of headaches, stomach aches, absence from school, crying, or other similar avoidant behavior. It is important for teachers and parents to recognize that anxiety may be the central issue when a student consistently displays such behavior in testing or other evaluative situations. This type of information about students can be solicited from teachers and parents through checklists or feedback questionnaires.

Designing Study-Skills Training Programs

Following the needs assessment, the next step in designing a program to improve study skills is identification of what needs to be accomplished. These goals may vary from school to school and depend largely upon which student needs have been identified through assessment. Comprehensive study training is the responsibility of school personnel, students, and parents. Examples of overall program goals are (a) to help students to become more effective and more efficient learners, (b) to improve the academic performance of students, and (c) to increase student comfort and ability to demonstrate knowledge on tests. Within the school, specific goals can be established by a team that includes the school psychologist, counselor, learning specialist, administrator, and perhaps a parent.

Ideally, to be helpful to as many students as possible, a comprehensive program to improve study and self-management skills includes both a developmental component and a remedial component. The focus of the developmental component is to teach appropriate skills and techniques at all grade levels, whereas the remedial component targets those students who need additional attention in order to acquire and use these skills.

Once goals are established, it is appropriate to consider how these goals can be accomplished and to make decisions about a time frame for implementation of the program. In this regard, there are many questions and issues to be addressed, such as how the program will be delivered, by whom, where and when, what resources are needed (these include human resources, program materials, and financial resources), what staff training will be required and who will provide it, and how the support and approval of the school authorities (e.g., school board or superintendent of schools) and parents will be obtained.

Within the developmental component (see Table 5.1, Phase III), students at all grade levels are taught study skills and general self-management techniques. Classroom teachers trained in these skills can instruct students in their use, and must allow for the practice that is crucial to skill acquisition. Initially, many study skills are learned as students learn to read (Salinger, 1983). As content areas expand, the study skills that address the particular achievement needs of these areas should be learned in conjunction with them (Tabberer, 1984). Some of the specific study skills that can be presented to students are reading, rereading, taking notes (both in class from a lecture and outside class from textbooks and other material), underlining, making an outline, defining terms, listing key words, writing summaries of important concepts, explaining similarities and differences between ideas, asking aloud and answering questions about the topic being studied, test-wiseness, study techniques such as SQ3R, and reviewing notes.

The self-management aspect (Table 5.1, Phase III) covers such areas as managing anxiety, concentrating, and time management. Anxiety management includes strategies such as relaxation, rewarding oneself, and self-talk. Time management includes planning, scheduling, identifying optimal study times, dealing with delay-avoidance, increasing the amount of time spent on a task and efficient use of time. These strategies are to be presented to students in the same manner as the specific study techniques have been taught.

Once the initial implementation of the study techniques and

self-management program has been completed, teachers, students, and parents can begin to assess to what extent students are applying what they have learned in this process. For most students, learning about these skills will be sufficient, and they will begin to apply them. There will be students, however, for whom exposure to these skills is not enough. It is at this point that the process of identifying students who are having difficulty can begin. Referral to the remedial component of the study-skills program is appropriate at this time (Table 5.1, Phase IV), and specific problems can be dealt with on an individual or small-group basis.

Materials

Selecting appropriate materials for teaching study skills and self-management is an important aspect of training. It is important to have materials available that define and explain each technique or strategy, both for staff training and for student instruction. Selection or development of study-training materials is best accomplished through the work of a multidisciplinary committee comprised of staff and parents.

The materials described in this section are just a few of the wide variety of resources and materials available for review and selection. One program designed to help coordinate study training from grade to grade and to integrate study skills into the regular course curriculum as basic skills is the hm Study Skills Program. Level I is designed for use in grades 5 through 7, Level II is for Grades 8 to 10, and the hm Math Study Skills Program is for pre-algebra students. This program is the result of a curriculum development project begun in 1977 by educators from the Bureau of Study Counsel at Harvard University (from which they are available) and the Milton Academy. More recently, the National Association of Secondary School Principals (NASSP), the National Association of Elementary School Principals (NAESP), and the National Council of Teachers of Mathematics have joined the project. The materials are currently published by NASSP (1904 Association Dr., Reston, VA 22091) and NAESP (1920 Association Dr., Reston, VA 22091).

Some materials more appropriate for secondary level students from which skill lessons can be drawn include *Quest: Academic Skills Program*, developed at the University of Michigan Reading and Learning Skills Center (Cohen, King, Knudsvig, Markel, Patton, Shtogren, & Wilhelm, 1973) and the *Reading Skills Lab Program* (Houghton Mifflin Publishing Co., 1970). Examples of materials geared directly toward students are study skills books such as *Study Skills: A Student's Guide for Survival* (Carman & Adams, 1972) and *Study Skills for Success* (Saleebey, 1981). Materials discussed earlier that focus on test-wiseness and test-taking skills include Form Z (Ferrell, 1977). Also available are the Test-Making Activity (McPhail, 1981), the SCORER system (Carman & Adams, 1972), and the Time-Use Chart (McCabe, 1982). These aids can be used with high school students; the forms could be adapted for use with younger children.

Staff Training

Staff training is essential to the successful implementation of any aspect of study training. Administrators, school psychologists, teachers, peer tutors, reading specialists, and counselors must all have a clear and comprehensive understanding of study skills and self-management techniques. When teachers are involved in and aware of study-skills training approaches, they can offer structured opportunities for students to practice and develop these techniques (Tabberer, 1984). Parents can also play an important role, in reinforcement and support of skill development, if they are provided with the appropriate knowledge. The scheduling of special meetings, to inform parents and solicit their support for the program, is a good way to increase parental involvement.

Guidelines for Facilitating Implementation

The importance of administrative support for the program cannot be overstated. Since comprehensive study training requires a multidisciplinary effort, communication among professionals is important. Informal discussions, department meetings, staffings, faculty meetings, and questionnaires are some ways to facilitate communication (Sanacore, 1982). Team teaching and consultation are also effective methods for enhancing a multidisciplinary approach.

Regarding the remedial component, it is important to stay aware of issues involving ethical practice, such as confidentiality and informed consent. Counselors and school psychologists should implement only those procedures for which they have adequate training. Both students and parents should give permission for any individualized treatment, and be kept apprised of progress or difficulties. Any limits to the privacy of information should be made explicit.

Evaluation

Evaluation is an important part of every school program. It is important not only for determining the effectiveness of what has been done, but also for the value it has for revising goals and planning future programs. Evaluation can be accomplished in a variety of ways and can be conducted at several points in the program. Any evaluation strategies will, of course, be based on the goals and objectives of the study-training components, as well as on overall program goals. For example, a program goal of increased test-taking competence could have as its intended outcome an increase in standardized test scores.

As the study and self-management material is taught to students, teachers should evaluate briefly after each instructional session. This short evaluation could consist of making note of what material was covered, the teacher's sense of how the lesson went, and the reactions the teacher observed on the part of the students.

Posttesting on any of the instruments used in the initial assessment process is a very important means of evaluating progress in study training. If adequate baseline data have been collected during the program development phase, criteria such as performance on classroom tests or standardized achievement tests, and grades may be examined. It is important to build in strategies for evaluating program goals and objectives from the initial development phase, so that evaluation can be seen as an integral part of the program. *The Evaluator's Handbook* (Morris & Fitz-Gibbon, 1978) is a helpful and practical guide to developing program evaluations.

ANNOTATED BIBLIOGRAPHY

Markel, G. (1981). Improving test-taking skills of LD adolescents. *Academic Therapy, 16,* 333–342.

Identifies academic problems common to LD adolescents and procedures that can be used to solve these problems. The author presents five categories of skills: anxiety-management skills, interpersonal skills, problem-solving skills, study and test-taking skills, and self-management skills. Outlines specific difficulties in each category and provides recommendations for designing interventions. Educators and parents alike will find this information valuable.

Saleebey, W. M. (1981). *Study skills for success.* Black Hills, SD: National Publishers of the Black Hills.

Concise workbook suitable for an age range from junior high school students to adult. Explains major principles of effective studying in an easy-to-read style. Stresses responsibility for learning and discusses the crucial role of attitudes. Includes many practical suggestions that can be used by students, teachers, and parents.

Sarason, I. G. (Ed.). (1980). *Test anxiety: Theory, research, and applications.* Hillsdale, NJ: Erlbaum.

Addresses research, theory and their application to test anxiety. Test anxiety has become the most widely studied of the specific anxieties, and this source book contains theoretical frameworks for organizing knowledge about this phenomenon as well as clinical and educational applications for remediation.

Thompson, M. E. (1981). *Study habits: Advice to students, parents, and teachers from research data.* (Report No. CG–017–230).(ERIC Document Reproduction Service No. ED 239 183)

This guide is written for parents, teachers, and students. Main purpose is to help students identify and to understand their study problems. Presents and discusses considerable research in an easily understandable format. Provides specific suggestions for both parents and students to aid the resolution of study problems.

Towle, M. (1982). Learning how to be a student when you have a learning disability. *Journal of Learning Disabilities, 15* (2), 90–92.

Presents a four-step model of studying that applies to all grade levels. Within each step of this process are specific cognitive strategies that students can utilize. Analyzes the skills required for various forms of organizing information. Teachers and parents can use this model to assist students in the learning process.

REFERENCES

Allen, G. (1971). Effectiveness of study counseling and desensitization in alleviating test anxiety in college students. *Journal of Abnormal Psychology, 77*, 282–289.

Archer, J., Jr., & Neubauer, T. (1981). Study skills on a shoestring. *NASPA Journal, 18*(3), 48–52.

Barron, B. G., McCoy, J., Cuevas, P., Cuevas, S., & Rachal, G. (1983). Study skills: A new look. *Reading Improvement, 20*, 329–332.

Brown, W. F., & Holtzman, W. H. (1967) *Surveys of study habits and attitudes.* New York: Psychological Corporation.

Carman, R. A., & Adams, W. R. (1972). *Study skills: A student's guide for survival.* New York: Wiley.

Champlin, S. M., & Karoly, P. (1975). Role of contract negotiation in self-management of study time: A preliminary investigation. *Psychological Reports, 37* 724–726.

Cohen, R., King, W., Knudsvig, G., Markel, G. P., Patton, D., Shtogren, J., & Wilhelm, R. M. (1973). *Quest: Academic skills program.* New York: Harcourt Brace Jovanovich.

Dean, J. (1977). Study skills: Learning how to learn. *Education, 5*, 9–11.

Dean, M. R., Malott, R. W., & Fulton, B. (1983). The effects of self-management training on academic performance. *Teaching of Psychology, 10*(2), 77–81.

Diggs, V. M. (1973). The relative effectiveness of the SQ3R method: A mechanized approach and a combination method for teaching remedial reading to college freshmen (Doctoral dissertation, West Virginia University, 1972). *Dissertation Abstracts International, 33*, 5964A.

Donald, S. M. (1967). The SQ3R method in grade seven. *Journal of Reading, 11*, 33–35, 43.

Dunn, R., Dunn, K., & Price, G. E. (1978). *Learning style inventory manual.* Lawrence, KS: Price Systems.

Ferrell, G. (1977). *Development and use of a test of test-wiseness.* Paper presented at Western College Reading Association annual meeting, Denver, CO. (ERIC Document Reproduction Service No. ED 154 374)

Gaudry, E., & Spielberger, C. D. (1971). *Anxiety and educational achievement.* Sydney, Australia: Wiley.

Greiner, J. M., & Karoly, P. (1976). Effects of self control training on study activity and academic performance: An analysis of self-monitoring, self-reward, and systematic-planning components. *Journal of Counseling Psychology, 23*, 495–502.

Griggs, S. (1985). Counseling for individual learning styles. *Journal of Counseling and Development, 64*, 202–205.

Gurrola, S. (1975). Determination of the relative effectiveness and efficiency of selected combinations of SQ3R study method components (Doctoral dissertation, New Mexico State University, 1974). *Dissertations Abstracts International, 44*, 1042A.

Hill, K. T. (1972). Anxiety in the evaluative context. In W. W. Hartup, (Ed.), *The young child* (Vol. 2). Washington, DC: National Association for the Education of Young Children.

Katahn, M., Strenger, S., & Cherry, N. (1966). Group counseling and behavior therapy with test anxious college students. *Journal of Counseling Psychology, 30*, 544–549.

Kirby, P. (1979). *Cognitive style, learning style, and transfer skill acquisition.* Columbus, OH: National Center for Research in Vocational Education, Ohio State University.

Lingren, H. C. (1969). *The psychology of college success.* New York: Wiley.

Mandler, G., & Sarason, S. (1952). A study of anxiety and learning. *Journal of Abnormal & Social Psychology, 47*, 166–173.

Markel, G. (1981). Improving test-taking skills of LD adolescents. *Academic Therapy, 16*(3), 333–342.

Marshak, D., & Burkle, C. R. (1981). Learning to study: A basic skill. *Principal, 61*(2), 38–40.

McAndrew, D. (1983). Underlining and notetaking: Some suggestions from research. *Journal of Reading, 27*(2), 103–108.

McCabe, D. (1982). Developing study skills: The LD high school student. *Academic Therapy, 18*, 197–201.

McManus, C. (1971). Group desensitization of text anxiety. *Behavior Research & Therapy, 9*, 51–56.

McPhail, I. (1981). Why teach test-wiseness? *Journal of Reading, 25,* 32–38.

Miller, A., & Gimpl, M. P. (1972). Operant verbal self-control of studying. *Psychological Reports, 30,* 495–498.

Millman, J., Bishop, C. H., & Ebel, R. (1965). An analysis of test-wiseness. *Educational and Psychological Measurement, XXV*(3), 707–726.

Mitchell, K., & Ng, K. (1972). Effects of group counseling and behavior therapy on the academic achievement of test anxious students. *Journal of Counseling Psychology, 19,* 491–497.

Moore, J. C. Schutz, R. E., & Baker, R. L. (1966). The application of a self-instruction technique to develop a test-taking strategy. *American Education Research Journal, III,* 13–17.

Morris, L., & Fitz-Gibbon, C. (1978). *Evaluator's handbook.* Beverly Hills, CA: Sage.

Pauk, W., & Cassel, R. (1971) *Manual for the Cornell Learning and Study Skills Inventory.* Jacksonville, IL: Psychologists and Educators Press.

Phillips, B. N. (1978) *School stress and anxiety.* New York: Human Sciences Press.

Richards, C. S., McReynolds, W. T., Holt, S., & Sexton, T. (1976). The effects of information feedback and self-administered consequences on self-monitoring study behavior. *Journal of Counseling Psychology, 23,* 316–321.

Robinson, F. P. (1961). *Effective study* (rev. ed.). New York: Crowell.

Robyak, J. E., & Downey, R. G. (1979). A discriminant analysis of the study skills and personality types of underachieving and nonunderachieving study skills students. *Journal of College Student Personnel, 20,* 306–309.

Rogers, D. (1984). Assessing study skills. *Journal of Reading, 27*(4), 346–354.

Ruebush, B. K. (1963). Anxiety. In H. W. Stevenson, J. Kagan, & C. Spiker (Eds.), *Sixty-Second Yearbook of the National Society for the Study of Education, Part I: Child Psychology.* Chicago: University of Chicago Press.

Saleebey, W. M. (1981) *Study skills for success.* Black Hills, SD: National Publishers of the Black Hills.

Salinger, T. (1983). Study skills: A "basic" in elementary reading instruction. *Reading Improvement, 20*(4), 333–337.

Sanacore, J. (1982). Transferring SPQ4R—study procedure: Administrative concerns. *The Clearing House, 55,* 234–236.

Sarason, I. (Ed.). (1980) *Test anxiety: Theory, research, and applications.* Hillsdale, NJ: Erlbaum.

Slakter, M., Koehler, R., & Hampton, S. (1970 Summer). Grade level, sex, and selection aspects of test-wiseness. *Journal of Educational Measurement, VII,* 119–22.

Tabberer, R. (1984). Introducing study skills at 16 to 19. *Educational Research, 26,* 1–6.

Thompson, M. E. (1981). *Study habits: Advice to students, parents and teachers from research data* (ERIC Document Reproduction Service No. ED 239 183).

Tichenor, J. L. (1977). Self-monitoring and self-reinforcement of studying by college students. *Psychological Reports, 40,* 103–108.

Towle, M. (1982). Learning how to be a student when you have a learning disability. *Journal of Learning Disabilities, 15*(2), 90–93.

Tryon, G. (1980). The measurement and treatment of test anxiety. *Review of Educational Research, 50*(2), 243–272.

Wilmore, D. J. (1966). A comparison of four methods of studying a college textbook (Doctoral dissertation, University of Minnesota, 1966). *Dissertation Abstracts International, 27,* 2413A–2414A.

Wooster, G. F. (1958). Teaching the SQ3R method of study: An investigation of the instructional approach (Doctoral dissertation, The Ohio State University, 1958). *Dissertation Abstracts International, 18,* 2067A–2068A.

Zaner-Bloser, Inc. (1979). *The Swassing-Barbe Modality Index: Directions for administration and scoring.* Columbus, OH: Author.

6 Peer-Influenced Academic Interventions

JANICE A. MILLER and DAVID W. PETERSON[1]

The primary focus of many school interventions is to accommodate the differing instructional needs of all the students within a single classroom. While these interventions commonly involve adult-directed interactions with students, emphasis in this chapter will be on student-to-student interactions designed to promote academic-skills acquisition. The term *peer-influenced academic interventions* represents a variety of structured interactions between two or more students, designed or planned by a school staff member, to achieve academic (primary) and social–emotional (secondary) goals. Although other peer-influenced interventions are utilized in school settings (e.g., peer counseling), this chapter focuses upon interventions designed primarily to increase academic performance. The common feature among these instructional interventions is the increased opportunity for instruction and assistance from and to peers. For example, in cross-age or peer tutoring, helping and teaching behaviors are often explicitly programmed and the learning of an individual student is emphasized. In cooperative learning, another alternative, specific helping behaviors can also be trained or rewarded, but the emphasis is on the simultaneous learning of individual students, mediated by the achievement of group goals or group rewards.

The effectiveness of both peer tutoring and cooperative learning has been well established through applied research (e.g., Cohen, Kulik, & Kulik, 1982; Johnson & Johnson, 1978), while practical use of these methods is also supported by allocated learning time research (Rossenshine & Berliner, 1978). Moreover, increased achievement has been correlated with instructional settings in which students are actively engaged in academic tasks with a high rate of success (Fisher et al., 1978; Greenwood & Delquardi, 1982). Peer-influenced interventions can allow for many student-response opportunities and can be structured to assure that the content of the curriculum is at the student's instructional level.

Peer tutoring and cooperative learning may also be effective in

[1] Both authors contributed equally to the preparation of this chapter.
Grateful appreciation is extended to Julie Phelps for assistance in preparation of this chapter.

prereferral intervention systems to prevent inappropriate special education placements (Graden, Casey, & Christensen, 1985). Because a major element in these peer-mediated interventions is the use of peers in teaching roles, there may be less need to refer students to special education programs in order to meet their instructional needs. An additional advantage of peer-influenced interventions may be that once teachers learn how to implement peer tutoring or cooperative learning strategies, they can apply this knowledge across a broad range of curriculum areas. Also, consultation to support implementation of these interventions can be provided by a variety of school personnel including school psychologists, school social workers, counselors, special and remedial teachers, and other regular education teachers.

Peer-mediated interventions may also facilitate the mainstreaming of handicapped students into less restrictive settings (Ballard, Corman, Gottlieb, & Kaufman, 1977; Cooper, Johnson, Johnson, & Wilderson, 1980). Teachers can use these student-to-student learning structures to provide appropriate academic instruction and practice. These structures can provide students opportunities to develop and to practice social and problem-solving skills.

This chapter defines and describes cross-age and peer tutoring as well as various models of cooperative learning. First, conceptual and theoretical bases of these student-to-student interactions are discussed and relevant research highlighted. Next are discussed the variables that should be considered in planning and selecting an appropriate peer-influenced intervention, given specific goals and student populations. Then, the implementation steps and associated problems of peer and cross-age tutoring as well as cooperative learning methods are presented. Also described is an approach to the evaluation of peer tutoring and cooperative learning strategies. Finally, an annotated bibliography identifies further sources of information regarding these interventions.

THEORY AND RESEARCH ON PEER-INFLUENCED ACADEMIC INTERVENTIONS

Cooperative Learning

Cooperative learning includes a variety of methods used to structure student-to-student academic interactions within a classroom. The more common cooperative learning methods are summarized in Table 6.1. In some methods students are required or encouraged to work together to achieve a common goal (e.g., Learning Together, Jigsaw, and Group Investigation). In other cooperative learning methods, students may not work together on the same task, but they are rewarded for their achievements based on the performances of each member of their group (e.g., team-assisted individualization). Finally, there are cooperative learning methods in which students work together on a common task and are rewarded based on individual group members' performances (e.g., Student Teams: Achievement Division, Teams-Games-Tournaments, and Jigsaw II). Two components, the group task and the group-based reward, differentiate cooperative learning structures from other types of instructional arrangements typically observed in classrooms.

TABLE 6.1 Summary Description of Cooperative Learning Methods

Student Teams: Achievement Division (STAD) (Slavin, 1978)

Four to five students are assigned to heterogeneous learning teams. The teacher introduces the material to be learned and then provides study worksheets to team members. Students study the material with their team members until everyone understands the material. Next, students take individual quizzes, but the scores are used to compute a team score. The contribution each student can make to the team score is based on improvement as compared with past quiz averages. High-scoring teams and high-performing students are recognized in a weekly class newsletter.

Teams—Games—Tournaments (TGT) (DeVries, Slavin, Fennessey, Edwards, & Lombardo, 1980)

This method of cooperative learning uses the same team structure and instructional format as in STAD. In addition, students play in weekly tournament games with students of comparable ability from other teams in the classroom. Assignments are changed every week, with the high and low scorers of each table moved to the next highest or lowest table respectively in order to maintain fair competition. Students can contribute to their team score based on their performance in the weekly tournaments. Again, a class newsletter is used to recognize high-scoring teams and individual tournament winners.

Team Assisted Individualization (TAI) (Slavin, Leavy, & Madden, 1982)

In TAI, the focus is on mathematics instruction. Heterogeneous teams of 4 to 5 students are formed. Based on a diagnostic test, each student is given an individually prescribed set of materials. For each unit, students read an instruction sheet, complete skillsheets, take checkouts, and finally take a test. Working in pairs, students check each other's worksheets and checkouts. When a checkout has been passed with a score of 80% or better, the student takes the test and the results are scored by a student monitor. Teams receive certificates for exceeding preset standards on the tests and for completing units.

Jigsaw (Aronson, 1978)

Students are assigned to six-member teams and each team member is given one section of a five-part academic unit. Two students share a section as a precaution in case of absenteeism. Expert groups are composed of team members from different groups who share the same academic material. The expert groups meet to discuss their material before returning to teach it to their group. After being taught each section by the team members, students take individual quizzes and are graded on their performance on the quiz.

Jigsaw II (Slavin, 1980)

In this modification of Jigsaw, students are formed into four- to five-member heterogeneous teams. Every student studies all of the material, but is given a section in which to become an expert. As in the original Jigsaw, students meet in expert groups, teach their fellow team members, and take individual quizes. However, individual scores are computed based on improvements and these become a group score. A class newsletter is used to recognize high-scoring teams and individuals.

Learning Together (Johnson & Johnson, 1975)

Students work in four- to five-member heterogeneous teams on assignment sheets. A single product from the group is expected and the group members may self-evaluate how well they worked together as a group at the end of the session. The teacher's role is to monitor the groups and

Table 6.1 continued

praise the students when they demonstrate cooperative behavior. In some applications of this method there is an incentive system incorporated, such as group grades.

Group Investigation (Sharan & Sharan, 1976)

In this method, students self-select their cooperative group of two to six members. The group chooses a topic from a unit being studied by the class and then decides who will study and prepare information on subtopics of the unit for a final report. Students are encouraged to use a variety of materials, engage in discussion with each other, and seek information from many sources. The groups present their projects to the class, and evaluation of the group and/or individuals is completed.

Cooperative learning methods are often contrasted to individual and competitive learning structures (Johnson & Johnson, 1975). An individual learning structure is one in which a student works alone and the evaluation and rewards assigned to the student's performance are independent of how other students in the class perform. As an example of an individualistic learning structure, a teacher gives students a math worksheet to complete as independent seatwork, and rewards with a star any student who completes it with 90% accuracy.

In a competitive learning structure, however, a student again works alone, but the evaluation and rewards assigned to the student's performance are mitigated by those given to other students' performance. For example, given the math seatwork activity just mentioned, the instructional setting would change to a competitive one if the teacher gave a star only to the student who had the most accurate paper.

Empirical research has been conducted to compare the relative effects of various cooperative learning methods—in contrast to more traditional competitive and individualistic learning situations—on such measures as achievement, intergroup relationships, self-esteem, locus of control, time on–task, liking of class, feelings about classmates, and perspective taking. The most attention, however, has been given to studying the effects of cooperative learning methods on student achievement.

Achievement outcomes

In a meta-analysis of 122 studies, Johnson, Maruyama, Johnson, Nelson, and Skon (1981) compared the effects of cooperative, competitive, and individualistic instructional settings on student achievement and productivity. Their results indicated the superiority of cooperative learning methods, either with or without competition among cooperative groups, over either competitive or individualistic structures. They found the results applicable to all subject areas, age groups, and for any task other than one requiring rote-decoding and correcting skills.

However, Slavin (1980 a & b, 1983) viewed the relationship between cooperative structuring and achievement as more complex. The suggested examination of the following components:

1. *Type of task*: How cognitively complex is the task?
2. *Group rewards*: Is a reward or recognition given based on individual learning and not just on the completion of a group product?
3. *Task specialization*: Are students required to share their information or to instruct their fellow group members?
4. *Group competition*: Are cooperative groups competing with each other for reward or recognition?
5. *Equal-opportunity scoring*: Are all students of varying ability levels in the group able to contribute to the group's total score?

Following his examination of field studies on cooperative learning, Slavin (1980 a & b, 1983) enumerated the components that are most strongly related to achievement.

1. On lower level tasks, the incorporation of individual accountability and a group-reward system improves academic performance, whereas on higher level cognitive tasks, less structured, more student-autonomous structures may be more effective in increasing achievement.
2. In general, the assignment of group rewards based on individual learning in cooperative groups increases achievement more than individual or competitive structures.
3. Competition among cooperative groups is one way to provide a basis for group rewards that improve student performance.
4. In cooperative learning structures, the achievement of blacks and Hispanics improves more than that of whites.

In contrast, Slavin found that the results of studies that examined the effects of task specialization and of equal-opportunity scoring on achievement have been inconclusive or inconsistent.

Slavin (1983) proposed theoretical models to explain how the group structure and the reward system may affect academic performance. He posited that it is the cooperative reward structure, that is, the provision of group rewards based on individual learning, and not the group structure or the process of student interaction in groups, that primarily is responsible for achievement effects. Because students are rewarded for their efforts, they are more motivated to perform and thus their achievement increases.

Most current research strongly supports Slavin's position, but more examination of the role that student interaction within cooperative groups has on achievement is needed. Webb (1982) suggested that student interaction may be an important variable to consider in understanding the relationship between achievement and cooperative structuring. For example, she reported that giving help was positively correlated with greater achievement, but that the effects of receiving help were more complex.

Students who received explanations from other students in response to their requests demonstrated greater achievement, but those who were given answers without explanation or who did not receive help in response to their request for assistance demonstrated lower achievement.

Social-emotional outcomes

Regardless of the cooperative learning method used, racially heterogeneous groups of students working collaboratively promoted long-lasting, cross-ethnic friendships. Although there has been concern that cooperative grouping might highlight performance differences and negate positive interrelationships, studies have not provided a basis for this concern (Sharan, 1980).

Cooperative learning methods have also been used to integrate mainstreamed handicapped students into regular classrooms. Field studies have indicated positive effects on cross-handicap relationships and achievement of normal class peers (Johnson & Johnson, 1980). Further, the effects of cooperative learning methods on self-esteem, locus of control, time on task, liking of class or school, feelings about classmates, and perspective taking have been evaluated. Overall, the studies indicate the positive impact of all cooperative learning methods on these variables (Slavin, 1980 a & b, 1983).

Based on the research cited, it is clear that cooperative learning methods can achieve both academic and nonacademic goals. Further research is needed to determine whether there are differences in results that are dependent on the characteristics of the students or the characteristics of the class, on the subject area being taught, or on which components of cooperative learning are employed. More data are also necessary to assess noncognitive outcomes. Finally, further study may clarify the long-term benefits of various cooperative learning methods (Slavin, 1983)

Peer and Cross-Age Tutoring

Similar to cooperative learning, peer and cross-age tutoring programs utilize reciprocal interaction among students as the primary vehicle for the delivery of academic instruction. In contrast to cooperative learning, peer and cross-age tutoring interventions accomplish instructional goals within structured dyads in which one student serves as the instructor (tutor) and the other as the learner (tutee). The tutor provides regularly scheduled instruction to the tutee, usually on a daily basis, using materials and procedures prepared by those responsible for implementing the program (e.g., teacher, school psychologist, resource teacher). The tutee's progress is measured regularly, and tutors are carefully trained and monitored to ensure appropriate teaching behaviors.

The theoretical foundations of peer and cross-age tutoring are diverse, and no unifying theoretical framework is readily evident from the literature. The lack of a framework may well limit the cohesiveness of existing research (Devin-Sheehan, Feldman, & Allen, 1976). However, several authors have discussed the interactional aspects of the tutor–tutee relationship, applying social identify theory (Sarbin, 1976), ethological perspectives (Hartup, 1976), and verbal-learning research (Annis, 1983). Cohen (1986), in an analysis of peer and cross-age tutoring, examined motivational, social, and teaching processes as well as their implications for program implementation. Recent research in instructional effectiveness and academic-engaged time (Rosenshine & Berliner, 1978) may offer fruitful bases for analysis of the effectiveness of different tutoring models. Social learning theory and research on modeling also offer explanatory constructs to guide future research.

Studies of various dimensions of tutoring have examined the effects of different program structures, the impact of varying tutor and tutee characteristics (e.g., age and sex differentials within pairs, handicapped vs. nonhandicapped) and, most important, the academic and affective benefits of different types of programs. Several major reviews of the research on peer and cross-age tutoring have been conducted. Cohen, Kulik, and Kulik (1982) reported results of a meta-analysis of 65 methodologically sound studies, and concluded that peer, and cross-tutoring programs have substantial and positive effects on both achievement and attitude toward subject matter for both tutees and tutors. This effect was somewhat stronger in mathematics than in reading. They also reported that the studies did not demonstrate significant changes in self-concept for either tutors or tutees. In addition, greater benefits were found in more highly structured programs, a finding confirmed in a review conducted by Rosenshine and Furst (1969).

Devin-Sheehan et al. (1976) reviewed structured versus unstructured tutoring programs and a number of personal characteristics that affect tutoring outcomes. They found that tutoring programs of varying structure produced significant academic gains in tutees and gains of a lesser degree in tutors. However, confident generalizations regarding the effect of sex, age, and skill differences within tutoring dyads on program effectiveness were not possible. In addition, because of insufficient data, generalizations were not made regarding the relationship of socioeconomic status and ethnic affiliation to tutoring outcomes. Other research assessing age and skill differences within tutoring dyads suggested that tutors who are older and more academically competent than their tutees may be more effective (Linton, 1973). Although studies comparing peer and cross-age tutoring with other forms of instruction are rare, some tutoring programs have demonstrated superiority over teacher-led interventions (Jenkins, Mayhall, Peschka, & Jenkins, 1974).

The benefits of tutoring for handicapped populations have also been demonstrated. Scruggs and Richter (1985) reviewed 22 studies that used learning-disabled, and in some cases, behavior-disordered students as both tutors and tutees. They concluded that tutoring was a powerful intervention in promoting academic gains with these populations, but reported that hard evidence regarding affective benefits was less compelling. Little conclusive research regarding the effectiveness of tutoring relative to other interventions is available for special populations.

Many studies on peer and cross-age tutoring have been criticized because of technical or methodological failings (Devin-Sheehan et al., 1976). However, existing research has clearly established that peer and cross-age tutoring can result in significant academic gain in a relatively cost-effective fashion (Maher, 1986). Although most studies are conducted in the schools and do not readily lend themselves to vigorous research designs (Scruggs & Richter, 1985), future research efforts need to identify and to isolate the critical variables that contribute the most to successful tutoring programs (Feldman, Devin-Sheehan, & Allen, 1976), and to examine in more detail the process components of tutor–tutee interaction (Kalfus, 1984). More conclusive information is also needed in regard to the affective and social benefits of tutoring (Scruggs & Richter, 1985), its relative effects in comparison with other interventions, the differing effects of tutoring on different types of student populations, and the extent to which student gains are generalized over time into other settings. Maher (1986) also identified the need to determine the organizational and ecological variables that promote effective tutoring programs.

GUIDELINES FOR PLANNING AND IMPLEMENTING PEER-INFLUENCED ACADEMIC INTERVENTIONS

Program Planning

The planning and implementation of peer-influenced academic interventions should be completed within the context of the entire educational services system. Successful implementation may well be dependent upon a thorough and reliable assessment of student and staff needs, as well as an assessment of a variety of organizational variables.

The first step in program planning involves conducting a needs assessment to determine instructional goals. In this regard, specific questions that are important to address include: What students require additional instruction? How many are involved and at what grade levels? What specific skill deficits do they have? In what skills do they require additional instruction? Are these needs a result of skill or performance deficits? Data to answer these questions are available through means such as curriculum-based assessments (Deno, 1985; Glickling & Havertape, 1981), reviews of standardized test results, evaluations of daily work, and from observations by the students' teachers.

The needs of teachers and other support staff who may be involved in program implementation also require assessment. What additional resources do they feel are needed for target students? What level of information do they have about peer-influenced interventions, and what kinds of resources (e.g., time) are they willing to commit? The extent to which the planned intervention responds to needs identified by school staff may well influence the eventual success or failure of the program.

Finally, the readiness of the organization (school, district, or agency) in which the interventions may be implemented should be considered as a part of the needs assessment. How willing are administrators to commit personnel and fiscal resources? Will parents be supportive of the program? What obstacles to successful program implementation exist, and how can these be dealt with? Administrators or parents who lack information about peer tutoring and/or cooperative learning may inadvertently view them as detracting from the basic academic program and will need to receive information regarding the potential benefits. Maher and Bennett (1984) outlined a systematic method of assessing the organizational readiness of school systems that enables the planner to conduct a thorough review of relevant system variables and to design appropriate program components.

The next step in program planning involves the establishment of program goals and objectives. Unless goals are clearly established, implementation of the program will be hampered by a lack of clear understanding as to what the program is designed to accomplish. Depending upon the results of the preceding needs assessment, goals may address student achievement needs and behavioral and affective issues. Goal specification not only assures a solid foundation for program development, but also enables program planners to design evaluation activities that will enable them to assess the impact of the intervention on students, staff, and the school.

Finally, the decision to select either a cooperative learning or a peer or cross-age tutoring intervention should be based upon an analysis of the goals established for the interventions, the learning and affective needs of the target students, the type of academic tasks to be taught, and the number of students to be involved. For example, if an entire class of students needs to acquire a specific set of skills, a cooperative learning intervention might be recommended, rather than peer or cross-age tutoring, because of the former's greater time efficiency. Conversely, if only a few students require additional instruction, peer or cross-age tutoring may be the intervention of choice.

Highly structured academic tasks involving considerable drill and practice (sight word reading, math facts) readily lend themselves to peer tutoring formats, while more complex tasks that involve higher-order cognitive skills may be better suited for cooperative learning programs. Both peer tutoring and cooperative learning interventions have been demonstrated to provide affective as well as academic gains for participants. However, the research literature provides little guidance in choosing between cooperative learning and peer tutoring, and those who plan interventions are advised to examine the instructional and affective needs of the identified student populations and to match these with the interventions they determine to be most likely to produce the desired results.

Implementing Cooperative Learning Programs

Before implementing a cooperative structure, consideration should be given to a number of issues. These include supporting the introduction and maintenance of cooperative learning methods in a classroom; selecting the most appropriate method; encouraging helping behaviors among students; promoting individual accountability within a cooperative group; and determining group composition and size.

Introduction and maintenance

The effective implementation of cooperative learning methods requires a change by staff members in their role, from that of providing direct teaching to students to that of directing requests for assistance and support back to the group. If student interdependence is to be achieved, staff members must view their role as that of facilitator and monitor of the group process. Moskowitz, Malvin, Schaeffer and Schaps (1983), in their evaluation of the implementation of Jigsaw (see Table 6.1) in elementary classrooms, hypothesized that such a role change may be very difficult for many teachers. Consequently, teachers implementing these approaches may make modifications that negate the integrity of the method. Staff self-selection in implementing cooperative learning methods, on-site consultation and support from consultants and special services providers may lessen this problem.

Selecting a cooperative learning method

The selection of a cooperative learning method to use in the classroom is dependent on the subject matter studied, the complexity of the material, and the maturity of the students. Cooperative learning methods that involve group study of a topic have been used primarily in content areas such as social studies or science, and for tasks that include activities at the higher cognitive levels of Bloom's (1964) taxonomy (e.g., interpretation, synthesis, and application of knowledge). In contrast, more explicit peer tutoring has generally been applied to curriculum areas in which the content is more prescribed by the teacher, and in which the emphasis is on the acquisition of basic skills and information. Because of the differences in the degree of structure and control provided by the teacher in each of these types of cooperative learning methods, the group investigation approach may be especially useful for more mature learners, whereas the peer tutoring methods can be applied at all grade levels.

Encouraging helping behaviors among students

There is a variety of ways to encourage students to assist each other. Slavin (1983) suggested that helping behaviors can be promoted by structuring the task so that peer tutoring is encouraged or is inherent in the task. For example, in Jigsaw (see Table 6.1) students become experts on one aspect of the task and teach their fellow team members so that they are prepared for individual quizzes. This task specialization can be used on tasks that can be broken into subtasks. In social studies, science, or literature, students may self-select a subtopic to learn or study. Upon completion of their individual studies, they would share their information with the other members of their group or combine their information with that of others into a final group report. The advantage of task specialization is that it increases interdependence among group members.

In other cooperative learning methods, helping behavior may be facilitated by highlighting the group's goals and the means of achieving them. Staff who implement the program should specify the group goals and the criterion-referenced evaluation system that will be the basis of the group reward. It is important to emphasize that the goal of working together in cooperative groups is not only to accomplish the task, but also to promote effective collaboration. Helping behavior in groups can be encouraged and facilitated by assigning specific activity roles within the group, by monitoring student interactions, by scheduling time at the end of the task for the group to discuss their interaction, and by rewarding groups for productive group behavior (Johnson & Johnson, 1978).

Promoting individual accountability among students

One goal of using cooperative learning methods is to encourage interdependence and helping behavior among students, but it is also important to structure the learning process to ensure that individual students are learning as well. A cooperative group may be very productive as the result of the efforts of one or more group members, and yet the individual learning of each of its members may or may not be enhanced through cooperative structuring of the task. In order to counteract this problem, Slavin (1983) suggested that it is important to establish and maintain a group norm toward continuing individual performance. It is important to make individual contributions visible, thus allowing other members of the group to monitor individual performance. This monitoring can occur in a cooperative group by acknowledging the individual's contribution to the group project. Individual efforts can also be quantified, such as in Teams —Games—Tournaments (Table 6.1), in which an individual earns points through competition with students from other cooperative groups.

Making the group reward-dependent on the efforts or contributions of each member also increases the likelihood that all members of the group will be encouraged or pressed to perform. The implementor of the cooperative learning method can establish the criteria for the group reward in a variety of ways. The criteria can include individual learning outcomes, (e.g., everyone in the group has to achieve 80% accuracy), some kind of aggregation of individual efforts (e.g., an average of individual improvement of scores, the assignment of a group grade based on the average of the three lowest individual grades, etc.), or each member's contribution to the final group product. Whatever criteria are selected, it is important to ensure that every member of the group has a reasonable opportunity to contribute to the group's final score or evaluation. It is for this reason that individual improvement scores are often selected as at least part of the total evaluation system used to determine the group's reward.

Determining group composition and size

The number of students assigned to each group should be determined by the age or cooperative experience of the students, with younger or less experienced students initially assigned to smaller groups. Groups should be as heterogeneous as possible, and random assignment may help to ensure this type of composition (Johnson & Johnson, 1978).

Implementing Peer and Cross-Age Tutoring Programs

Careful consideration of important program components will help to assure the success of peer and cross-age tutoring programs. Such program components include program supervision and management; determination of lesson content and format; scheduling of the sessions; selection of tutors and tutees to establish working pairs; training the tutors; and developing procedures for program monitoring and maintenance.

Program management and supervision

The first task in implementing a peer or cross-age tutoring program involves designating the person or persons who will be responsible for managing and supervising the program. If the program is to be implemented in one classroom, the teacher of that class may well be the obvious choice. If the intervention involves coordinating responsibilities among a number of classrooms, consideration may be given to choosing an educational professional such as a school psychologist, social worker, or special education resource teacher to serve as the manager. If tasks are to be shared among several staff, it is important to specify staff responsibilities in order to avoid duplication or confusion.

Management responsibilities involve ongoing program maintenance tasks and daily supervision and evaluation of tutors. Maintenance responsibilities include scheduling, securing appropriate tutors and tutees and matching them into compatible pairs, collating student performance data, and keeping administrators and others with an investment in the program regularly apprised of its status. The program manager may wish to provide brief weekly status reports to school staff.

Daily supervision is especially important and can include direct supervision of tutor–tutee pairs in order to provide praise for appropriate teaching and on-task behaviors, to model appropriate teaching behaviors, and to provide immediate assistance when problems arise. Tutoring programs that use such supervision have been shown to be more effective than those that do not provide structured supervision (Mayhall et al., 1975). If possible, the program supervisor should circulate among the tutor–tutee pairs to facilitate the teaching process and provide assistance if questions or problems arise. On-site supervisors can also assist in daily collection of data on student progress by monitoring tutor assessment activities and compiling tutee performance data.

Determining lesson content and format

Lesson content should be directly related to the specific objectives established when the program was designed. When possible, lessons should be derived from or directly related to the curriculum and academic tasks taught regularly in the classroom. This may well facilitate generalization, and increase the likelihood that tutees will maintain the skills that they acquire during tutoring sessions in other academic settings (Jenkins & Jenkins, 1985).

Peer or cross-age tutoring should provide added instruction, repetition, or practice in materials currently being studied, or clarification of concepts (Jenkins & Jenkins, 1985). Tasks should be chosen to reinforce materials currently being presented. Drill and practice tasks are especially suited to young children, but almost any material is adaptable to a peer tutoring format. Particularly with young children, attempts should be made to structure tasks as much as possible, and lesson content should be specified and should be prepared ahead of time.

Scheduling sessions

The scheduling of tutoring sessions involves consideration of practical issues, including existing classroom schedules and the availability of tutors and tutees, and involves research on the length and frequency of sessions.

Sessions need to be scheduled so that they do not disrupt the existing instructional program and, if possible, they should be arranged to enable the program monitor to circulate among the pairs during the sessions. Although efforts should be made to minimize conflicts with preexisting activities, the program manager should recognize that tutees have special needs and may profit more from the increased instructional time afforded to them in peer tutoring than from traditional seatwork.

While empirical investigation of scheduling variables is limited, available studies suggest that daily 30-minute sessions may be more effective than less frequent sessions (Mayhall & Jenkins, 1977). The length of the sessions should, of course, also be based upon observations of the tutees' ability to remain on task. Experience suggests that primary-age students profit from daily sessions and can remain on task for sessions of up to 20 minutes in length.

Selecting tutors, tutees, and establishing compatible pairs

When the program's goals are primarily academic in nature, older students of at least average ability who are academically competent in the subject matter to be caught can be selected as tutors (Ehly, 1986; Jenkins & Jenkins, 1981). However, the diversity of the academic skills of tutors, as reported in the literature, and the successful use of learning-disabled tutors indicates that academic competence need not be an ironclad criterion for selection (Scruggs & Osguthorpe, 1986). If the tutors selected have skill deficits in the subject areas to be taught, it is suggested that they tutor younger students in order to minimize the effect of subject-matter deficits (Jenkins & Jenkins, 1981).

Some authors have suggested that interest and social characteristics represent the most important considerations in tutor selection (Ehly, 1986). Tutors who demonstrate sensitivity, responsibility, appropriate social skills, and the ability to remain on task will be able to master and maintain necessary tutoring skills. However, research is at best equivocal on this matter, and if tutor availability or program goals require utilization of less socially adept tutors, the program can be attempted if tutor training is highly structured and the tutors' skills are carefully monitored during implementation.

Selection of tutees should be based primarily on the match between the planned program's instructional content and potential target students' needs. Successful programs have involved tutees of a wide range of ages (primary grades through college) and abilities. Students with poor attending skills and inappropriate social behaviors may be less likely to succeed, but programs that include such students have been successful (Scruggs & Osguthorpe, 1986).

Tutor training

The effectiveness of peer and cross-age tutoring programs is at least partially dependent upon the quality of training provided to the tutors (Harrison, 1976; Osguthorpe & Harrison, 1976). It is also clear, especially with younger tutors, that provision of a structured training program can help to assure that tutors use effective instructional techniques and that they avoid teaching behaviors that discourage progress and that hamper positive social interactions.

A number of authors have described important considerations and specific components of an effective tutoring program (Deterline, 1970; Ehly, 1986, Ehly & Larsen, 1980; Jenkins & Jenkins, 1981, 1985; Lippit, 1976; Pierce, Stahlbrand, & Armstrong, 1984). These authors suggest that the tutor be able to:

1. Locate, organize, and use efficiently the prepared tutoring materials;
2. Secure and maintain the tutee's attention during the tutoring sessions;
3. Provide concise directions and clear expectations for the tutee's behavior and for learning expected during the sessions;
4. Provide tutee with clear directions for responses;
5. Provide contingent verbal praise for correct responses and intermittent tangible reinforcers when appropriate;
6. Utilize consistent and effective error-correction procedures (for example, modeling, leading, and testing);
7. Avoid punishing interactions during tutoring;
8. Use cues, shaping, and prompting appropriately to encourage correct responses;
9. Assess tutee mastery or a lesson or of a unit of instruction.
10. Maintain accurate records regarding tutee progress; and
11. Allocate time effectively during tutoring sessions.

The duration of training sessions will vary based upon the skills tutors have already acquired, the tutors' ages, and the complexity of the material to be taught. Training should include careful explanation of the tutoring process and of the supervisor's expectations, modeling of appropriate tutoring behaviors, and role playing with feedback to enhance acquisition of the competencies listed above.

EVALUATING PEER-INFLUENCED ACADEMIC INTERVENTIONS

Evaluation of peer-influenced academic interventions can include assessment of student achievement; measurement of affective variables; evaluation of group process data; collection of information on teacher/ administrator/parent satisfaction; examination of cost-effectiveness information; and determination of the extent to which different program components have been implemented and maintained. The focus of evaluation activities upon each of these variables depends, naturally, upon the program's goals and objectives, the scope of the project, and the resources available to conduct the evaluation.

At a minimum, both peer tutoring and cooperative learning interventions should include an assessment of student achievement. Although a number of studies report traditional norm-referenced achievement data, it is important to use direct, and if possible, daily measurements of academic skills closely related to the material being taught (Jenkins & Jenkins, 1985). Carver (1974) and Jenkins and Pany (1978) discuss what they consider to be the inadequacies and relative measurement insensitivity of norm-referenced assessment for the measurement of student growth. Curriculum-based measures (Deno, 1985; Gickling & Havertape, 1981) and daily performance measures (Jenkins & Jenkins, 1981) provide data that are most likely to measure student growth accurately; can be used formatively to modify interventions while they are occurring; and can be reported summatively at the conclusion of a program.

If affective variables are included in the program goals, evaluators may wish to measure self-concept, attitude toward the intervention's subject matter, and student attitude toward school or classmates. Such variables can be assessed through existing published instruments such as the Piers-Harris Children's Self-Concept Scale (Piers & Harris, 1969), through questionnaires developed by program staff, or by structured student interviews. The evaluator may also wish to collect direct observational data with which to assess the rate of student's on-task behavior or to evaluate the nature and quality of verbal interactions that occur among students who participate in the intervention. Finally, the impact of peer-influenced intervention on other constituent groups within the school system or building may be investigated. Questionnaires or interviews may be conducted with teachers, administrators, parents, and other school staff to determine their attitudes toward and their evaluations of the interventions.

Maher (1986) has described a comprehensive evaluation format that includes the measurement of a number of discrete cross-age tutoring program components, such as the percentage of training, planning and tutoring sessions completed, the collection of cost data, the rate of assignment completion, test performance, attendance, and attitudinal data. Those who evaluate cooperative learning interventions may also want to include pre-post assessment of group-process data.

Once the data have been collected and analyzed, the results should be reported to all relevant groups within the system. Students should be given direct feedback on their performance. School staff and administrators should receive a report on the impact of the program. If appropriate, evaluation information should also be provided to parents and other members of the school community. Such accountability will foster credibility and increase the likelihood that future program efforts will receive support.

SUMMARY, CONCLUSIONS, AND FUTURE DIRECTIONS

Use of the peer-influenced intervention strategies discussed in this chapter offers to educators and to special service providers viable ways to increase allocated learning time and to improve students' academic skills in a time-efficient and cost-effective manner. Cooperative learning strategies involve simultaneous learning by students, in groups, that are mediated by the achievement of group goals; whereas peer tutoring incorporates explicitly programmed teaching behaviors in tutor–tutee dyads, with an emphasis on indvidual learning. Considerable research exists in support of the effectiveness of these interventions within different student populations. To further enhance effectiveness, those responsible for planning and implementing the interventions should establish goals carefully, based upon an assessment of both system needs and student needs. They should select appropriate interventions based upon those goals and needs, and evaluate their effectiveness.

The implementation of cooperative learning interventions involves the introduction and selection of an appropriate method, the encouragement of helping behavior among students, and the promotion of accountability within the group. The implementation of peer and cross-age tutoring programs requires careful selection and training of tutors, close and consistent supervision of tutor–tutee pairs, selection of instructional content and format of tutoring sessions, scheduling the sessions, and establishment of compatible dyads. Evaluation of either of these interventions should include curriculum-based measurement of academic progress and, when appropriate, assessment of the affective outcomes of the interventions, as well as impact of the program on the educational systems in which they are implemented.

Existing empirical research provides the practitioner with a number of well-established generalizations that, if incorporated into the interventions' implementation, will enhance the probability of success. However, many legitimate questions exist regarding cooperative learning and peer and cross-age tutoring.

Future research should examine ecological effects of these interventions to determine whether student gains are maintained within the classroom. Additional data are needed with respect to process components of the interactions among students and to a variety of mediating variables, such as student age and ability. Research must also examine the relative effectiveness of these interventions in comparison with other available techniques. It is perhaps most important to conduct research to determine methods for encouraging school personnel to utilize these interventions on a consistent basis.

Although it is clear that peer-influenced interventions can be effective and offer increased instructional opportunities, they are not regularly incorporated into most educational settings. Perhaps the current zeitgeist of educational reform and concurrent emphasis on rediscovering what works in education will prompt additional practitioners from all arenas to take advantage of these potentially powerful educational technologies.

ANNOTATED BIBLIOGRAPHY

Ehly, S. (1986). *Peer tutoring: A guide for school psychologists.* Washington, DC: National Association of School Psychologists.

Provides a practical how-to approach to peer and cross-age tutoring. Offers an overview of critical components of effective tutoring programs, and includes a section on programs involving special populations. An accompanying 30-minute videotape (available from the publisher) can be used to assist in training others in tutoring. The section on tutor training will be especially useful to those establishing tutoring programs.

Ehly, S. W., & Larsen, S. C. (1980). *Peer tutoring for individualized instruction.* Boston: Allyn & Bacon.

One of few comprehensive texts on peer and cross-age tutoring. Provides a thorough treatment of this type of intervention. Includes history and research, establishing and structuring a peer-tutoring program, developing instructional content, and variations of peer tutoring with nontraditional populations.

Jenkins, J. R., & Jenkins, L.M. (1981). *Cross age and peer tutoring: Help for children with learning problems.* Reston, VA: Council for Exceptional Children.

This brief (87 pages) but relatively comprehensive text provides an excellent and practical overview of important components of successful peer and cross-age tutoring programs. Practical and proven advice on tutor training and selection, tutoring curriculum, and measurement is provided. Also reviews relevant research on effective tutoring programs and advocate for daily, performance based measures of tutor progress.

Johnson, D. W., & Johnson, R. J. (1975). *Learning together and alone: Cooperation, competition, and individualization.* Englewood Cliffs, NJ: Prentice-Hall.

Outlines and distinguishes among the basic instructional goal structures that operate in schools today: cooperative, competitive, and individualistic. Advocates the incorporation of cooperative learning structure in schools and discusses the theoretical basis and empirical evidence for their position. Provides practical suggestions for staff who are interested in implementing cooperative learning in the classroom. School personnel may find the chapter "Monitoring Your Classroom: Listening, Watching and Reflecting" particularly helpful in evaluating the implementation of this method.

Slavin, R. E. (1983). *Cooperative learning.* London: Longman.

Effective summary of the theory and research that supports the development and implementation of cooperative learning methods. Provides a brief overview of various cooperative learning methods, but its primary value to practitioners is not as a source of information to guide the implementation of a specific method in a classroom, but as an excellent source of references on the major approaches to cooperative goal structuring. For researchers, there is a thoughtful chapter on directions for further study.

REFERENCES

Annis, L. (1983). Processes and effects of peer tutoring. *Human Learning, 2,* 39–47.

Aronson, E. (1978). *The jigsaw classroom.* Beverly Hills, CA: Sage Publications.

Ballard, M., Corman, L., Gottlieb, J., & Kaufman, M. (1977). Improving the social status of mainstreamed retarded children. *Journal of Educational Psychology, 69,* 605–611.

Bloom, B. S. (1964). *Stability and change in human characteristics.* New York: Wiley.

Carver, R. (1974). Two dimensions of tests: Psychometric and edumetric. *American Psychologist, 29,* 512–518.

Cohen, J. (1986). Theoretical considerations of peer tutoring. *Psychology in the Schools, 23,* 175–186.

Cohen, P. A., Kulik, J. A., & Kulik, C. C. (1982). Educational outcomes of tutoring: A meta-analysis of findings. *American Educational Research Journal, 19,* 237–248.

Cooper, L., Johnson, D. W., Johnson, R., & Wilderson, F. (1980). Effects of cooperative, competitive, and individualistic experiences on interpersonal attraction among heterogeneous peers. *Journal of Social Pscyhology, 111,* 243–252.

Deno, S. L. (1985). Curriculum-based measurement: The emerging alternative. *Exceptional Children, 52,* 219–252.

Deterline, W. A. (1970). *Training and management of student tutors: Final report.* (ERIC Document Reproduction Service No. ED 048 133)

Devin-Sheehan, L., Feldman, R., & Allen, V. (1976). Research on children tutoring children: A critical review. *Review of Educational Research, 46,* 355–385.

DeVries, D., Slavin, R., Fennessey, G., Edwards, K., & Lombardo, M. (1980). *Teams-games-tournaments: The team learning approach.* Englewood Cliffs, NJ: Educational Technology Publications.

Ehly, S. (1986). *Peer tutoring: A guide for school psychologists.* Washington, DC: National Association of School Psychologists.

Ehly, S. W., & Larsen, S. C. (1980). *Peer tutoring for individualized instruction.* Boston: Allyn & Bacon.

Feldman, R. S., Devin-Sheehan, L., & Allen, V. L. (1976). Children tutoring children: A critical review of research. In V. A. Allen (Ed.), *Children as teachers: Theory and research on tutoring* (pp. 235–252). New York: Academic Press.

Fischer, C., Felby, N., Marleave, R., Cohen, L., Dishaw, M., Moore, J., & Berliner, D. (1978). *Teaching and learning in the elementary school: A summary of the beginning teacher evaluation study.* San Francisco: Far West Laboratory.

Gickling, E. E., & Havertape, J. F. (1981). Curriculum-based assessment. In J. A. Tucker (Ed.), *Non-test based assessment* (pp. S1–S23). Minneapolis, MN: The National School Psychology Inservice Training Network, University of Minnesota.

Graden, J. L., Casey, A., & Christensen, S. L. (1985). Implementing a prereferral intervention system: Part I. The model. *Exceptional Children, 51,* 377–384.

Greenwood, C., & Delquardi, J. (1982, September). *The opportunity to respond and student academic performance in school.* Paper presented at the Conference on Behavior Analysis in Education, Ohio State University, Columbus, OH.

Harrison, G. V. (1976). Structured tutoring: Antidote for low achievement. In V. A. Allen (Ed.), *Children as teachers: Theory and research on tutoring* (pp. 169–177). New York: Academic Press.

Hartup, W. W. (1976). Cross-age versus same-age peer interaction: Ethological and cross cultural perspectives. In V. A. Allen (Ed.), *Children as teachers: Theory and research on tutoring* (pp. 41–55). New York: Academic Press.

Jenkins, J. R., & Jenkins, L. M. (1981). *Cross age and peer tutoring: Help for children with learning problems.* Reston, VA: Council for Exceptional Children.

Jenkins, J., & Jenkins, L. (1985). Peer tutoring in elementary and secondary programs. *Focus on Exceptional Children, 17,* 1–12.

Jenkins, J. R., Mayhall, W. F., Peschka, C., & Jenkins, L. M. (1974). Comparing small group and tutorial instruction in resource rooms. *Exceptional Children, 40,* 245–250.

Kenkins, J., & Pany, D. (1978). Standardized achievement tests: How useful for education? *Exceptional Children, 34,* 448–453.

Johnson, D., & Johnson, R. (1978). Cooperative, competitive and individualistic learning. *Journal of Research and Development in Education, 12* (1), 3–15.

Johnson, D., & Johnson, R. (1980). Integrating handicapped students into the mainstream. *Exceptional Children, 47,* 90–98.

Johnson, D., & Johnson, R. (1975). *Learning together and alone.* Englewood Cliffs, NJ: Prentice-Hall.

Johnson, D., Maruyama, G., Johnson, R., Nelson, D., & Skon, L. (1981). The effects of cooperative, competitive and individualistic goal structures on achievement: A meta-analysis. *Psychological Bulletin, 89,* 47–62.

Kalfus, G. (1984). Peer mediated interventions: A critical review. *Child and Family Behavior Therapy, 6,* 17–43.

Linton, T. (1973). The effects of grade displacement between student tutors and students tutored. *Dissertation Abstracts International, 33,* 4091–A. (University Microfilms No. 72–32, 034.)

Lippitt, P. (1976). Learning through cross-age helping: Why and how. In V. A. Allen (Ed.), *Children as teachers: Theory and research on tutoring* (pp. 157–168). New York: Academic Press.

Maher, C. A. (1986). Direct replication of a cross age tutoring program involving handicapped adolescents and children. *School Psychology Review, 15,* 100–118.

Maher, C. A., & Bennett, R. E. (1984). *Planning and evaluating special education services.* Englewood Cliffs, NJ: Prentice-Hall.

Mayhall, W. F., & Jenkins, J. R. (1977). Scheduling daily or less-than-daily instruction: Implications for resources programs. *Journal of Learning Disabilities, 10,* 3, 159–163.

Mayhall, W. R., Jenkins, J. R., Chestnut, N., Rose, F., Schroeder, K., & Jordan, B. (1975). Supervision and site of instruction as factors in tutorial programs. *Exceptional Children, 43,* 151–154.

Moskowitz, J., Malvin, J., Schaeffer, G., & Schaps, E. (1983). Evaluation of a cooperative learning strategy. *American Educational Research Journal, 20,* 687–696.

Osguthorpe, R. T., & Harrison, G. V. (1976). Training parents in a personalized system of reading instruction. *Improving Human Performance Quarterly, 5,* 62–68.

Pierce, M. M., Stahlbrand, K., & Armstrong, S. B. (1984). *Increasing student productivity through peer tutoring programs.* Austin, TX: Pro-Ed.

Piers, E. V., & Harris, D. B. (1969). *The Piers-Harris children's self-concept scale (the way I feel about myself).* Nashville, TN: Counselor Recordings and Tests.

Rosenshine, B. V., & Berliner, D. C. (1978). Academic engaged time. *British Journal of Teacher Education, 4,* 3–16.

Rosenshine, B., & Furst, N. (1969). *The effects of tutoring upon pupil achievement: A research review.* Washington, DC: Office of Education. (ERIC Document Reproduction Service No. ED 064 462)

Sarbin, T. R. (1976). Cross-age tutoring and social identity. In V. A. Allen (Ed.), *Children as teachers: Theory and research on tutoring* (pp. 29–40). New York: Academic Press.

Scruggs, T. E., & Osguthorpe, R. T. (1986). Tutoring interventions within special education settings: A comparison of cross-age and peer tutoring. *Psychology in the Schools, 23,* 187–193.

Scruggs, T. E., & Richter, L. (1985). Tutoring learning disabled students: A critical review. *Learning Disability Quarterly, 8,* 286–298.

Sharan, S. (1980). Cooperative learning in small groups: Recent methods and effects on achievement, attitudes, and ethnic relations. *Review of Educational Research, 50*(2), 241–271.

Sharan, S., & Sharan, Y. (1976). *Small-group teaching.* Englewood Cliffs, NJ: Educational Technology Publications.

Slavin, R. (1978). Student teams and achievement divisions. *Journal of Research and Development in Education, 12,* 39–49.

Slavin, R. (1980a). Cooperative learning. *Review of Educational Research, 50,* 315–342.

Slavin, R. (1980b). *Using student team learning* (rev. ed.). Baltimore, MD: Center for Social Organization of Schools, John Hopkins University.

Slavin, R. (1983). *Cooperative learning.* London: Longman.

Slavin, R. E., Madden, N. A., & Leavey, M. (1982, April). *Effects of student teams and individualized instruction on student mathematics achievement, attitudes, and behaviors.* Paper presented at the annual meeting of the American Educational Research Association, New York.

Webb, N. (1982). Student interaction and learning in small groups. *Review of Educational Research, 52,* 421–445.

7 School-Based Counseling

CHARLES A. MAHER and JUDITH SPRINGER

School professionals are increasingly called upon to help students learn skills to cope with developmental milestones, learning problems, and social stressors (Reynolds, Gutkin, Elliott, & Witt, 1984). One important avenue for providing such instruction and support is *school-based counseling*. School-based counseling may be defined as the direct face-to-face provision of information, advice, or guidance by a counselor to an individual student or a group of students (Maher & Forman, 1987). Several distinguishing features, summarized and discussed in more detail below, characterize school-based counseling.

Distinguishing features of school-based counseling:
1. School-based counseling provides an opportunity to counsel students in a natural setting.
2. It is provided over a finite period of time and within circumscribed time parameters.
3. It is targeted to a clearly defined set of school-related goals.
4. It can be provided both in one-to-one or in group modes.
5. It can be provided by a range of different school personnel.
6. It has limited confidentiality.
7. It involves assisting some involuntary clients.

DISTINGUISHING FEATURES OF SCHOOL-BASED COUNSELING

School-based counseling is provided in the natural context of the school, with numerous opportunities available for observing students while they interact with teachers and peers, and for consulting with significant people in the student environment. As such, counseling interventions can be planned to complement effectively other psychoeducational interventions (e.g., study-skills training), thereby increasing potential benefits to students.

School-based counseling is necessarily provided within the time constraints imposed by the hours of the school day, by the minutes in a class period, and by the length of the school year, and occurs over a finite period such as a semester. Consequently, it is important that school-based counselors attend diligently to the logistics of arranging counseling sessions around complex and sometimes competing priorities that include students' academic classes, provision of special subjects, and mandatory assemblies.

Due to the time-limited focus, school-based counseling is necessarily and most usefully targeted to a clearly defined set of goals in one or more areas of a student's functioning. These areas typically include educational problems and concerns, academic/vocational/career decision making, cognitive and behavioral competence, and social and emotional functioning. Achievement of these kinds of goals may be indicated by a student's increased understanding of a topic or an issue, by an increase in positive attitudes about something or someone, or by the development of proficiency in certain tasks or behaviors. Counseling goal attainment may be realized through counseling provided to an individual student (one-to-one mode) or to more than one student at a time (group mode).

Counseling in schools can be provided by a range of school personnel, including psychologists, guidance counselors, social workers, nurses, administrators, and other students. In this chapter, however, focus is on the provision of counseling services by school professionals, henceforth referred to as *counselors*. For a complete discussion of peer-mediated approaches, the reader is referred to chapter 6.

School-based counseling is not a strictly confidential relationship. As a school employee, it is essential for the school-based counselor to abide by local district policy and state and federal regulations governing educational services provision. More specifically, counselors are under an obligation to report the intent of students to harm either themselves or others (e.g., suicidal thoughts, substance abuse, venereal disease) as well as to report any indication that a student has been the victim of child abuse (Wilson, 1981). Accordingly, school-based counselors have an ethical obligation to inform students of the limits of confidentiality at the very onset of counseling. Moreover, it is generally accepted practice to inform parents that a student is to be counseled, prior to initiation of counseling activities (Shaffer, 1985).

Practitioners of school-based counseling are often asked to assist at least some involuntary clients. Since many counseling approaches are based on the premise of a cooperative client (Ritchie, 1986), an involuntary-client situation poses special problems for the practitioner. In particular, the counselor may find it difficult to collaborate with the student in defining the student's priority concerns, and to involve the counselee in setting his or her own goals for the counseling intervention.

Rationale for School-Based Counseling

It is fundamental for success in school that all students, both normal and exceptional, learn to make a range of educational decisions that affect their immediate and long-range futures. Many students experience developmental-milestone problems and life crises, especially in our increasingly complex society (Achenbach, 1982). Schools can be another major source of stress for students, due to the multiple performance and social demands inherent in school settings (Forman & O'Malley, 1984). Students who experience learning problems encounter a special set of related social and emotional difficulties, such as poor peer relationships and low self-esteem. A special responsibility exists, therefore, for the provision of counseling as a related service to students classified as handicapped under the provisions of the Education for All Handicapped Children Act (PL 94–142). Fortunately, counselors in schools are in the unique position of being able to provide instruction and support to all of these students in the very setting where students experience much of their life stress.

Purpose of Chapter

The purpose of this chapter is threefold: (a) to review selectively the important research and concepts that have influenced school-based counseling and that are likely to do so in the future; (b) to consider practical guidelines for planning, implementing, and evaluating counseling programs in schools; and (c) to identify directions for future research and practice as well as to provide important resources for additional reading.

PERTINENT RESEARCH AND CONCEPTS

Practitioners of school-based counseling who seek effective short-term interventions for diverse student populations encounter a potentially bewildering array of counseling theories, methods, and techniques. Although conventional counseling texts (e.g., Dinkmeyer, 1968; Gazda, 1978) may offer insight into particular philosophies, theories, and interpersonal processes involved in counseling, most of these publications provide little practical guidance for planning, implementing, or evaluating student counseling interventions and programs. Although a good portion of reported applied empirical research on counseling documents potentially worthwhile interventions, it is characterized by conspicuous lack of either procedural detail or guidelines for adapting and implementing the interventions in local school settings.

Discussion in this section of the chapter is designed to complement material, presented in other chapters of this volume, about psychoeducational interventions in schools. As such, only three types of counseling interventions will be discussed selectively here: (a) vocational or career counseling, (b) cognitive–emotive counseling, and (c) relaxation training.

Vocational or Career Counseling

School-based counseling that focuses on vocational and career goals of students has traditionally occurred almost exclusively within the domain of secondary school guidance departments. Additionally, a paucity of reported empirical research exists in the area (Illback, 1987). The few school-based vocational or career counseling studies that have been reported have addressed issues of career decision making and of career maturity. Outcome assessment poses particular problems in this area because of the difficulty in assessing outcome quality (e.g., What constitutes a good career decision?). Egner and Jackson (1978), for example, developed a ten-week program to improve both career decision-making (defined as the ability to apply a decision-making strategy to assess hypothetical career choices) and career maturity (defined as career awareness and exploration) of 11th-grade students. Students in the program demonstrated significantly increased career maturity scores relative to a no-treatment control group, and career maturity was found to be significantly related to career decision-making ability. However, it must be noted that students were voluntary participants and did not, therefore, constitute a random, representative sample. Therefore, generalizability of the results to a more heterogenous student population is not clear.

Another study regarding career decisionmaking involved a relatively brief counseling intervention. Warner and Jepon (1979) grouped high school juniors by conceptual ability (high and low) and provided them with a 5½ hour counseling experience. Students were randomly assigned to one of two formats: the first format was directed toward students' own career decisions, while the second group simulated career decisions for a hypothetical student. Contrary to the authors' expectations, high conceptual-level students scored higher on choice-basis complexity when they participated in the simulation rather than the experiential groups. Due to the extreme brevity of the intervention and the small sample of students, the investigators appropriately presented their results as tentative.

Generally, the applied empirical research literature on school-based vocational and career counseling indicates that the area is underdeveloped, but is important for future research (Illback, 1987). The few reported studies in the area have been compromised by methodological problems such as overly brief interventions, small sample sizes, and non-random selection of subjects.

Cognitive–Emotional Approaches

Long-standing empirical evidence indicates that the cognitive–emotional approaches of Beck (1976) and Ellis (Ellis, 1979; Ellis & Harper, 1975) are effective in treating anxiety, fears, and depression with adult populations

(Lahey, 1982). However, it has been only since the early 1970s that the utility of cognitive–emotional approaches with children has begun to be addressed through research (Bernard & Joyce, 1984). Two cognitive–emotive approaches that have been investigated extensively with a child population are Rational–Emotive Therapy and its educational counterpart, Rational–Emotive Education (Knaus, 1974). (For discussions of two important allied approaches, social problem-solving and self-instruction, see chapters 3 and 10 respectively.) Rational–Emotive Therapy (RET) and Rational–Emotive Education (REE) reflect the view that people's irrational beliefs about events, rather than the events themselves, lead to excessive emotional distress. Major interventions derived from this base include RET and REE group counseling and preventively-oriented affective education programs. The basic techniques used in these approaches are educational in nature and include guided discovery, didactic presentation, homework assignments, and structured role play (Bernard & Joyce, 1984).

In their comprehensive review of the research on the effectiveness of RET and REE with school-age populations, Bernard and Joyce (1984) caution about generalizing to various child and adolescent populations from extant research because of methodological problems with those studies. Problems include small sample sizes, brief treatments, high within-group variability, lack of follow-up data, lack of replication studies and, in some cases, posttest-only designs and lack of attention–placebo control groups. Given these types of limitations, the results of several interventions are presented below as representative of relevant research.

An application of REE as a school-based preventive mental health intervention was undertaken by DiGuiseppe and Kassinove (1976). Fifteen weekly sessions of REE were provided to fourth- and eighth-grade classes. An alternate mental health program, consisting of human relations classes, was provided to other fourth- and eighth-grade classes, and no-treatment control students attended regular health classes. After the intervention, all REE classes scored significantly higher than other groups on a test of rational ideas, but only the fourth-grade classes scored significantly higher on independent measures of emotional adjustment. These mixed results, while interesting, are difficult to interpret, especially in light of the post-test-only design, the use of several RET-oriented dependent measures, and the possibility of experimenter bias.

Block (1978) addressed the pressing educational problems of failure- and misconduct-prone black and Hispanic high school students. In a commendable effort to apply naturalistic and important scholastic outcome criteria, Block examined the effectiveness of rational–emotive discussion groups on the students' grade point average, number of class cuts, and incidents of disruptive behavior. Alternate-treatment controls received a human relations program, while no-treatment controls were placed on a waiting list. Pretreatment comparisons demonstrated that the groups did not originally differ significantly on the dependent measures. Treatment groups met for 45 minutes daily over twelve weeks. At both posttreatment comparisons and at follow-up, rational–emotive groups showed the greatest improvement on all dependent measures.

Another group of students with school-related problems was the focus of a study by M. M. Omizo, Cobberly, and S. A. Omizo (1985). These investigators examined the effects of REE group counseling on the self-concept and locus of control (i.e., the degree to which individuals believe they can control their fate) of learning-disabled children. Sixty students, ages 8 to 11 years, were assigned randomly to either REE or placebo-control groups. No significant differences were found when participants were pretested on the dependent measures. Treatment groups met for 1 hour twice a week for 12 weeks. Posttreatment testing revealed significant differences in favor of the REE group on several subscales of the self-concept measure as well as a significantly more internal locus of control.

Finally, efforts have been made to alleviate the anxiety and to improve the test performance of test-anxious students. Reviews of studies in this area by Forman and O'Malley (1984) and Dendato and Diener (1986) indicate general decreases in self-reported anxiety, but rarely indicate improvements in test performance.

Although the overall current status of RET and REE research with children remains equivocal, the positive results of some applied empirical research are encouraging for school-based counseling. A strong and consistent finding, noted by Bernard and Joyce (1984) in their comprehensive review, is that children can learn the content of RET and REE lessons as measured by tests of irrational ideas, but that such changes have not generally resulted in large-scale behavior change, such as increasing assertiveness or reducing aggression.

Relaxation Training

Whereas cognitive–emotive approaches are designed to help students learn to control their irrational cognitive responses to stressful situations, relaxation training is intended to help pupils monitor and regulate their physiological responses to stressors. Well-controlled studies on the efficacy of relaxation training with children are both unusual and relatively recent (Richter, 1984). Major relaxation-training interventions with children and adolescents have addressed behavior problems in hyperactive and emotionally disturbed children, as well as the problem of test anxiety. In this discussion, the emphasis will be on relaxation techniques that can be implemented by school personnel—in school settings, without technical aid or special equipment.

Generally, relaxation-training studies have involved instruction in progressive relaxation, which employs the alternate tensing and relaxing of various muscle groups, and/or instruction in guided imagery. Training has been individual and in groups, with either taped or live presentations of instructions. As noted by Richter, the literature regarding the treatment of hyperactive children is quite contradictory, due in part to lack of precision and consistency in the criteria for subject selection. Hyperactive children may be residents of a treatment center, teacher-referred, or physician-diagnosed. Other problems include lack of comparability among dependent measures in different studies, brief treatment periods, and insufficient follow-up data.

A pilot study of a home-based audio taped relaxation program for 6- to 10-year-old minimal-brain-injured children is described by Lupin, L. M. Braud, W. Braud, and Duer (1976). After a three-month treatment period, consistent improvement was found on parent ratings, classroom observations, and psychometric data. Due to the small sample size and lack of any control group, these results should be considered only as suggestive.

Comparing the effects of relaxation training and exercise on the matching-task performance of third-grade hyperactive boys, Klein and Deffenbacher (1977) found that both treatments resulted in significantly better performance than a no-treatment control group. Interpretation of these findings is clouded, however, by methodological insufficiences such as the brevity of the treatment and the posttest-only design of the study.

In another intervention with hyperactive male students (age 7 to 13 years), Putre, Loffio, Chorost, Marx, and Gilbert (1977) compared the effectiveness of listening to commercially available progressive relaxation tapes with the effectiveness of listening to control tapes of children's adventure stories for ten minutes daily for two weeks. Both groups significantly decreased muscle tension as measured by electromyographic (EMG) pretests and posttests of forehead muscle tension. Simply listening to tapes may have a relaxing effect on hyperactive children, but the possibility remains that the decrease may have been due at least in part to habituation with the measuring instrument.

A comprehensive study by Braud (1978) employed both EMG-biofeedback and progressive relaxation exercises with a population of physician-diagnosed hyperactive children between the ages of 6 and 13 years. Both approaches resulted in significant reductions on multiple measures, including measures of muscular tension, hyperactivity, emotionality, excitability, and impulsivity. Although EMG-biofeedback resulted in significantly greater decreases in forehead muscle tension than did relaxation, it did not result in significantly greater improvement on behavioral ratings or psychological tests. This finding is particularly important since relaxation training is easier, less expensive, and more practical than biofeedback training. Additionally, students can practice the techniques in any setting, which may facilitate generalization and maintenance.

Vacc and Greenleaf (1980) applied relaxation training with a population of 6- to 12-year-olds classified as emotionally handicapped. They compared the effects of a 4-week program of relaxation training, with and without covert reinforcement, on the behavior ratings and the self-reported anxiety of the students. Neither intervention resulted in significant effects, and it was concluded that younger emotionally handicapped children may need more structure and more repetition than was provided in this study.

A study by K. M. Denkowski and G. C. Denkowski (1984) compared group progressive relaxation and guided fantasy exercises with and without individual EMG-biofeedback. They examined differential effects of these variations on the academic achievement and self-control of 45 teacher-referred hyperactive elementary children. Treatment consisted of eight weekly 25-minute sessions for the treatment groups, whereas a placebo control group listened to taped children's stories. No significant differences were found among the three groups when all dependent variables were considered together, but locus of control was found to be significantly more internal for the progressive-relaxation-only group.

Another major focus of relaxation training interventions has been treatment of test anxiety. Schuchman (1977) compared the effectiveness of progressive relaxation with EMG-assisted relaxation and non directive counseling high-school students. All three groups experienced a significant decline in anxiety and significant increases in Scholastic Aptitude Test (SAT) scores. However, in other studies (e.g., Little & Jackson, 1974), self-reported test anxiety has been reduced without an accompanying improvement in actual test performance.

It has been suggested that test anxiety is comprised of two aspects: (a) emotionality, a physiological component, and (b) worry, which is cognitive (Schuchman, 1977). Dendato and Diener (1986) proposed another element, a preparation deficit resulting from poor study and test-taking skills. In a study designed to tap all these aspects, the investigators compared effects of a relaxation-training–RET treatment, a study-skills treatment, and a combination treatment on both the test anxiety and the classroom test performance of test-anxious undergraduates (mean age = 19). The relaxation-RET treatment effectively reduced anxiety, but failed to improve classroom test scores; study-skills training had no effect on either measure. However, the combined treatment both reduced anxiety and improved classroom performance significantly more than did either treatment alone.

In a comprehensive review of efficacy studies employing relaxation training with school-age children, Richter (1984) concluded that relaxation training has been effective when used over an extended period of time and accompanied by additional supports (e.g., parental or teacher involvement) or other interventions. Relaxation training was found to be most effective with target behaviors that could be clearly defined and meaningfully measured. However, relaxation training was found to have "dubious utility" when used as an isolated treatment for vaguely defined or longstanding problems.

Relaxation training appears to be an effective adjunct to other forms of intervention for the alleviation of some behavior problems and for anxiety reduction. Moreover, it is cost effective, free of negative side effects, and relatively easy to implement within a school setting.

In this section, research regarding three very different types of school-based interventions has been reviewed. Familiarity with the wide range of available interventions can help the practitioner with the processes of planning and implementation of counseling programs.

GUIDELINES FOR PLANNING AND EVALUATION

Throughout this volume, a number of school-based psychoeducational interventions are presented. The goal of this section is to provide guidelines for how and when such counseling interventions can be implemented in schools. Four separate, yet interrelated, processes will be discussed: (a) assessing the need for counseling; (b) designing counseling programs and interventions; (c) implementing programs and interventions; and (d) evaluating effectiveness.

Assessing the Need for Counseling

Students who are likely to be considered for school-based counseling are ones whose behavioral, emotional, and/or interpersonal functioning causes distress to themselves or others and interferes with their development and learning (Tharinger, 1985). Comprehensive, ongoing assessment of the psychoeducational needs of each student who is considered for counseling is essential in order to ensure the best possible match between those needs and the specific forms of counseling interventions to be employed (Maher & Forman, 1987).

Assessment of a student's psychoeducational needs, as a basis for counseling, requires a clear and parsimonious framework with which to guide the counselor in assessment activities. Such a framework reflects three potentially relevant assessment domains:

- *Knowledge* necessary to plan and act effectively and appropriately
- *Attitudes* necessary to succeed in school
- *Skills* necessary to plan, act, and succeed

Assessment is guided by the following question: What areas of weakness or need are interfering with this student's ability to obtain maximum benefit from his or her schooling? Functioning within the three domains is systematically examined, in the form of further questions: (a) Does this student lack information that would permit more successful functioning (e.g., career information)?; (b) Do attitudes or beliefs of the student impede success in school (e.g., low self-esteem)?; (c) Does the student have the prerequisite skills for application of both knowledge and attitudes to effective school performance (e.g., study skills, assertive skills)?

Thorough assessment of a student's competencies within the three domains of knowledge, attitude, and skill can readily occur through a broad-based, behavioral assessment approach. In this kind of approach, various methods must be utilized to obtain relevant assessment information: interviews with students, teachers, parents, and other significant parties; direct observation; behavior-rating scales and checklists; sociometric data; psychoeducational measures; and reviews of permanent products such as records of grades and attendance.

After initial assessment and relevant information gathering, hypotheses may be formulated regarding the student's strengths and weaknesses within the three domains. For example, the counselor may determine that a student possesses the necessary knowledge and skills for school success, but that the student is hindered by an attitude that schoolwork is for wimps. Then a variety of potential interventions can be considered appropriately, depending upon the availability of resources. These interventions may include a change in placement or classroom; a classroom-behavior management program; consultation with the teacher or parent; consideration for special education assistance; referral for family counseling; referral for medical examination and consultation; and school-based individual or group counseling (Tharinger, 1985). If school-based counseling is determined to be potentially beneficial by the counselor, the student, the parent(s), and other significant parties, then the process of program design is initiated. If counseling is deemed inappropriate, other types of interventions would be selected.

Designing Counseling Programs and Interventions

The importance of linking student needs with appropriate interventions cannot be overstressed, not only in terms of maximizing student benefit, but also with respect to minimizing the risks (e.g., school failure, dropping out, misconduct) posed by failing to apply appropriate interventions. It is therefore solid practice for counselors in schools to guide their selection of interventions, using both developmental theory and current research. In this way, practitioners can evaluate the appropriateness of the interventions for the level of cognitive development and emotional maturity of the student. Illustratively, the authors and others (e.g., Kendall & Braswell, 1985) have found that some impulsive emotionally-disturbed children below the age of 12 or 13 years may have considerable difficulty reflecting on the content of their thoughts. For such students, an intervention—such as a program to reduce impulsivity—which emphasizes more concrete behaviors, may be more effective.

A practical, structured approach to program design, described by Maher and Bennett (1984), indicates four design elements to be considered by the counselor: (a) purpose and goals of the counseling program or intervention; (b) counseling methods, materials, and activities; (c) roles, relationships, and responsibilities of counselor, student, and significant others; and (d) evaluation planning.

In all aspects of program design, it is important to involve, to the extent possible, the student, parents, and school staff in design efforts. It has been demonstrated that such involvement increases the counseling goal attainment of students (Barbrack & Maher, 1984) and the program satisfaction of students, parents, and school staff (Maher, 1981).

Program and intervention design efforts can be guided by a series of questions to be raised and addressed systematically with the student and/or others, depending on the age and maturity of the student and the nature of the problem. These questions are as follows:

1. What is to be accomplished as a result of counseling (e.g., higher grades, increased school attendance)?
    (a) Has need for and relevance of the accomplishment(s) been established?
    (b) Are the students and others aware of what is to be accomplished?
2. For the stated accomplishments to be realized, what knowledge, skills, and attitudes are important for the student to acquire and develop (e.g., study skills, understanding of school rules and penalties)?
    (a) Has need for and relevance of these student qualities been established?
    (b) Are the students and others aware of the importance of these qualities?
3. For the stated accomplishments to be realized and student qualities to be acquired and developed, what particular interventions can be applied by the practitioner?
    (a) Has a rationale for use of particular interventions been established?
    (b) Are the students and others aware of the rationale?
4. For the particular interventions to be applied, what will be the roles, responsibilities and relationships of the parties involved?
5. How can it be determined if the interventions were applied, accomplishments were realized, and student qualities acquired and developed?

The case example below illustrates this recommended approach to program design.

A ninth-grade boy is referred for counseling because of his poor test performance and low motivation. Through a broad-based assessment procedure, the counselor has determined that this student has above-average intellectual ability, but has poor study skills, high test anxiety, and considers himself to be "dumb." At this juncture, the counselor meets with the student (and his parents and teachers) to determine what is to be accomplished through counseling. Together, they decide that an appropriate goal would be to improve test grades. With this goal in mind, the participants determine the knowledge, attitude, and skills required to enable the student to attain his goal (e.g., information regarding the most efficient test-taking strategies and study techniques; the attitude that effort can improve performance; skills to reduce anxiety through physical relaxation and control of irrational thoughts). Appropriate interventions are then selected. In this instance, appropriate activities include study-skills instruction, relaxation training, and cognitive–emotive education.

After appropriate interventions are selected, the roles, responsibilities and relationships of involved parties are determined. The classroom teacher initiates a program of study-skills instruction for this student and for other students in need of this service, with consultative services to be provided by the counselor. Anxiety-management training is provided by the counselor according to a specified schedule. Student responsibilities include practicing relaxation techniques and attending all scheduled counseling sessions.

Finally, an approach for monitoring and evaluating progress toward the counseling goal is selected (e.g., monthly review of test grades).

Evaluation of counseling effectiveness is considered in detail in a later section of this chapter.

Implementing Programs and Interventions

Specific, purposeful efforts by counselors can serve to facilitate and monitor the implementation of their programs and interventions. Efforts of this nature document how services are delivered, by describing the conditions under which counseling services are provided, who is receiving the services, the activities occuring within sessions, and difficulties that have been encountered. This kind of information helps in making decisions about the revision of ongoing counseling, and aids in the interpretation of outcome assessment.

One useful approach to program implementation, identified by the acronym DURABLE (Maher & Bennett, 1984), fosters program implementation by encouraging frequent and purposeful interactions with staff. Particular aspects of the DURABLE approach that are especially useful in implementation of counseling programs and interventions include discussing, understanding, rewarding, adapting, and evaluating the implementation:

1. *Discussion.* Teachers, parents, and secondary school students should participate in discussions with the counselor of the nature, scope, and anticipated outcome of the counseling program prior to implementation.

2. *Understanding*. Review and consideration of major concerns of staff and students about the counseling program occur in this aspect.
3. *Rewarding*. To maintain staff cooperation (e.g., sending students to scheduled counseling sessions), teachers are reinforced verbally and in writing.
4. *Adapting*. Implementation problems are addressed in this aspect.
5. *Evaluating implementation*. This kind of evaluation documents the extent to which the counseling program has been carried out as planned and indicates aspects (e.g., number of sessions) of the program that may require revision.

Evaluating the Effectiveness of Counseling Programs and Interventions

A variety of indicators of school-based counseling program effectiveness can be used, including counselor perception of student progress; students' own perceptions of progress; teacher perceptions of student progress; satisfaction of students, teachers, and parents; and student attainment of goals to a predetermined level. For the purposes of this chapter, two frequently used, practical approaches to the evaluation of counseling effectiveness in schools will be discussed: (a) goal-attainment evaluation and (b) the single-case design.

Goal-attainment evaluation involves preprogram and postprogram assessment. This approach, which is especially applicable when students, teachers, and parents are all involved in counseling-program planning and evaluation, is selected at the time the intervention is being designed. After counseling goals are set, a goal attainment scale is developed. Goals are operationalized by specifying measurable criteria that allow assessment of degree of goal attainment to be made at specified time intervals. An example of a goal attainment scale is shown in Table 7.1. More detailed information about goal-attainment scaling, including a formula for computation, may be found in Maher (1981) and in Maher and Barbrack (1985).

The single-case design approach is especially helpful in evaluating whether counseling interventions are responsible for observed outcomes. Single-case designs require the recording of multiple observations before, during, and after an intervention. Treatment effects are assessed by visually or statistically analyzing differences between a student's baseline performance and performance after the intervention has been applied (Fagley, 1984). The basic difference between this kind of evaluation and a preprogram–postprogram evaluation design is the collection of data at many more points, prior to and during the intervention. This approach helps to rule out competing explanations for observed outcomes, because increases in goal attainment due to maturation, the effects of other

TABLE 7.1 Example of a Completed Goal Attainment Scale (all goals were weighted equally)

Goal Attainment Scale Categories	Improved School Attendance	Improved Classroom Productivity	Improved School Socialization
Best anticipated success (+2)	100% daily attendance	90–100% completion of academic classroom assignments in all academic classes	0–1 disciplinary referrals to vice-principal
More than anticipated success (+1)	90–99% daily attendance*	80–89% completion of academic classroom assignments	2–4 disciplinary referrals to vice-principal*
Expected level of success (0)	80–89% daily attendance (based on school attendance records)	70–79% completion of academic classroom assignments (based on teacher record books)*	5–6 disciplinary referrals to vice-principal (based on office records)
Less than expected success (−1)	60–79% daily attendance √	50–69% completion of academic classroom assignments	7–10 disciplinary referrals to vice-principal
Most unfavorable outcome thought likely (−2)	Less than 60% daily attendance	Less than 50% completion of academic classroom assignments √	More than 10 disciplinary referrals to vice-principal √

Note: Date of IEP implementation: January 15, 1979
Date of IEP evaluation: March 15, 1979
    Goal Attainment Score at January 15 = 30.8
    Goal Attainment Score at March 15   = 61.2

    Goal Attainment Change Score   = 30.4
√ = level of pupil attainment at IEP implementation
* = level of pupil attainment at IEP evaluation

Note: From "Evaluating individual counseling of conduct problem adolescents: The goal attainment scaling method" by C. A. Maher and C. R. Barbrack, 1984, *Journal of School Psychology, 23*, p. 288. Copyright 1985 by Pergamon Press. Reprinted by permission.

programs, or repeated testing would be expected to show themselves equally over both baseline and intervention periods (Maher & Bennett, 1984). For further information on single-case designs, the reader is referred to Kazdin (1982).

SUMMARY AND CONCLUSIONS

This chapter delineated the distinguishing features of school-based counseling and proposed a rationale for its application. A selective review of representative research efforts in three areas of school-based counseling (vocational and career counseling, cognitive–emotional approaches, and relaxation training) was presented. Methodological problems that characterize much of the currently available research were described.

Practical guidelines for planning, implementing, and evaluating school-based counseling programs were provided. Four interrelated processes were described: (a) assessing student need for counseling; (b) designing counseling programs and interventions; (c) implementing counseling; and (d) evaluating its effectiveness. Particular emphasis was placed on the necessity of conducting broad-based behavioral assessments, the importance of matching student needs with appropriate interventions, and the desirability of involving students, staff, and parents in the planning, implementation, and evaluation of counseling programs.

Considerable further research is needed in order to establish the efficacy of particular treatments for specific types of student problems. In this respect, the accumulation of results from carefully designed single-case studies would be particularly helpful. Such studies should aim toward positive changes in socially valid outcome criteria, in order to provide maximum benefit to the student population that is served by school-based counseling.

ANNOTATED BIBLIOGRAPHY

Bernard, M. E., & Joyce, M. R. (1984). *Rational-emotive therapy with children and adolescents: Theory, treatment strategies, preventative methods.* New York: Wiley.

Provides an excellent background for the prospective practitioner of RET/REE in schools. Includes an objective, critical review of the literature regarding RET efficacy studies with children, analyses of specific childhood problems from an RET perspective, systematic and practical guidelines for RET interventions with children, descriptions of allied cognitive – behavioral methods, approaches to working with teachers and parents, and actual counseling lesson plans for various age groups.

Kendall, P. C., & Braswell, L. (1985). *Cognitive behavior therapy for impulsive children.* New York: Guildford Press.

Offers an extensive review and discussion of self-instructional and problem-solving approaches with children, along with valuable information regarding the characteristics of the non-self-controlled, impulsive child, and the assessment of cognitive and behavioral change. Presents explicit strategies for self-control training with impulsive children. Integral aspects of the program include: (a) a problem-solving approach (b) self-instructional training (c) behavioral contingencies (d) modeling (e) affective education, and (f) role-play exercises. A specific-treatment manual is presented in the appendix.

Lahey, B. B., & Straus, C. C. (1982). Some considerations in evaluating the clinical utility of cognitive-behavior therapy with children. *School Psychology Review, 11*, 67–74.

Provides a framework for the critical evaluation of cognitive-behavior therapy treatment studies. Proposes eight criteria by which to judge treatment methods, and suggests that the bottom line should be whether treatments result in socially valued changes (e.g., improvements in academic achievement).

Maher, C. A., & Bennett, R. E. (1984). *Planning and evaluating special education services.* Englewood Cliffs, NJ: Prentice-Hall.

This concise guide presents an approach to planning and evaluation that enables school personnel to develop programs targeted to the needs of their own school or school district. Planning and evaluation are depicted as ongoing activities relating to the development and improvement of assessment, instruction, delivery of related services (such as counseling), personnel development, and administration.

Richter, N. C. (1984). The efficacy of relaxation training with children. *Journal of Abnormal Child Psychology, 12*, 319–344.

Examines the efficacy of relaxation-training methods used by school personnel with children in a school setting, without additional help or equipment. Discusses methodological problems encountered in research in this area, and presents a selection of supportable findings.

REFERENCES

Achenbach, T. M. (1982). *Developmental psychopathology* (2nd ed.). New York: Wiley.

Barbrack, R. R., & Maher, C. A. (1984). Effects of involving conduct problems adolescents in the setting of counseling goals. *Child and Family Behavior Therapy, 6*, 33–43.

Beck, A. T. (1976). *Cognitive therapy and the emotional disorders*. New York: New American Library.

Bernard, M. E., & Joyce, M. R. (1984). *Rational–emotive therapy with children and adolescents: Theory, treatment strategies, preventative methods*. New York: Wiley.

Block, J. (1978). Effects of a rational–emotive mental health program on poorly achieving, disruptive high school students. *Journal of Counseling Psychology, 25*, 61–65.

Braud, L. W. (1978). The effects of frontal EMG biofeedback and progressive relaxation upon hyperactivity and its behavioral concomitants. *Biofeedback and Self-Regulation, 3*, 69–89.

Dendato, K. M., & Diener, D. (1986). Effectiveness of cognitive/relaxation and study-skills training in reducing the self-reported anxiety and improving the academic performance of test-anxious students. *Journal of Counseling Psychology, 33*, 131–135.

Denkowski, K. M., & Denkowski, G. C. (1984). Is group progressive relaxation training as effective with hyperactive children as individual EMC biofeedback treatment? *Biofeedback and Self-Regulation, 9*, 353–364.

DiGiuseppe, R., & Kassinove, H. (1976). Effects of a rational–emotive school mental health program on childlren's emotional adjustment. *Journal of Community Psychology, 4*, 382–387.

Dinkmeyer, D. C. (Ed.). (1968) *Guidance and counseling in the elementary school*. New York: Holt, Rinehart & Winston.

Egner, J. R., & Jackson, D. J. (1978). Effectiveness of a counseling intervention program for teaching career decision-making skills. *Journal of Counseling Psychology, 25*, 45–52.

Ellis, A. (1979). Rational–emotive therapy: Research data that support the clinical and personality hypotheses of RET and other modes of cognitive behavior therapy. In A. Ellis & J. M. Whitely (Eds.), *Theoretical and empirical foundations of rational–emotive therapy* (pp. 101–173) Monterey, CA: Brooks/Cole.

Ellis, A., & Harper, R. A. (1975). *A new guide to rational living*. Englewood Cliffs, NJ: Prentice-Hall, Inc.

Fagley, N. S. (1984). Behavioral assessment in the schools: Obtaining and evaluating information for individualized programming. *Special Services in the Schools, 1*, (2), 45–57.

Forman, S. G., & O'Malley, P. L. (1984). School stress and anxiety interventions. *School Psychology Review, 13*, 162–170.

Gazda, G. M. (1978). *Group counseling: A developmental approach* (2nd ed.). Boston. Allyn & Bacon.

Illback, R. J. (1987). Vocational education. In C. A. Maher & S. G. Forman (Eds.), *A behavioral approach to the education of children and youth* (pp. 171–184) Hillsdale, NJ: Erlbaum.

Kazdin, A. E. (1982). *Single-case research designs: Methods for clinical and applied settings*. New York: Oxford University Press.

Kendall, P. C., & Braswell, L. (1985). *Cognitive behavior therapy for impulsive children*. New York: Guilford Press.

Klein, S. A., & Deffenbacher, J. L. (1977). Relaxation and exercise for hyperactive impulsive children. *Perceptual and Motor Skills, 45*, 1159–1162.

Knaus, W. J. (1974). *Rational–emotive education: A manual for elementary school teachers*. New York: Institute for Rational Living.

Lahey, B. B., & Strauss, C. C. (1982). Some considerations in evaluating the clinical utility of cognitive-behavior therapy with children. *School Psychology Review, 11*, 67–74.

Little, S., & Jackson, B. (1974). The treatment of test anxiety through attentional and relaxation training. *Psychotherapy: Theory, Research, and Practice, 11*, 175–178.

Lupin, M., Braud, L. M., Braud, W., & Duer, W. F. (1976). Children, parents, and relaxation tapes. *Academic Therapy*, *12*, 105–113.

Maher, C. A. (1981). Developing and implementing effective individualized education programs for conduct-problem adolescents: The goal-oriented approach to learning. *Child Behavior Therapy*, *3*, 1–11.

Maher, C. A., & Barbrack, C. R. (1982). Preventing high school maladjustment: Effectiveness of professional and cross-age behavioral group counseling. *Behavior Therapy*, *13*, 259–270.

Maher, C. A., & Barbrack, C. R. (1984). Evaluating individual counseling of conduct problem adolescents: The goal attainment scaling method pp. 162–176. *Journal of School Psychology*, *23*.

Maher, C. A., & Bennett, R. E. (1984). *Planning and evaluating special education services*. Englewood Cliffs, NJ: Prentice-Hall.

Maher, C. A., & Forman, S. G. (1987). Overview of a behavioral approach to the education of children and youth. In C. A. Maher & S. G. Forman (Eds.), *A behavioral approach to the education of children and youth* (pp. 7–14). Hillsdale, NJ: Erlbaum.

Omizo, M. M., Cubberly, W.E., & Omizo, S. A. (1985). The effects of rational–emotive education groups in self-concept and locus of control among learning disabled children. *The Exceptional Child*, *32*, 13–19.

Putre, W., Loffio, K., Chorost, S., Marx, V., & Gilbert, C. (1977). An effectiveness study of relaxation tape with hyperactive children. *Behavior Therapy*, *8*, 355–359.

Reynolds, C. R., Gutkin, T. B., Elliott, S. N., & Witt, J. C. (1984). *School psychology: Essentials of theory and practice*. New York: Wiley.

Richter, N. C. (1984). The efficacy of relaxation training with children. *Journal of Abnormal Child Psychology*, *12*, 319–344.

Ritchie, M. H. (1986). Counseling the involuntary client. *Journal of Counseling and Development*, *64*, 516–518.

Shaffer, M. B. (1985). Best practices in counseling senior high school students. In A. Thomas & J. Grimes (Eds.), *Best practices in school psychology* (pp. 393–400). Washington, DC: National Association of School Psychologists.

Schuchman, M. C. (1977). A comparison of three techniques for reducing Scholastic Aptitude Test anxiety. *Dissertation Abstracts International*, *38*(4A), 2010.

Tharinger, D. (1985). Best practices in counseling elementary students. In A. Thomas & J. Grimes (Eds.), *Best practices in school psychology* (pp. 447–457). Washington, DC: National Association of School Psychologists.

Vacc, N. A., & Greenleaf, S. M. (1980). Relaxation training and covert positive reinforcement with elementary school children. *Elementary School Guidance and Counseling*, *14*, 232–235.

Wilson, L.S. (1981). The inmate's therapist: Application of the rules of confidentiality in the correctional setting. *New Jersey Psychologist*, *31*, 22–25.

Warner, S. G., & Jepon, D. A. (1979). Differential effects of conceptual level and group counseling format on adolescent career decision-making processes. *Journal of Counseling Psychology*, *26*, 497–503.

8 School-Based Interventions for Discipline Problems

HOWARD M. KNOFF

Discipline problems in the classroom represent one of the more prevalent, most concerning, yet least researched areas in all of education and educational psychology (Jones & Tanner, 1981). A national survey of teachers, for example, revealed that 9 of 10 respondents believe that student misbehavior interferes with the teaching process; 25% of the teachers think that it presents a significant interference (National Education Association [NEA] 1981). From parental and public perspectives, discipline has been rated consistently the most critical problem faced by the schools over the past fifteen years (Elam, 1983; Gallup, 1983). Clearly, mental health and special services practitioners who work in schools or interact with school-aged children need to be aware of the scope of discipline problems, the range of potential interventions either to prevent or to treat these problems, and the decision-making processes available for choosing effective and efficient interventions. Researchers, meanwhile, should be aware that this area requires substantially more empirical attention and representation.

Discipline as a mode of intervention relates primarily to student misbehavior. Misbehavior may be defined as an observable action that is judged by another individual (e.g., a teacher or administrator), usually in an authority position, to be inappropriate to a given context, time, or setting (Charles, 1985). For the purpose of this chapter, children who exhibit discipline problems are students who are not emotionally disturbed or so behaviorally disordered that a special education placement is warranted (although education students may still manifest discipline problems at times). Thus, the concern here is with the disturbing, not the disturbed child: the child who consciously or not exhibits the behaviors—talking without permission, daydreaming, wandering around the classroom or school hallways, swearing, disobeying the requests of school staff, insolence and rudeness, not being prepared for class—that comprise the vast majority of school discipline problems (Jones, 1979).

Discipline is defined best by considering the characteristics of one's society, community, school, and classroom. Often, the philosophies and values of individuals in each of these ecological systems will influence what

118

discipline interventions are appropriate, when they are considered necessary, how they are chosen and used, and who implements them. More generally, however, three primary definitions of discipline apply: (a) discipline as a punitive intervention; (b) discipline as a means of suppressing or eliminating inappropriate behavior, of teaching or reinforcing appropriate behavior, and of redirecting potentially inappropriate behavior toward acceptable ends; and (c) discipline as a process of self-control whereby the (potentially) misbehaving student applies techniques that interrupt inappropriate behavior, and that replace it with acceptable behavior. Although this chapter will emphasize the last two definitions, which involve positive, best-practices approaches toward solving discipline problems, the issues and practices resulting from the first definition will be considered first in the context of corporal punishment.

Corporal punishment is defined as "the intentional infliction of physical pain, physical restraint, and/or discomfort upon a student as a disciplinary technique . . . [it] does not include use of reasonable and necessary physical force: (a) to quell a disturbance that threatens physical injury to any person or destruction of property; (b) to obtain possession of a weapon or other dangerous objects within a pupil's control; and (c) for the purpose of self-defense of others" (National Association of School Psychologists [NASP], 1986, p. 1). To date in the United States, corporal punishment has been supported by the Supreme Court (*Ingraham v. Wright*, 1977) and is legally permitted in 42 states. Empirically, corporal punishment has not been found to reduce discipline problems; it does not facilitate positive learning environments; it models and may encourage additional violence; it does not teach appropriate, adaptive behavior and self-discipline; and it has been used in inequitable and discriminatory ways. Finally, its availability in the schools appears to discourage staff to learn and to use other more positive and effective discipline techniques and approaches (Hyman, McDowell, & Raines, 1977).

Despite these facts, corporal punishment inexplicably continues to be used. Whether this reflects the lack of training, knowledge, or skill of those who must discipline school-aged children or the reality of our violent society, such punishment has no moral or ethical rationale and should be legislated out of existence. Indeed, this has been recommended by such organizations as the American Bar Association, American Medical Association, American Psychological Association, National Association of School Psychologists, National Education Association, and the National Parent-Teachers Association. At this time, special services professionals must be aware not only of the statutory implications of corporal or other punishment approaches, but also of the psychological implications and actual versus desired results of such punishment. With such knowledge, it is clear that the two non-punitive approaches of discipline noted above should be the most favored, implemented, and successful.

Given this perspective on punishment, this chapter will emphasize those discipline interventions that involve the elimination of students' inappropriate behavior and the training, redirection, or self-application of appropriate behavior. Despite this focus on intervention and change, discipline must be conceptualized as a comprehensive process that, to be most effective, encompasses both systematic problem-solving and preventive services delivery (Knoff, 1984a, 1985a). Taken together, these two components outline a process that may identify the most appropriate discipline interventions for specific misbehaving students and indicates ways to broaden the scope and perspective of discipline so that some child-specific problems can truly be prevented. This approach addresses many of the concerns of parents and teachers cited above, and may result in schools that devote more time to the teaching and learning process and in children who are able to experience the excitement of academic and social development and success.

This problem-solving and preventive services conceptualization, then, will be used to structure this chapter's review of the literature and guidelines for planning and evaluation. Within this context, specific discussions will include: (a) the problem-solving process, (b) the three preventive programming perspectives, (c) selected discipline interventions and their theoretical and empirical support, (d) methods of planning and evaluating comprehensive interventions, and (e) some legal and ethical issues relevant to the topic. Rather than duplicate information in other chapters of this book, it will be noted here that social problem-solving (chapter 3), social-skills training (chapter 9), and behavioral self-management approaches (chapter 10) could be integrated easily into a comprehensive discipline-intervention program that would prevent school children's misbehavior problems. Respectively these approaches might help students (a) to understand the social consequences of their misbehavior and to plan more appropriate problem-solving actions, (b) to develop more appropriate social interaction skills so that socially inept behaviors are not perceived by teachers as misbehavior, and (c) to apply self-monitoring strategies that encourage acceptable behavior and interfere with or interrupt unacceptable behavior. The individual and group counseling approaches discussed in chapter 7 might also become important components of a discipline-intervention plan, and study-skills training approaches (chapter 5) might prevent misbehavior when they decrease a student's academic failure or frustration in the classroom.

REVIEW OF THE LITERATURE ON SCHOOL DISCIPLINE

Conceptually, the systematic problem-solving approach toward addressing and preventing discipline problems involves four broad, interacting components: problem identification, problem analysis, intervention based on the first two components, and an evaluation of the intervention and its intended effects (Knoff, 1984a). This heuristic model summarizes much of the psychological literature addressing discipline. To date, no empirically derived guidelines have been generated with which to address discipline problems. Indeed, no actuarial or other decision model exists at this time to determine which specific intervention theory or model to embrace or to implement, and under what circumstances. Guided by the conceptual, problem-solving model described below, this is clearly an area for future research.

Problem identification determines primarily whether a referred discipline problem is an actual problem, specific to the student in question. At times, a perceived discipline problem may be (a) a reflection of rigid or zealous community norms; (b) due to a teacher's lack of confidence, knowledge, skill, training, and/or objectivity; (c) an actual discipline problem, but one that involves a group of individuals exhibiting the same or similar difficulties in one classroom or building; or (d) an actual problem specific to the targeted student. Even before analyzing the referred problem, therefore, the special services practitioner must determine "who owns the problem." When done ecologically, this question may have multiple answers. That is, the student may be misbehaving, yet the student's teacher, family members, and peer group may also be contributing to, supporting, or reinforcing the problem.

Two important perspectives that clarify who owns the problem and whether the referred student has been correctly identified are the *normative* and the *developmental* perspectives. Briefly, the normative perspective compares the referred student with others in the classroom or school building in order to validate the misbehavior, given local norms, and to determine if the student is the only one with the problem. The developmental perspective compares the student to accepted norms for behavioral, psychological, and social-emotional development to determine if the manifested behavior is expected and acceptable given the student's chronological age or developmental maturity. Naturally, these perspectives can be expanded by other, more theoretical perspectives. Clearly, for example, Rogers, Adler, Skinner, and Bandura all have their own definitions of typical behavior, misbehavior, and emotionally or behaviorally disturbed behavior. A number of these theoretical perspectives will be considered.

Assuming that the referred student has been identified correctly as exhibiting a discipline problem, problem analysis must be completed in preparation for and to ensure an appropriate intervention program. Four interdependent analysis procedures, reflecting a summarization of the literature, can guide this process: the *ecological/systems*, *group process/ social psychological*, *developmental/psychoeducational*, and *theoretical/ psychological* procedures.

The ecological/systems procedures involve analyses of the various classroom, building, district, family, and community systems that may be interdependently influencing the discipline problem and require attention as part of a multimodal intervention. The group process/social psychological analyses focus particularly on the referred student's classroom, its group development, and its interpersonal processes and norms; this may further clarify the discipline problem and classroom reactions and responses to it. The developmental/psychoeducational procedures analyze the comprehensive impact of childhood development in general and of the interaction of cognition, learning and behavior in particular as it relates to the referred behavior. And, finally, the theoretical/psychological procedures involve analyses consistent with the many theoretical explanations of misbehavior, its causes, and its effects. All of these analyses should be focused on a comprehensive understanding of the discipline problem and the determination of which intervention directions to pursue. A problem analysis using only one of these areas may be satisfactory for some discipline problems; for others the analysis may require all four areas before a full understanding of the dynamics and interrelationships specific to the problem is apparent.

With respect to intervention, three broad areas have been identified: the "effective teacher," student/self-management, and theoretical/psychological interventions. Briefly, the effective teacher interventions involve best-practice strategies that are supported both theoretically and empirically and intervene directly and efficiently with misbehavior, often preventing its recurrence. The student/self-management interventions are strategies that interrupt, interfere with, or prevent misbehavior, and result in appropriate, often prosocial behavior. Misbehaving students are taught to implement these strategies by themselves at appropriate times. The theoretical/psych-
ological interventions are theorist-generated strategies (e.g., from Harris, Dreikurs, or Goldstein) that may or may not have empirical support, but that are consistent within a described framework and conception of normal versus abnormal behavior. Specific strategies and approaches from these three intervention areas will be discussed below from primary, secondary, and tertiary prevention perspectives.

Specific to the evaluation of the intervention program should be the investigation of both intended and unintended effects relative to the referred student's ecological system. Further, this evaluation should include both process and product evaluations and formative and summative evaluations. The process evaluation simply evaluates teachers' satisfaction with the implementation and results of the intervention; the product evaluation assesses whether there has been an actual decrease in the referred misbehavior. The formative evaluation occurs while the intervention is actually being implemented, and determines its progress and the necessity of any fine-tuning; the summative evaluation occurs once the intervention has been terminated, and determines its overall success and what improvements might have increased its effectiveness and impact. All four types of evaluation are important, as they determine the overall validity and utility of the problem-solving process and of the intervention program. Significantly, evaluation should not be planned after the intervention has been implemented. Rather, it should be fully integrated into the problem-solving process. The problem identification and problem analysis steps must be used to develop baselines for the process and product evaluations, and using the discussions that outline the intervention program as a time to plan criteria and methodologies for the formative and summative evaluations, respectively. Additional information on the evaluative process is available in Maher and Bennett (1984).

The preventive aspect of the systematic problem-solving approach involves primary, secondary, and tertiary prevention programming. Primary prevention programs are generally proactive, community- or school district-wide activities, aimed at increasing awareness and coordinating action toward minimizing all student misbehavior before it occurs. Secondary prevention programs focus on clearly identified subgroups of students who demonstrate characteristics or precursor behaviors that make them at risk for discipline problems and on interventions implemented to ensure that these problems do not occur. Tertiary prevention programs are reactive interventions developed to address already-existing discipline problems and are implemented to decrease or to eliminate their future occurrences. Conceptually, these three preventive approaches can interact with the four problem-solving components to guide the resolution of any discipline-related problem (see Figure 8.1). For example, a problem requiring a primary prevention program would be addressed best by first identifying the problem, then analyzing it fully, next developing and implementing a comprehensive intervention plan, and finally evaluting its multifaceted effects. Adding an ecological/systems perspective, it also should be emphasized that, to be maximally successful, some preventive intervention programs will involve more than the misbehaving student; they also may involve the student's peers, school teachers, support staff, administrators, classroom, school district, home, and community.

A review of primary, secondary, and tertiary prevention interventions suggests that a great deal more empirical research is needed in all areas. Although some areas have substantial empirical support (e.g., the behavior modification/therapy interventions in the tertiary prevention area), other areas are represented primarily by theoretical conceptualizations and interventions with relatively little attendant experimental testing and support. Below, a number of specific discipline interventions are described within each of the three preventive approaches.

FIGURE 8.1 A comprehensive model of discipline in the schools:
A consultation problem-solving model

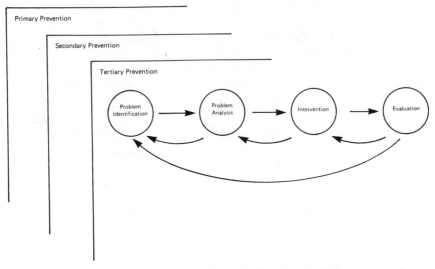

Note. This model must also take into account the student's ecology, including peers, teachers, school support staff and administrators, conditions and characteristics at home and in the community, as well as general community values.

Primary Prevention Interventions

Because they focus on all students before they have exhibited discipline problems, many primary prevention programs depend on home, school, and community cooperation and coordination. For example, a comprehensive primary mental health project in Connecticut (Allen, Chinsky, Larcen, Lochman, & Selinger, 1976) coordinated its school and community resources by teaching the students in an entire school district to successfully use independent problem-solving skills through a classroom-based curriculum. In Rochester, New York, the Primary Mental Health Project (Cowen, 1982) has developed community, family, and school training programs focused on children's socialization and problem-solving skills, by teaching parents and others how to nurture these skills before negative behaviors and habits arise. Finally, other parent-training curricula, such as Active Parenting (Popkin, 1983) and Parent Effectiveness Training (Gordon, 1970), have developed effective parenting philosophies, skills, and general practices that counteract misbehavior and foster increased parent–child communication and understanding.

Although additional research is needed to further identify the specific variables that make these programs successful, they have demonstrated that communities can coordinate and implement successful, comprehensive programs that decrease school discipline problems. Further, many of these primary prevention programs have provided effective interventions for use in secondary and tertiary prevention programs. This is an important point. Although this chapter has created artificial boundaries (e.g., separating primary, secondary, and tertiary prevention strategies) for organization's sake, many primary prevention program components can be adapted and implemented within secondary or tertiary programs, making the resultant program significantly more successful and effective. Special services professionals are urged to explore these generalization potentials; and they should not limit themselves to the necessarily abridged indications appearing throughout this chapter.

From a school perspective, the development of a well-defined, school-wide discipline policy may be the best preventive program available to encourage appropriate school behavior. Such a policy should be sensitive to students' developmental changes across the age span, and it should clearly identify expected behavior, inappropriate behavior, and the consequences of both types of behavior at various age or grade levels. Significantly, by emphasizing expected behaviors, the policy can become a teaching tool whereby students can learn new, prosocial behaviors instead of simply being told what "not to do." The policy also should specify (a) how and when school officials above the teacher (e.g., the principal, the superintendent) will become involved in a discipline problem, and (b) what exclusionary interventions will be available to school staff (e.g., in-school suspension, detention, expulsion), when they can be used, and what appeal or due process rights are available to the students involved. Finally, the discipline policy will have its greatest impact when supported by parents, students, and school personnel, including the paraprofessional and maintenance staff (e.g., custodians, cafeteria workers).

In addition to the discipline policy, primary prevention research has identified interventions that can decrease the misbehavior of most school children. Many of these interventions involve effective-teacher techniques (see above); the children are often passive recipients of these interventions. Below is a summary of the empirically derived teacher characteristics or actions known to facilitate the management of student conduct (Florida Coalition for the Development of a Performance Evaluation System, 1983):

1. *Rule specification, clarification, practice, and monitoring* (Greenwood, Hops, Delquardi, & Guild, 1974; Herman & Traymontana, 1971). When classroom rules are explicitly outlined for students, are modeled and practiced for and by them, and are enforced by positive reinforcement for compliance and specific feedback for non-compliance, then misbehavior generally decreases while on-task behavior and academic achievement increases.

2. *Teacher withitness* (Borg, 1975; Brophy & Everston, 1976; Kounin,

1977). When teachers identify the precursors and initial incidences of misbehavior and intervene with the most critical elements of that misbehavior to prevent its exacerbation and its spread to other students, and provide incompatible, acceptable alternatives, then misbehavior generally decreases.

3. *Teacher attentiveness and intervention preparedness* (Kounin, 1977; O'Leary, Kaufman, Kass, & Drabman, 1970). This point refers to the teacher's ability to monitor concurrent situations when one involves a potential for student misbehavior, and to intervene if necessary without affecting the other ongoing activity or situation. When intervention is necessary, the teacher is able to identify misbehaving students, to specify the inappropriate behaviors or circumstances and why they are unacceptable, and to suggest acceptable behaviors using quiet reprimands and proximity control. This entire process generally decreases misbehavior and prevents other students from increasing their agitation and subsequent disruptiveness.

4. *Teacher interaction: facilitating participation/performance and maintaining teaching pace* (Kounin, 1977). A teacher's ability to: (a) keep students positively involved in oral learning activities (e.g., preparing them with questions before calling on them for answers; alerting them that anyone may be called on at any time), and (b) avoid irrelevant interruptions, content redundancies, and the unnecessary use of small group activities will help in maintaining the momentum of a classroom lesson or lecture, while also decreasing opportunities for student misbehavior.

5. *Effective praise* (Becker & Armstrong, 1968; Brophy, 1981). General and noncontingent teacher praise effectively increases primary grade students' appropriate behavior. For older students, however, praise should be specific, low key, sincere, and contingent. In general, the most effective praise has these latter characteristics. Additional characteristics of the most effective praise are that its delivery is varied over time; it rewards specified performance criteria; it provides students with feedback about their competence or the value of their accomplishments; and it relates the present good performance to past good performances (Brophy, 1981).

Even though effective teaching interventions are indirectly applied to children (i.e., they are not taught directly to them), some primary prevention programs do target school children as their primary, active participants. Many of these programs teach societal, affective, and/or personal values (e.g., Values Clarification as developed by Raths, Harmin, & Simon, 1966; Simon, Howe, & Kirschenbaum, 1978), social problem-solving skills (e.g., Gesten & Weissberg, chapter 3 of this volume), and/or appropriate behavioral responses to difficult interactive situations or dilemmas. These programs assume that knowledge of these skills will help children (a) to avoid situations that could result in appropriate behavioral responses, and (b) to consider the consequences of their actions in all situations so that misbehavior is not considered a viable option at any time. Although student self-management is the primary goal, some of these programs are built upon specific theoretical tenets and perspectives. Special services professionals should investigate the theoretical under-pinnings of any potential primary prevention curriculum to ensure that it is consistent with the needs of the specific target group and with the philosophies of those who implement the program.

The revised Developing Understanding of Self and Others (DUSO; D. Dinkmeyer & D. Dinkmeyer, Jr., 1982) and the Toward Affective De-velopment (TAD; Dupont, Gardner, & Brody, 1974) curricula exemplify two primary prevention, affective education programs (see Baskin & Hess, 1980, for a critical, comprehensive review). Collectively, these approaches consist of many structured classroom activities that address such topics as friendship; communication; individual differences; feelings, problem solving and consequences; relaxation; and social-behavioral interrela-tionships. Generally, these programs provide an internally determined chronology of socialization and social skills development; focus on one skill or construct requiring less than 1 hour of classroom time per week; provide the teacher with a detailed lesson plan of relevant stories, activities, and visual aids; recommend generalization strategies for use throughout the week; and are developed as an ongoing curricular activity spanning the entire school year. DUSO 1 and DUSO 2 were developed for pre-kindergarten through fourth-grade students, while TAD is used primarily in the fourth through sixth grades. On the secondary prevention level, these curricula could be used with identified groups of students who are participating in counseling or socialization groups because of their poor interactive and social skills.

Secondary Prevention Interventions

Because they focus on at-risk populations and the early identification of potential discipline problems, secondary prevention interventions target the following types of student groups: (a) low achievers whose academic frustration leads to acting-out behavior; (b) students whose familial dis-cipline styles have not prepared them behaviorally for the external structure of the school setting; and (c) individuals who are influenced negatively by their own or older peer groups toward misbehavior, defiance of adults or authorities, or other attention-seeking behaviors. These targeted students often need exposure and training in specific skills and interactions that inhibit inappropriate behavior and encourage pro-social behavior. One example of a secondary prevention program, in this context, is the Structured Learning Therapy (SLT) program (Goldstein, Sprafkin, Gershaw, & Klein, 1980; McGinnis, Goldstein, Sprafkin, & Gershaw, 1984).

The multidimensional, skillstreaming approach of SLT targets handicapped and nonhandicapped children and adolescents who lack prosocial, interpersonal, stress-management, and planning skills. These are the individuals who often manifest the aggressive, immature, and developmentally inappropriate behaviors that exist as or contribute to discipline problems. Although many of the elementary-aged and adolescent skillstreaming areas of focus have the same labels, they vary according to the unique developmental needs, levels, and issues inherent in each age group. The elementary-age skillstreaming areas (with specific examples) involve: Classroom Survival Skills (listening, asking for help, following instructions); Friendship-Making Skills (beginning a conversation, sharing, apologizing); Skills for Dealing with Feelings (expressing feelings, recognizing others' feelings, dealing with anger); Skill Alternatives to Aggression (using self-control and problem solving, accepting consequences); and Skills for Dealing with Stress (showing sportsmanship, responding to failure, saying no). The adolescent skillstreaming areas involve: Beginning Social Skills; Advanced Social Skills; Skills for Dealing with Feelings; Skill Alternatives to Aggression; Skills for Dealing with Stress; and Planning Skills.

Each skillstreaming skill is taught systematically, practiced, and reinforced in a group format using SLT, which consists of behavioral modeling, role playing, performance feedback, and transfer of training components. Each skill is taught by listing the title of the skill, helping students to identify the behavioral steps necessary to perform it, and posting a chart with these behavioral steps outlined for later student reference. The skill is then modeled for the students, showing them what to do through a live role play presented by the adult group leaders. After the relevance of the skill to the students is discussed, they are then shown how to perform the skill, each practicing the skill in their own role play. The students then receive individual feedback on their performance and are assigned homework to facilitate the generalization of the skill to other settings and circumstances. This homework is reviewed at the beginning of the next session, when the skill and its behavioral components are again reinforced.

Research investigating the skillstreaming/SLT program have supported both its component parts (i.e., modeling, role playing, transfer of training) and the program as a whole (Goldstein, 1981; Greenleaf, 1982; McGinnis et al., 1984). To date, most programmatic research on SLT has been with more seriously maladjusted or aggressive children and adolescents. Future research should investigate the program's effectiveness with more routine discipline problems, its implementation and utilization in typical school settings, and its use by teachers as well as psychologically trained professionals.

Tertiary Prevention Interventions

As noted above, there are three broad intervention areas within the problem-solving format. Significantly, many of the primary prevention effective-teacher strategies can be equally effective within tertiary prevention programs. For example, teacher-student proximity, rule specification, and contingent reinforcement and punishment have successfully curtailed active misbehavior in the classroom. The student/self-management interventions, meanwhile, generally are first taught to students by teachers or special service practitioners until they are independently applied by these referred students to prevent or interrupt their misbehavior. Examples of student/self-management strategies include cognitive behavioral techniques, relaxation or guided fantasy therapies, social problem-solving interventions, and direct or vicarious modeling approaches. Some of these are discussed further in chapter 10. Finally, there are innumerable theoretical/psychological interventions in the tertiary prevention area. Below, these interventions will be particularly emphasized through a conceptual model and specific, successfully documented strategies.

Wolfgang and Glickman (1986) have organized the tertiary theoretical/psychological interventions into three broad conceptual areas. Theories and interventions in the *non-interventionist* area generally posit that children can solve their own discipline problems and realize their potential of appropriate behavior if given a nurturing, nonjudgmental, reflective environment, with a teacher who facilitates their social development and maturation. Theories and interventions in the *interactionalist* area believe that misbehaving students need to be responsible for their inappropriate behavior and its change, and that if change does not occur with teacher supervision, then teachers must make the individual assume responsibility. Theories and interventions in the *interventionist* area assume that teachers must structure the misbehaving student's environment and reinforcement contingencies so that appropriate behavior is shaped and reinforced, and inappropriate behavior is extinguished or punished. Specific theorists and examples of their intervention strategies, within these conceptual areas, are summarized in Table 8.1 and a representative sample is described in greater detail below.

TABLE 8.1 Primary, Secondary, and Tertiary Discipline Interventions Across the
Teacher Effectiveness, Student Self-Management, and Psychological/Theoretical
Components of the Problem-Solving Model

	Components		
Level	*Teacher Effectiveness*	*Student Self-Management*	*Psychological/ Theoretical*
Primary	School discipline code Community, family, school preventive, socialization, and problem-solving programs Classroom rule specification Teacher/staff withitness Teacher/staff preparedness Teacher/staff interaction Effective praise	Social-skills training Problem-solving training Self-control training Study-skills training	Developing Understanding of Self and Others (DUSO) Toward Affective Development (TAD) Active Parenting Parent Effectiveness Training Values Clarification
Secondary	Same strategies as above focused on an at-risk or early identified population	Structured Learning Therapy (SLT) Social problem solving (see chapter 3) Social-skills training (see chapter 9) Behavioral self-management approaches (see chapter 10) Study-skills training (see chapter 5)	Same strategies as above focused on an at-risk or early identified population
Tertiary	Same strategies as above focused on preventing, interfering, or stopping student misbehavior that has occurred and continues to occur	Same strategies as above focused on preventing, interfering, or stopping student misbehavior that has occurred or continues to occur Relaxation therapy Behavioral/cognitive thought stopping Systematic desensitization Behaviorial self-monitoring techniques	*Non-Interventionist Strategies:* Parent/Teacher Effectiveness Training Transactional Analysis Values Clarification *Interactionalist Strategies:* Dreikurs' Social Discipline Model Glasser's Reality Therapy Redl's Influence Techniques *Interventionist Strategies* Social Learning Theory approaches Behavior Modification techniques Assertive Discipline approach Corporal and other punishment techniques Other approaches and strategies above which are grounded by psychological/ theoretical tenets.

Non-Interventionist: Thomas Gordon

Gordon, who developed the Teacher-Effectiveness Training (TET) approach (Gordon, 1974), which is based on many of Carl Rogers' humanistic notions, believes that misbehavior reflects a student's underlying unhappiness or frustration. By using *active listening*, a process of critical listening with reflections on thought or feeling, the student is helped to realize that the teacher is concerned with helping to specify and to solve the problem. After achieving rapport, the teacher further supports the student's own problem-solving capacities and developing, positive self-concept. Throughout this process, however, the teacher also communicates his or her own feelings and expectations to the student using *I-messages* (e.g., "Mary, I don't like it when you talk out in class because it disrupts my train of thought and the ability of others to listen to me."). Ultimately, the teacher and the student develop a mutually acceptable plan (a "win-win" plan) to eliminate the problem. This plan is developed by (a) defining the problem, (b) generating possible solutions, (c) evaluating and deciding on final solutions, and (d) implementing and evaluating these solutions.

Research evaluting TET has been relatively limited, and has focused generally on only one or two components of the program. Although teachers' I-messages (Carducci, 1975) have reduced students' disruptive behavior, and the overall TET program has resulted in more positive student-teacher relationships (Galloway, Thornton, & Evans, 1976), far more sophisticated and controlled research is needed.

Interactionalist: Rudolph Dreikurs

Dreikurs, who is significantly influenced by Alfred Adler, believes that there are four primary, conscious goals that motivate children's misbehavior: the need for attention; the need for power and control; revenge; and to compensate for feelings of helplessness, inadequacy, and frustration. To decrease misbehavior, the teacher must determine which underlying motivation is causing the behavior and then work to change the child's goal. Specific suggests of techniques that teachers can use for dealing with each of these categories of misbehavior include:

1. *Attention*: Discuss the situation with the student and work out a plan for change; reinforce positive behavior while ignoring misbehavior; catch the student being good and reinforce that behavior; develop a plan of logical consequences and handle through class discussions.
2. *Power*: Avoid giving in to the student by getting into a power struggle; diffuse the student–teacher power struggle by giving an unexpected, friendly response to the power-seeking behavior;

identify the power goal to the student; acknowledge that the teacher really cannot force the student to acquiesce to adult demands; allow the defiance (so long as no one else is disrupted), yet apply logical consequences; give the student acceptable power through class jobs; reinforce student cooperation; allow the class to react to the student's behavior.

3. *Revenge*: Confront the student with the underlying goal, and offer to develop a joint plan for change; provide boundaries to the behavior (e.g., that hurting self and others will not be accepted); maintain empathic and supportive communication; help the student to be more accepted by the class through group support activities.

4. *Helplessness and inadequacy*: Identify the underlying goal to the student and encourage the student to keep trying; plan academic and other activities that allow the student opportunities to experience success; plan activities that provide the student with group support and encouragement; and offer ongoing assistance and availability.

Dreikurs also recommends that teachers demonstrate and practice respect for students, kindness, firmness and clear classroom limits; democratic teaching approaches with shared responsibility and joint problem solving or decision-making; encouragement rather than reinforcement or praise; and emphases on natural and logical consequences (Dreikurs & Grey, 1968). Natural consequences are environmental consequences that occur by themselves due to a student's own behavior; they are not set up by the teacher (e.g., a student who rushes to hand in a paper may get a low mark due to errors made in haste). Logical consequences are arranged with the student in advance by a teacher in order to respond to that student's misbehavior; these consequences are linked conceptually with the misbehavior (e.g., a student who constantly taps his pencil may lose the pencil for the remainder of the activity and then have to make up his work during recess or at home).

Hyman, Flanagan, and Smith (1982) identified 10 reasonably adequate studies that investigated aspects of Dreikur's (and Adler's) classroom discipline approaches. Results included some generally positive programmatic and case study applications; support for indirect rather than direct or non-intervention approaches to address student misbehavior; and one high school program that significantly decreased violent disciplinary incidents. Overall, however, the research support was not compelling (more is needed), and the difficulty of discriminating which facets of the Dreikurs program were responsible for its success was apparent.

Interactionalist: William Glasser

Glasser believes that: (a) students can control their own behavior; (b) classroom rules must be explicit and enforced, and make students responsible for their own behavior; (c) students choose to misbehave and that this is not acceptable; and (d) teachers should deal with students' here-and-now behavior, and not accept excuses. While, at first glance, this may sound very teacher-directed and authoritative, this approach actually requires that students take charge of their own behavior and, if more direct intervention is needed, that teachers force students to retain responsibility over any necessary behavioral changes (Charles, 1985). One of Glasser's specific interventions involves the development of a *behavioral plan.*

The behavioral plan is written by the student who has exhibited persistent misbehavior; the teacher decides to force the student to take full responsibility for both the misbehavior and its appropriate change. This plan consists of a statement of the problem, a specific, positive plan of action to change the problem, a list of positive consequences (if the behavior is changed) and negative consequences (if the misbehavior persists) and a written and signed commitment by the student that this plan is acceptable and will be enacted in good faith. Minimally, the plan's development may be a problem-solving technique for the student toward changing his or her own behavior and an intervention that will resolve the problem in a positive manner. If the plan is unsuccessful, Glasser ultimately recommends stronger, "reality-oriented" interventions: in-school suspension, out-of-school suspension, and alternative education or institutional settings.

Reviews of studies evaluating Glasser's classroom approaches (Clarizio & McCoy, 1983; Hyman, et al., 1982) identified both positive and unremarkable successes. Although some studies reported improvement in student attitude and self-concept, other studies have noted no improvement in these areas subsequent to teacher in-service programs and classroom implementation. Again, the relative lack of studies that controlled specific variables and utilized sound methodological designs suggests the need for more research, rather than a rejection of this approach and its component intervention procedures.

Interventionists: Behavior Modification

Of the four predominant behavioral intervention areas (classical or Pavlovian conditioning, operant or Skinnerian conditioning, social learning theory, and cognitive), the operant conditioning area has most addressed discipline or behaviorial management problems. The operant paradigm views behavior as a function of critical, discriminated stimuli (available and observable in the environment), reinforcements (e.g., token, social, activity-oriented, and primary or biologically based), and stimulus-reinforcement contingencies (positive, aversive, and punishing). Misbehavior, then, occurs when a stimulus (e.g., a child's desire to receive teacher attention similar to other peers) elicits, voluntarily or by chance, a behavioral response (noisily clowning around, which indeed does draw the teacher's attention) that establishes a contingency ("When I clown around, I can get the teacher to notice me").

A vast number of behavior modification interventions at the tertiary prevention level have been developed and empirically validated. A comprehensive review involving positive reinforcement approaches, aversive procedures, and punishment procedures is beyond the focus of this chapter (see Sulzer-Azaroff & Mayer, 1986, for an extensive discussion). Briefly, however, positive approaches teach and/or reinforce behaviors that are acceptable and are incompatible with misbehavior, and reinforce absence or decrease of misbehavior. Interventions in this area include: (a) behavioral shaping and chaining, (b) reinforcing differential rates of alternate (Alt-R) or incompatible behaviors (DRI), (c) reinforcing differentially low rates of behavior (DRL), (d) reinforcing differential rates of diminishing behavior (DRD), and (e) reinforcing differential rates of nonoccurring behavior (DRO).

Aversive procedures involve the contingent withdrawal of a negative stimulus or of a (potential) positive reinforcement when an inappropriate behavior is discontinued. Two primary aversive procedures, *response cost* and *timeout*, have effectively decreased specific types of student misbehavior. Significantly, if timeout is not discontinued when a student's misbehavior has stopped, then it may be considered punishment. Punishment involves the application of an aversive stimulus after an inappropriate response in order to decrease or eliminate that response. *Overcorrection* exemplifies another behaviorial punishment technique.

Interventionist: Lee Canter

Canter's assertive discipline approach combines teachers' verbal assertiveness with a systematic program of behavioral rewards and punishments. Its underlying assumptions emphasize the teacher's right to establish a working classroom structure, disciplinary order, and behaviorial expectations that students must follow—all supported by administration and parents (L. Canter & M. Canter, 1976). Assertive discipline involves five important steps: the teacher (a) recognizes and removes any initial barriers that might undermine this disciplinary approach, (b) learns to set rules and boundaries for students, (c) is openly assertive when responding to discipline problems, (d) follows through on classroom rules, and (e) identifies and reinforces positive and appropriate behavior. Behaviorial interventions that are often integrated into this approach include (a) for misbehavior, timeout, loss of privileges and preferred activities, detentions, visits to the principal, and home consequences; and (b) for appropriate behavior, attention, special awards and privileges, positive feedback to parents, and group reinforcements. Although assertive discipline uses a number of empirically tested behaviorial interventions, its overall program requires additional field validation and differential evaluation.

As is evident, there are numerous tertiary prevention interventions for misbehavior, many of them with research support. Clearly, however, additional research is necessary not just to validate the effectiveness of each approach, but also to address when the questions of certain approaches should be used and how they should be used and how they should be implemented and applied. Procedures to help in this implementation process are currently available from Knoff (1984a), Maher (1981), and Wolfgang and Glickman (1986). This process, though, involves more than the teacher and the misbehaving child; often it involves a comprehensive organizational perspective. The next section provides this perspective through an introduction to planning and to evaluating discipline interventions.

GUIDELINES FOR PLANNING AND EVALUATION

Organizationally, a significant amount of cooperation and coordination is necessary to implement a school-wide preventive discipline program — from the school board down to the teaching staff. From a planning perspective, every school agent must recognize that there are at least two components of a discipline program: the administrative component, often overseen by the superintendent and including the curriculum and program chairs, as well as building principals, and the service delivery component, which is often the responsibility of the classroom teacher and of the special services professionals. To ensure a successful program, these two sometimes distinctly different components need to be explored, discussed, and understood by both administrators and by service delivery staff. Ultimately, success will be determined by the ability of both these professional groups to resolve critical differences, to agree to disagree at times, and to commit to a program that may not be perfect but is optimal under existing conditions. The organizational development of a preventive discipline program is critical to its success; further information in this area is available from Furtwengler and Konnert (1982).

Two ways to implement successful discipline interventions and to address both administrative and service delivery components of program development involve inservice programming and consultation processes. Knoff (1985b), describing the goals of a discipline inservice program, focused on teachers' abilities (a) to distinguish among misbehavior and conduct-disordered, emotionally disturbed, and maturationally delayed behaviors; (b) to identify their own disciplinary philosophies, styles, biases, strengths, and weaknesses; (c) to apply the conceptual problem-solving model toward solving discipline problems; and (d) to understand and to move toward more preventive programming in the areas of classroom management. Ultimately, the program and its follow-up consultation strives to increase teachers' knowledge and skills in this area so that they solve discipline problems in the classroom more independently. The in-service session is divided into four interacting units: value clarification and group process analysis, review of the problem-solving process above, study of special clinical techniques and issues, and problem-solving practice through case study analysis. The initial unit utilizes various value clarification and organizational psychology exercises as well as discussion in order to address some of the administrative issues delineated above, and the latter three units deal primarily with service-delivery practices. Knoff (1985b) described the in-service program as a 10-unit sequence, yet it could be adapted easily to fit the needs of any school district. While this approach has not been empirically evaluated, it has been used in a number of workshops and consultations throughout the nation.

Consultation processes are closely aligned with the inservice approach and with the entire process of discipline intervention. Clearly, the inservice program used alone provides at best fundamental information, and limited skill-building and case-study practice. To maximize the effects of the inservice program, administrators and teachers must receive ongoing supervision and consultation as they use their new knowledge and skills for their respective building, district, or classroom problems. As its practitioners become more expert and successful, this professional consultation may be decreased to an on-call or as-needed basis. The extensive consultation literature cannot of course be fully reviewed here (see Conoley, 1981, and Knoff, 1984b, for reviews). However, it appears that the process and organization development models of consultation may be best suited to facilitate the administrative component of discipline program development, whereas the behavioral, mental health, and psychoeducational models can address the service delivery component. All of the consultation models should be used in a multimodal fashion, similar to the multimethod assessment and multimodal intervention approaches alluded to throughout this chapter.

Regardless of the administrative or service delivery components involved, discipline interventions involve ethical issues and procedures that must be practiced in a manner consistent with any other educational or mental health oriented intervention. For special services practitioners, the ethical codes of the American Psychological Association (1981) and of the National Association of School Psychologists (1984) provide representative structure and direction. Inherent in both of these documents is the need for professional responsibility and competence, specific training in those interventions that are recommended and implemented, and special care to uphold assiduously the welfare of the student. Because many of the discipline interventions discussed have only preliminary empirical support, practitioners should evaluate any intervention continually so that it can be discontinued if negative or unintended effects are observed. Finally, the ethics of using punishing techniques when other effective, positive approaches are available should be seriously questioned. Practitioners should consult state legal statutes in this area especially; some states have specific guidelines and criteria for the use of punishment and aversive behavioral techniques.

Even more specific to discipline and in contrast to corporal punishment, one lower court decision (*in re Gault*, 1967) and two Supreme Court decisions (*Goss v. Lopez*, 1975; *Wood v. Strickland*, 1975) guarantee public school students some form of due process (usually a hearing) before a school suspension of any length can be instituted. The latter case also noted that school board members could be held accountable for any unfair expulsion of a student. Special services professionals have the legal and ethical responsibility to be aware of these and future decisions and to ensure their implementation in the schools. Ignoring such responsibility could result in a professional's inclusion in a civil suit filed against a school district's board or its administrative leaders. Special services professionals also have the responsibility to monitor any disciplinary and behavior-change techniques in order to ensure that they are practiced professionally, ethically, and effectively.

SUMMARY

This chapter has described various discipline intervention approaches designed for classroom use. Initially defining student misbehavior and discipline and outlining a problem-solving model of discipline, a preventive approach to solving discipline problems was emphasized. Given the non-empirical nature of many discipline interventions, future research should address (a) the variables and characteristics underlying successful discipline interventions, (b) the programmatic success of the various discipline models and their interventions, (c) the components of the problem-solving process, and (d) those decision-making mechanisms that identify specific analysis and intervention approaches for specific types and circumstances of discipline problems. The chapter concluded with guidelines for planning and evaluation, suggestions for facilitating the administrative and service delivery implementation of discipline programs, and a brief consideration of ethical and legal issues and practices.

ANNOTATED BIBLIOGRAPHY

Dreikurs, R., Grunwald, B. B., & Pepper, F. C. (1982). *Maintaining sanity in the classroom: Classroom management techniques* (2nd ed.). New York: Harper & Row.

An excellent summary of the theory and techniques of Dreikurs and his social discipline perspective. Dreikurs advocates the democratic classroom and blends a child-oriented view of education with the realities and responsibilities that children need. Discusses ways to work with discipline referrals, logical consequences and their utility, and ways to cope with special academic and behavioral problems.

Glasser, W. (1969). *Schools without failure*. New York: Harper & Row.

Glasser's classic book outlines his reality therapy approach to discipline problems and their resolution. Discussed are the many educational practices and characteristics that help children to fail in school and to develop negative self-expectations and self-concepts. The reality therapy steps that help students to take responsibility for their own behavior are outlined, as well as are the three types of classroom meetings and possible activities and topics for discussion.

Millman, H. L., Schaefer, C. E., & Cohen, J. J. (1980). *Therapies for school behavior problems*. San Francisco, CA: Jossey-Bass.

Reviews the recent literature across a number of common referral problems and concerns. Annotated bibliographies encapsulate the most important studies. Included in the review are interventions for classroom management problems, immature behaviors, habit disorders, disturbed peer relationships, and disturbed relationships with teachers.

Sulzer-Azaroff, B., & Mayer, G. R. (1986). *Achieving educational excellence: Using behavioral strategies*. New York: Holt, Rinehart & Winston.

A comprehensive volume that discusses the major behavior modification principles, elements, and techniques in the field. Provides pragmatic examples of past research that exemplify best practices in dealing with discipline and other behavioral concerns. The discussion includes the principles and procedures for motivating, instructing, and managing behavior; applications toward improving instruction and conduct; and organizational management strategies, all as they apply to the classroom and the educational process.

Wolfgang, C. H., & Glickman, C. D. (1986). *Solving discipline problems: Strategies for classroom teachers* (2nd ed.). Boston: Allyn & Bacon.

Practical, clearly written, providing a conceptual model of discipline that integrates a number of important theorists and their strategies. Includes reviews of teacher-effectiveness training, transactional analysis, values clarification, Dreikurs social discipline, reality therapy, behavior modification and punishment, and assertive discipline. Guidelines for teacher planning and integration strengthen the generalizability of this volume.

REFERENCES

Allen, G. J., Chinskey, J. M., Larcen, S. W., Lochman, J. E., & Selinger, H. V. (1976). *Community psychology and the schools: A behaviorally oriented multilevel preventive approach*. Hillsdale, NJ: Erlbaum.

American Psychological Association. (1981). *Ethical principles of psychologists*. Washington, DC: Author.

Baskin, E. J., & Hess, R. D. (1980). Does affective education work? A review of seven programs. *Journal of School Psychology, 18*, 40–50.

Becker, W. C., & Armstrong, W. R. (1968). Production and elimination of disruptive classroom behavior by systematically varying teacher's behavior. *Journal of Applied Behavior Analysis, 1*, 35–45.

Borg, W. R. (1975). Teacher classroom management skills and pupil behavior. *Journal of Experimental Education, 44*, 52–58.

Brophy, J. (1981). Teacher praise: A functional analysis. *Review of Educational Research, 51*, 5–32.

Brophy, J., & Everston, C. M. (1976). *Learning from teaching*. Boston: Allyn & Bacon.

Canter, L., & Canter, M. (1976). *Assertive discipline: A take-charge approach for today's educators*. Seal Beach, CA: Canter & Associates.

Carducci, R. A. (1975). *A comparison of I-messages with commands in the control of disruptive classroom behavior.* Unpublished doctoral dissertation, University of Nevada.

Charles, C. M. (1985). *Building classroom discipline: From models to practice* (2nd ed.). New York: Longman.

Clarizio, H. F., & McCoy, G. F. (1983). *Behavior disorders in children* (3rd ed.). New York: Harper & Row.

Conoley, J. C. (Ed.). *Consultation in schools: Theory, research, procedures.* New York: Academic Press.

Cowen, E. L. (Ed.). (1982). Research in primary prevention in mental health [Special issue]. *American Journal of Community Psychology, 10.*

Dinkmeyer, D., & Dinkmeyer, D., Jr. (1982). *Developing understanding of self and others: (DUSO) 1 and 2* (rev. ed.). Circle Pines, N: American Guidance Service.

Dobson, J. (1970). *Dare to discipline.* Wheaton, IL: Tyndale House.

Dreikurs, R., & Grey, L. (1968). *A new approach to discipline: Logical consequences.* New York: Hawthorn Books.

Dreikurs, R., Grunwald, B. B., & Pepper, F. C. (1982). *Maintaining sanity in the classroom: Classroom management techniques* (2nd ed.). New York: Harper & Row.

Dupont, H., Gardner, O.S., & Brody, D. S. (1974). *The tasks of affective development.* Circle Pines, MN: American Guidance Service.

Elam, S. M. (1983). The Gallup education surveys: Impressions of a poll watcher. *Phi Delta Kappan, 65,* 26–32.

Florida Coalition for the Development of a Performance Evaluation System. (1983). *Domains: Knowledge base of the Florida Performance Measurement System.* Tallahassee, FL: Office of Teacher Education, Certification, and Inservice Staff Development.

Furtwengler, W. J., & Konnert, W. (1982). *Improving school discipline: An administrator's guide.* Boston: Allyn & Bacon.

Galloway, N., Thorton, R. W., & Evans, J. H. (1976). *Student/teacher interaction as a function of teacher training.* (*ERIC Document Reproduction Services* No. ED 124 525).

Gallup, G. H. (1983). Fifteenth annual Gallup Poll of the public attitudes toward the public schools. *Phi Delta Kappan, 65,* 33–47.

Goldstein, A. P. (1981). *Psychological skill training.* Elsmford, NY: Pergamon Press.

Goldstein, A. P., Sprafkin, R. P., Gershaw, N. J., & Klein, P. (1980). *Skillstreaming the adolescent: A structured learning approach to teaching prosocial skills.* Champaign, IL: Research Press.

Gordon, T. (1970). *PET: Parent effectiveness training.* New York: Wyden.

Gordon, T. (1974). *TET: Teacher effectiveness training.* New York: McKay.

Goss v. Lopez, 419 U.S. 565 (1975).

Greenleaf, D. O. (1982). The use of structured learning therapy and transfer programming with disruptive adolescents in a school setting. *Journal of School Psychology, 20,* 122–130.

Greenwood, C. R., Hops, H., Delquardi, J., & Guild, J. (1974). Group contingencies for group consequences in classroom mananagement: A further analysis. *Journal of Applied Behavior Analysis, 7,* 413–425.

Herman, S. H., & Traymontana, J. (1971). Instructions and group versus individual reinforcement in modifying disruptive group behavior. *Journal of Applied Behavior Analysis, 4,* 113–119.

Hyman, I., Flanagan, D., & Smith, K. (1982). Discipline in the schools. In C. R. Reynolds & T. B. Gutkin (Eds.), *The handbook of school psychology* (p. 454–480). New York: Wiley.

Hyman, I., McDowell, E., & Raines, B. (1977). Corporal punishment and alternatives in the schools: An overview of theoretical and practical issues. In J. Wise (Ed.), *Proceedings: Conference on corporal punishment in the schools.* Washington, DC: National Institute of Education.

In re Gault, 387 U.S.1, 87 S.Ct. 1428 (1967).

Ingraham v. Wright, 430 U.S. 651 (1977).

Jones, F. (1979). The gentle art of classroom discipline. *National Elementary Principal, 58,* 26–32.

Jones, R. S., & Tanner, L. N. (1981). Classroom discipline: The unclaimed legacy. *Phi Delta Kappan, 62,* 494–497.

Knoff, H. M. (1984a). A conceptual review of discipline in the schools: A consultation service model. *Journal of School Psychology, 22,* 335–345.

Knoff, H. M. (1984b). The practice of multimodal consultation: An integrating approach for consultation service delivery. *Psychology in the Schools, 21,* 83–91.

Knoff, H. M. (1985a). Best practices in dealing with discipline referrals. In A. Thomas & J. Grimes (Eds.), *Best practices in school psychology* (pp. 251–262). Washington, DC: National Association of School Psychologists.

Knoff, H. M. (1985b). Discipline in the schools: An inservice and consultation program for educational staffs. *The School Counselor, 32,* 211–218.

Kounin, J. S. (1977). *Discipline and group management in classrooms.* Huntington, NY: Krieger Publishing.

Maher, C. A. (1981). Decision analysis: An approach for multidisciplinary teams in planning special service programs. *Journal of School Psychology, 19,* 340–349.

Maher, C. A., & Bennett, R. E. (1984). *Planning and evaluating special education services.* Englewood Cliffs, NJ: Prentice-Hall.

McGinnis, E., Goldstein, A. P., Sprafkin, R. P., & Gershaw, N. J. (1984). *Skillstreaming the elementary school child: A guide for teaching prosocial skills.* Champaign, IL: Research Press.

National Association of School Psychologists. (1984). *Principles for professional ethics.* Washington, DC: Author.

National Association of School Psychologists. (1986). *Supporting paper on corporal punishment position statement.* Washington, DC: Author.

National Education Association. (1970). Corporal punishment: Teacher opinion. *National Education Association Research Bulletin, 48,* 48–49.

O'Leary, K. D., Kaufman, K. F., Kass, R. E., & Drabman, R. S. (1970). The effects of loud and soft reprimands on the behavior of disruptive students. *Exceptional Children, 37,* 145–155.

Popkin, M. H. (1983). *Active parenting handbook.* Atlanta, GA: Active Parenting.

Raths, L. E., Harmin, M., & Simon, S. B. (1966). *Values and teaching.* Columbus, OH: C. E. Merrill.

Simon, S. B., Howe, L. W., & Kirschenbaum, H. (1978). *Values clarification: A handbook of practical strategies for teachers and students* (rev. ed.). New York: Hart Publishing.

Sulzer-Azaroff, B., & Mayer, G. R. (1986). *Achieving educational excellence: Using behavioral strategies.* New York: Holt, Rinehart & Winston.

Wolfgang, C. H., & Glickman, C. D. (1986). *Solving discipline problems: Strategies for classroom teachers* (2nd ed.). Boston: Allyn & Bacon.

Wood v. Strickland, 95 S.Ct. 992; 420 U.S. 308 (1975).

9 Social-Skills Interventions: Research Findings and Training Techniques

STEPHEN N. ELLIOTT, FRANK M. GRESHAM, and ROBERT W. HEFFER

The acquisition of social skills is critical to the well being both of children and of the educational enterprise. This point is attested to by the recent volume of educational and psychological research on the development, assessment, and treatment of children's social behaviors. The reasons for this recent interest in children's social skills among educators and psychologists is based on research findings that emphasize the relationship between academic achievement and social skills (e.g., Feldhusen, Thurston, & Benning, 1970) and on the burgeoning belief that schools are an important environment for the development of socially competent individuals.

In this chapter, we review research on the classification, assessment, and treatment of children's social-skill problems and then focus on the implementation of interventions for children who experience a variety of social-skills deficits. As background for this discussion, we first examine some of the components of social skills to provide a definition and to suggest which students should be targeted for social-skills interventions.

COMPONENT BEHAVIORS AND DEFINITIONS OF SOCIAL SKILLS

Social skills have been described as the nexus between the individual and the environment, the tools used to initiate and maintain vital interpersonal relations (Phillips, 1978). Although many definitions of social skills have been offered, we believe that the following seven components, identified by Michelson, Sugai, Wood, and Kazdin (1983), are essential to a functional understanding of social skills.

1. Social skills are acquired primarily through learning (e.g., observation, modeling, rehearsal, and feedback).
2. Social skills comprise specific and discrete verbal and nonverbal behaviors.
3. Social skills entail both effective and appropriate initiations and responses.

4. Social skills maximize social reinforcement.
5. Social skills are interactive by nature and entail both effective and appropriate responsiveness.
6. Social skill performance is influenced by the characteristics of the environment.
7. Deficits and excesses in social performance can be specified and targeted for intervention. (p. 3)

Thus, social skills are learned behaviors that affect interpersonal relations with peers and adults. Importantly, we do not consider social skills as global personality traits. Rather, social skills are discrete, situationally specific behaviors that are affected by a person's age, sex, social status, and interactions with others.

IMPORTANCE OF SOCIAL SKILLS

A review of the research literature demonstrates convincingly that children who exhibit social-skills deficits appear to experience both short- and long-term negative consequences that appear to be precursors of more severe problems of adolescence and adulthood (Rinn & Markle, 1979). Social-skills deficits have also been related to numerous problems in adjusting to the normal classroom environment (Stumme, Gresham, & Scott, 1983). Socially unpopular children have been shown to lack a variety of social skills, such as communicating needs, cooperating, responding positively to peers, and making friends (Gottman, Gonso, & Rasmussen, 1975; LaGreca & Santogrossi, 1980). Research on classroom functioning has shown relationships between social-skills difficulties and measures of academic variables as well as between social-skills difficulties and other educationally related variables (Gresham, 1983a). Other studies have shown social skills to be related to teacher judgments of social status (LaGreca, 1981) and to teacher acceptance (Good & Brophy, 1978). As Gresham (1983b) summarized:

Children who possess adequate levels of social skills tend to demonstrate higher levels of academic performance, are viewed by teachers as enjoying higher sociometric status, attend to classroom tasks more frequently, ask more questions, and are better liked by teachers than socially unskilled children. (p. 163)

Coie (1985) asked, and answered empirically, "Who should be singled out for social-skills intervention?" Aggression and social withdrawal or isolation are the two behavioral criteria most frequently used to identify children at social risk. Coie analyzed past sociometric and observational research and concluded that the evidence indicated that children who are actively rejected by their peers are the group most at risk for future problems. These rejected children tended to continue to be rejected, both

across time and upon entering new peer groups, because the same pro-
vocative and disruptive behavior problems characterized interactions in
both old and new situations. Coie concluded "that rejected children are
more at risk for acting-out problems and are beleaguered by feelings of
lower self-worth and loneliness. The best available data would indicate this
is the group of children for whom preventive intervention programs are
most appropriate" (p. 148).

The remainder of this chapter will focus on methods of assessing and
treating social-skills deficits. As a means of summarizing the chapter, we
provide a four-category classification model of social-skills deficits that can
be used to select intervention methods.

METHODS OF ASSESSING SOCIAL SKILLS

A number of methods have been used to assess social skills of children
and adolescents. Recent reviews have identified the following assessment
procedures: (a) ratings by others, (b) sociometric techniques, (c) self-
report measures, (d) behavioral role-play measures, (e) behavioral interviews, and (f) naturalistic observations (Asher & Hymel, 1981; Foster &
Ritchey, 1979; Gresham, 1981, 1985a).

Assessment of social skills can be conceptualized as a series of
hypothesis-testing sequences. Hypotheses are generated in an attempt to
answer questions related to the following stages of assessment: (a)
identification/classification, (b) intervention, and (c) intervention
evaluation. Hypotheses are generated based on whatever information is
then available and then tested on subsequent occasions by gathering
additional information. Comprehensive social-skills assessments allow one
to identify and classify specific social-skill deficits, and evaluate the outcome of social-skills interventions.

A standard procedure for assessing social skills does not exist. Rather,
the hypotheses that are initially generated dictate the direction of subsequent assessment, as well as the questions to be answered and the
methods to be used. Assessment of social skills should proceed from that of
global behavioral information to that of specific behavioral information as
a means of selecting and planning intervention. By contrast, assessment for
the evaluation of intervention success typically proceeds in the opposite
direction, moving from behavior-specific outcomes to more global analyses
of important social outcomes (social validity).

Ideally, practitioners should assess using methods that possess reliability
(consistency of measurement), validity (capacity to answer a given
assessment question), and practicality (cost of collecting information)
(Gresham & Cavell, 1987). Unfortunately, few social-skills assessment
methods meet all three criteria of reliability, validity, and practicality.
Easily administered instruments (e.g., self-report scales), which are useful

for screening purposes, are of little help in designing interventions. Other methods that require considerably more effort from assessors and clients (e.g., naturalistic observations and self-monitoring) often have either equivocal or unknown psychometric properties (Dodge & Murphy, 1984; Gresham & Elliott, 1984). Moreover, there is a tendency for assessment data obtained from different sources to correlate moderately at best; more often, correlations are quite low (Matson, Esveldt-Dawson, & Kazdin, 1983). As a safeguard, multiple sources of information are required when assessing social skills.

The following assessment techniques were chosen primarily because they provide information on important targets of social-skill interventions for school practitioners and do so in a manner that is relatively reliable, valid, and practical.

Assessment for Identification and Classification

Several assessment procedures now in use generate information that determines the existence of social-skills problems. The most frequently used assessment procedures in this category are self-report measures, ratings by others, sociometric techniques, and behavioral role-play tasks (Gresham, 1985a; Gresham & Elliott, 1984). The majority of these assessment techniques are practical, given the ease of their administration and their relatively modest time consumption.

Teacher and parent ratings have been historically a prime source of information in the evaluation of behavior problems of children and adolescents (Edelbrock, 1983). Recently, ratings by adults, particularly teachers, have been used to assess social skills. The most comprehensive published teacher rating scale is the *Social Behavior Assessment* (SBA) developed by Stephens (1978). The SBA contains 136 social skills on which teachers rate children's behavior on a 3-point scale (i.e., *acceptable level*, *less than acceptable level*, or *never*). The literature concerning the SBA provides evidence for its reliability (interrater, internal consistency, and stability) and validity (content, criterion-related, and construct) (Gresham & Reschly, 1985; Stephens, 1980; Stumme, Gresham, & Scott, 1982, 1983).

Gresham and Elliott (Clark, Gresham, & Elliott, 1985; Gresham, Elliott, & Black, 1985) have recently developed the *Teacher Rating of Social Skills* (TROSS) scale. The TROSS is a 50-item rating scale on which teachers rate social behavior on a 3-point frequency dimension (*often true*, *sometimes true*, or *never true*). A unique feature of the TROSS is the inclusion of an importance dimension on which teachers specify whether each behavior is *critical* for classroom success, *important* for classroom success, or *unimportant* for classroom success. Having teachers evaluate behaviors using the importance criteria ensures the social validity of the behaviors being assessed and has implications for selecting target behaviors for intervention. For example, behaviors receiving a low frequency rating and a high importance rating should be top-priority behavior targets for social-skills interventions. Preliminary evidence on the TROSS indicates that it has a stable factor structure, adequate internal consistency ($r = .97$), and efficiency in discriminating mainstreamed mildly handicapped children from nonhandicapped children (Black, 1985; Clark et al., 1985; Gresham et al., 1985). The TROSS was designed to provide information comparable to that offered by the SBA, but to require less time for teachers to complete and to provide an importance dimension that facilitates the identification of target behaviors.

Sociometric techniques are useful in determining which children are poorly accepted, rejected, or unpopular. Two basic types of sociometric procedures commonly used are *peer nominations* and *peer ratings*. Both of these procedures can be keyed to nonbehavioral and behavioral criteria. Nonbehavioral criteria are based upon activities or attributes of children rather than on specific behaviors. As such, sociometrics that are keyed to nonbehavioral criteria are tapping children's attitudes toward or their preferences for engaging in certain activities with certain peers rather than their perceptions of peers' behavior. By contrast, behavioral criteria are based upon peers' perceptions of the specific behaviors of their peers. Peer nominations and ratings keyed to behavioral criteria may be more accurately termed *behavioral sociometrics*. A wealth of literature exists on children's sociometrics (see Asher & Hymel, 1981; Gresham, 1981; Hops & Greenwood, 1981, for reviews of the literature). This literature suggests that sociometric techniques provide reliable and valid indications of a child's social functioning. Self-report measures of children's social skills are not as frequently used as are teacher ratings or sociometrics, but they represent a potentially important source of assessment information. Most self-report measures have been ill-constructed modifications of adult assertion scales that are inappropriate for school-age children and that have not demonstrated adequate levels of reliability and validity (see Gresham, 1985b, for a review).

Assessment for Intervention

Some assessment techniques are suitable for obtaining information that is useful in designing social-skills training programs. The extent to which an assessment technique allows for a *functional analysis* of behavior determines its utility as an intervention-assessment method. That is, if the assessment procedure allows for the identification of antecedent, sequential, and consequent conditions surrounding problematic social behavior, it is an intervention-related social-skills assessment method. Two techniques for functional analysis are *behavioral interviews* and *naturalistic observations*.

Behavioral interviews are used to conduct functional analyses of social behavior (Gresham, 1983a). These interviews are useful for defining social behaviors in observable terms, identifying the antecedent, sequential, and consequent conditions surrounding target behaviors, and for designing observational systems that measure target behaviors.

Assessment of children's behavior in natural settings (e.g., classroom, playground, etc.) is the most ecologically valid method of assessing children's social skills. Naturalistic observations enable a functional analysis of behavior as it occurs in the natural setting. Determination of which behaviors are to be observed can be based upon teacher ratings of behavior frequency and importance. These determinations can then be operationalized through behavioral interviews.

Assessment for Intervention Evaluation

Evaluating the effects of social-skills interventions is an exercise in social validation. The question is: Does the quantity and quality of behavioral change make a difference in terms of an individual's functioning in society (Wolf, 1978)? In other words, do changes in targeted social behaviors predict an individual's standing in important social outcomes (Gresham, 1983b)? And what are the important social outcomes among children and adolescents? The vast literature on children's social development would suggest that among children and adolescents, socially valued outcomes include acceptance in the peer group, acceptance by significant adults (e.g., teachers and parents), school adjustment, mental health status, and lack of contact with the juvenile court system (see Asher, Oden, & Gottman, 1977).

Social-skills interventions should therefore produce changes in the desired direction of these outcomes. Thus, one way of evaluating treatment effects would be to track changes in these outcomes as a function of treatment. Evaluation can be cast into a norm-referenced framework, by comparing target children's functioning on these outcomes with the functioning of selected peers who do not require social-skills interventions. If the target child's status on important social outcomes is in the normal range of peer functioning, then the intervention has produced a socially important effect. Comprehensive treatments of the subject of social validation can be found in Kazdin (1977) and in Wolf (1978).

APPROACHES TO SOCIAL-SKILLS INTERVENTIONS

A large number of procedures have been identified as effective in social-skills training. These procedures can be classified under four major headings: (a) manipulation of antecedents, (b) manipulation of consequences, (c) modeling/coaching, and (d) combined procedures. In practice, most effective social-skills interventions use combined procedures rather than a single technique. Therefore, after reviewing these procedures separately, a general model of social-skills training will be presented in which a number of procedures are integrated into a problem-solving approach.

Manipulation of Antecedents

Some children experience difficulties in interpersonal relationships because their social environment is not structured in such a way that positive social exchanges are likely. Antecedent control of social behavior can set the occasion for positive social interactions, and it has the advantage of requiring less teacher time and teacher monitoring than do some other procedures (e.g., reinforcement-based procedures). It is important to note that antecedent-control procedures assume implicitly that the child possesses the requisite social skills but is not performing them at acceptable levels.

Strain and his colleagues (Strain, 1977; Strain, Shores, & Timm, 1977; Strain, & Timm, 1974) used a procedure that they termed *peer social initiations* to increase social-interaction rates of socially withdrawn children. The general procedure involved a trained peer confederate to initiate positive social interactions with the withdrawn child in a free-play environment. Peer confederates were coached prior to the intervention in how to initiate appropriately and to maintain social interactions. This procedure was effective in increasing the rates of social interactions in withdrawn children. Strain and Fox (1981) provide a comprehensive review of these procedures.

Another procedure that manipulates antecedent conditions in order to set the occasion for positive social interactions is termed *cooperative learning*. Cooperative learning has been used frequently to promote academic achievement gains in mildly handicapped children, as well as to increase the occurrence of positive social interactions between nonhandicapped and mildly handicapped students (see Madden & Slavin, 1983; and chapter 6 of this volume). Basically, in cooperative learning a group of students work together to complete an academic task. The group rather than the individual then receives a grade on the completed academic product. This procedure requires that students cooperate, share, and assist each other in completing the task and, as such, the procedure represents an effective technique for increasing positive social behaviors. Cooperative learning carries the assumption that children know how to cooperate, but that they are not doing so at desired levels (i.e., the targeted students have performance deficits).

Manipulation of Consequences

A number of operant-learning procedures have been used as means to increase the frequency of positive social behaviors and to decrease the frequency of negative social behaviors. All of the operant-learning procedures are based on the assumption that low rates of positive social interaction and high rates of negative social interaction result from the reinforcement contingencies (positive or negative) that occur subsequent to behavior. The further assumption implied in using these procedures is that the child knows how to perform the social behavior in question but is not doing so because of a lack of reinforcement for appropriate social behavior. From among the numerous studies in this area, three exemplary techniques will be reviewed: contingent social reinforcement, group contingencies, and differential reinforcement.

Contingent social reinforcement

In this technique, a teacher reinforces socially the appropriate school behaviors. For example, Allen, Hart, Buell, Harris, and Wolf (1964) instructed a teacher to reinforce socially a 4-year-old socially isolated girl whenever she interacted with other children. This procedure led to a sixfold increase in social-interaction rates over baseline levels. Variations of this basic procedure have been successful with elective mutes and in severely and profoundly mentally retarded populations (Mayhew, Enyart, & Anderson, 1978).

Contingent social reinforcement increases rates of positive social interaction. However, to be effective, it requires a great deal of teacher involvement on a consistent basis. Contingent social reinforcement is perhaps best used to maintain social interaction rates once they have been established through use of other social-skills intervention procedures.

Group contingencies

Group contingencies use the application of consequences for the group-behavior management of children in the classroom (Litow & Pumroy, 1975). Three types of group contingencies have been used to teach social skills: dependent, independent, and interdependent group contingency systems. Dependent group contingency systems are established when the same response contingencies are in effect simultaneously for all group members, but are applied in response to the performances of only one or more selected group members. Reinforcement for the group, therefore, depends upon the behavior of selected children rather than on the behavior of the entire group. Independent group contingencies are established when the same response contingencies are in effect concurrently for all group members, but are applied to behavioral performances on an individual basis. Thus, reinforcement for a given individual is independent of the behavior of others in the group. Interdependent group contingencies are established when the same response contingencies are in effect for all group members, but are applied on the basis of a group level of performance. Reinforcement, then, is interdependent upon the collective behavior of the group.

Gamble and Strain (1979) used two interdependent group contingency systems to increase the frequency of social skills in a self-contained classroom for emotionally disturbed children. Social skills included behaviors such as cooperation, compliance to request, sharing, saying "please" and "thank you," and verbal complimenting. Under the first interdepenedent contingency system, children earned reinforcement for the entire class if each child earned at least 20 "Smiley Faces" per week. Smiley Faces were awarded contingent upon the above-mentioned social skills, and could be traded in for back-up reinforcers. Under the second interdependent contingency system, a designated sum of Smiley Faces earned by the entire class resulted in reinforcement for the entire class at the end of the week. Both contingency systems were effective in increasing the social skills frequency of emotionally disturbed children.

Weinrott, Carson, and Wilchesky (1979) reported similar findings using a dependent group contingency, in which socially withdrawn children and their peers earned token reinforcement (points) for positive social interaction. Variations of group contingency systems have been used effectively to increase task-related social skills (Crouch, Gresham, & Wright, 1985; F. M. Gresham & G. N. Gresham, 1982) and to decrease negative social behaviors (Page & Edwards, 1978; Zwald & Gresham, 1982).

Group-oriented contingency systems are thus shown to be effective in teaching social skills in classroom settings. Their advantages are the savings in teacher time and effort in the administration of these programs and their use of children as behavior managers for themselves. Negative peer pressure is occasionally seen as a disadvantage.

Differential reinforcement

Differential reinforcement of other behavior (DRO) and differential reinforcement of low rate of responding (DRL) have been used to teach social skills in classroom settings. In DRO, reinforcement is presented after any behavior except the target behavior. The individual is reinforced only after a certain amount of time has elapsed without the performance of the target behavior. For example, if one wishes to decrease aggressive behavior and to increase positive social interactions, any behavior that is exhibited by the child, except aggressive behavior, is reinforced. This procedure has the effect of increasing all other responses and extinguishing aggressive behavior.

Pinkston, Reese, LeBlanc, and Baer (1973) used a DRO procedure to decrease the aggressive behavior of a preschool boy combined with contingent social reinforcement to increase positive social interaction. The DRO procedure consisted of the teachers reinforcing differentially positive peer interaction and ignoring aggressive behavior.

Differential reinforcement of low rates of behavior (DRL) involves the delivery of a reinforcer in response to reductions in performance of target behavior. Reinforcers may be delivered for reduction in the overall frequency of a response within a particular time period, or for an increase in the amount of time that elapses between responses (interresponse times). For example, if one wanted to decrease the frequency of talking-out behavior in a classroom, a reinforcement contingency could be specified so that reinforcement would only occur if the frequency of behavior was at or below a given criterion level. Dietz and Repp (1973) used a DRL schedule to reduce inappropriate talking in an entire Educable Mentally Retarded (EMR) classroom. During the DRL contingency, students could earn reinforcement if the entire class made five or fewer "talk outs" in a 50-minute period. This was also an interdependent group contingency because reinforcement was based upon the behavior of the class. This procedure was effective in decreasing inappropriate talking during class. A similar DRL procedure was used by Zwald and Gresham (1982) with emotionally disabled junior high school students.

DRO and DRL are effective in decreasing the frequency of negative social behaviors. These procedures are perhaps best used as adjuncts in social-skills interventions as a means of decreasing negative social behaviors while at the same time teaching positive social behaviors.

Modeling and Coaching

Modeling and coaching have the broadest base of empirical support for teaching social skills to children and adolescents (Gresham, 1985b; Wandless & Prinz, 1982). Modeling can be divided into two types: *live modeling*, in which the target child observes the social behaviors of models in naturalistic settings (e.g., the classroom) and *symbolic modeling*, in which a target child observes the social behaviors of a model via film or videotape. *Coaching* is a direct verbal-instruction technique that involves three steps. First, the child is presented with rules for or standards of behavior. Second, the targeted social skills are rehearsed behaviorally with the coach or peer partner. Third, the coach provides specific feedback during the behavior rehearsal and offers suggestions for future performance.

Both symbolic (filmed or videotaped) and live modeling have been effective in teaching social skills, although the majority of empirical studies have used symbolic modeling because of the experimental control afforded by filmed modeling. Live modeling may be a more flexible technique for classroom settings, because of the opportunity they afford to modify the modeling sequences based upon behavioral performance. In addition, live modeling does not require the use of videotape equipment.

Coaching has also received empirical support as a social-skills training technique. Oden and Asher (1977) used coaching to teach the social skills of participation, communication, cooperation, and peer reinforcement to third- and fourth-grade students. The coaching procedure involved three steps: (a) verbal instruction, (b) opportunity for skill rehearsal, and (c) feedback on skill performance. This procedure was effective in increasing the sociometric status of third- and fourth-grade students. Ladd (1981) obtained similar results using a coaching procedure as did Gottman, Gonso, and Schuler (1976).

Gresham and Nagle (1980) conducted the only published study in which modeling and coaching were compared. Third- and fourth-grade students were exposed to one of four conditions: (a) modeling, (b) coaching, (c) modeling and coaching, and (d) attention controls. The three treatment conditions were equally effective in increasing sociometric status and in increasing the frequency of positive social interactions. The treatments containing a coaching component were more effective in decreasing rates of negative social interactions than was modeling alone.

A Combined-Procedures Approach to Social-Skills Training

A general framework for social-skills training can be described by the acronym DATE. First, behaviors are *defined* and stated in observable terms. In addition, the conditions (antecedent and consequent) surrounding the behavior are also defined. Second, behaviors are *assessed* using the procedures described earlier in this chapter. Third, *teaching* strategies are prescribed to fit the student's needs as determined by the assessment. Fourth, the effects of the teaching procedures are *evaluated* empirically using the assessment methods by which students were selected for training. This Define-Assess-Teach-Evaluate (DATE) approach is applied continuously to each deficient social behavior that the student exhibits.

The DATE framework can be implemented through five steps: (a) establishing the need for performing the behavior, (b) identifying the specific behavioral components of the skill or task analysis, (c) modeling the behavior using either live or filmed procedures (symbolic modeling or coaching the behavior), (d) behavior rehearsal and response feedback, and (e) generalization training. These five steps represent an easily implemented and effective approach to teaching social behavior. They may also be supplemented by reinforcement-based techniques and by antecedent techniques described earlier that enhance skill performance and that promote generalization.

ISSUES IN PLANNING AND EVALUATING SOCIAL-SKILLS INTERVENTIONS

Classifying Social-Skills Difficulties and Selecting Interventions

Most authors agree that social incompetencies observed in children can result from both difficulties in response acquisition and from difficulties in response performance (Bandura, 1977). Kratochwill and French (1984), for example, remarked that response-acquisition (i.e., skill) deficits "occur when the individual has not learned skills that are necessary to exhibit a socially competent response," whereas, performance deficits "arise when the child fails to successfully perform behaviors he or she is capable of" (p. 332). Gresham and Elliott (1984) extended this two-way classification scheme to include four general areas of social-skills problems. As shown in Figure 9.1, this scheme of social-skills difficulties distinguishes whether a child knows how to perform the target skill and ascertains the presence of emotional-arousal responses (e.g., anxiety or impulsivity).

FIGURE 9.1 Conceptual classification system for children's social-skill problems. (Emotional arousal responses can be anxiety, fear, anger, or impulsivity that interfere with the acquisition or performance of appropriate social behaviors.)

	Acquisition Deficit	Performance Deficit
Emotional Arousal Response Absent	Social Skill Deficit	Social Performance Deficit
Emotional Arousal Response Present	Self-Control Skill Deficit	Self-Control Performance Deficit

Social-skill deficits

This social-skill problem characterizes both children who have not acquired the necessary social skills with which to interact appropriately with others and those children who have failed to learn a critical step in the performance of the skill. Direct instruction, modeling, behavioral rehearsal, and coaching are frequently used to remediate social-skill deficits (Gresham, 1982).

Social performance deficits

Children with social-performance deficits have appropriate social skills in their behavior repertoires, but they fail to perform them at acceptable levels. Typically, social-performance deficits have been modified by manipulating antecedents and consequences. Interventions have included peer initiations (Strain et al., 1977), contingent social reinforcement (Allen et al., 1964), and group contingencies (Gamble & Strain, 1979).

Self-control social-skills deficits

This social-skills problem is descriptive of a child for whom an emotional-arousal response has prevented skill acquisition. Anxiety is one such emotional-arousal response that has been shown to prevent acquisition of appropriate coping behaviors, particularly with respect to fears and phobias (Bandura, 1977). Hence, a child may not learn to interact effectively with others because social anxiety inhibits social approach behavior. Impulsivity (a tendency toward short response latencies) is another emotional-arousal response that can hinder social-skills acquisition (Kendall & Braswell, 1985). Two important criteria determine the existence of a self-control social-skills deficit: (a) the presence of an emotional-arousal response and (b) the child's not knowing or never performing the skill in question. Interventions designed to remediate this social-skills problem involve primarily emotional-arousal reduction techniques, such as desensitization or flooding, paired with self-control strategies, such as self-talk, self-monitoring, and self-reinforcement (Kendall & Braswell, 1985; Meichenbaum, 1977).

Self-control social-performance deficits

Children with self-control social-performance deficits have a particular social skill in their behavior repertoires, but their skill performance is hindered by both an emotional-arousal response and by problems of antecedent or consequent control. Identification of a self-control social-performance deficit rests on two criteria: (a) the presence of an emotional-arousal response and (b) inconsistent performance of the social skill in question. Self-control strategies to teach inhibition of inappropriate behavior, stimulus-control training to teach discrimination skills, and contingent reinforcement to increase display of appropriate social behavior are often used to ameliorate this social-skill problem (Bolstad & Johnson, 1977; Kendall & Braswell, 1985; Rosenbaum & Drabman, 1979).

Social Validity of Social-Skills Methods

The concept of social validity has become an important consideration in the assessment and treatment of children (Kazdin, 1977; Witt & Elliott, 1985; Wolf, 1978). With respect to social skills, assessment methods should reflect outcomes that social systems (e.g., schools) consider important, and intervention strategies should target behaviors that are valued by the child's social environment (e.g., parents, teachers). "Selecting a behavior that may not be important in a child's environment . . . would result in assessment and training focusing on social skills which are of minimal, if any, relevance to the child's *real* social interactions" (Michelson, 1983, p. 14). The most effective and socially valid methods for evaluating social skills include the tracking of the social-behavior changes that best predict a child's standing on socially important outcomes, such as changes in sociometric and teacher ratings (Gresham, 1983; Gresham & Elliott, 1984).

Programming for Generalization

To be truly effective, behaviors taught in social-skills training programs should generalize across time (maintenance), settings, individuals, and behaviors. Until recently, investigators interested in social-skills interventions have failed to address issues of generalization in their research. Berler, Gross, and Drabman (1982) recommended that social-skills interventions not to be considered valid unless generalization to the natural environment could be demonstrated. Other researchers have described social-skills interventions in which at least some maintenance and generalization of treatment effects were observed (e.g., Tofte-Tipps, Mendonica, & Peach, 1982).

Application of social skills outside the training setting does not occur naturally; rather, generalization must be programmed actively into the training program (Weissberg, 1985). Stokes and Baer (1977) and Michelson et al. (1983) discussed several procedures, referred to as *generalization facilitators*, that enhance generalization beyond the specific aspects of an intervention. Examples of generalization facilitators include: (a) teaching behaviors that are likely to be maintained by naturally occurring contingencies, (b) training across stimuli (e.g., persons, setting) common to the natural environment, (c) fading response contingencies to approximate naturally occurring consequences, (d) reinforcing application of skills to new and appropriate situations, and (e) including peers in training. By incorporating as many of these facilitators as possible into social-skills interventions, and by offering booster sessions at regular intervals, maintenance and generalization of skills are enhanced.

An Example of Social-Skills Training: Saying "Thank You"

Responding to a compliment, gift, or favor by saying "thank you" is an integral part of positive social behavior (e.g., it increases the likelihood of reciprocal positive interactions and of the delivery of compliments, gifts, or favors in the future). Although no empirical evidence exists to date, the notion that saying "thank you" properly reflects socially valued treatment goals and outcomes has intuitive appeal. Furthermore, expressing one's gratitude appears to be a behavior that has a high probability of support from the natural environment. Finally, recognition of situations in which responding with appreciation is appropriate appears to be a relatively simple discrimination task, thus enhancing maintenance and generalization of training effects. Presented in Table 9.1, is an outline of how one might remedy a social-skills deficit of verbalizing "thank you" appropriately.

TABLE 9.1 Training Model for a Social-Skills Deficit in Saying "Thank You"

An Example Rationale for Saying "Thank You"

1. It tells others you appreciate their behavior.
2. It makes others want to say or to do nice things for you again.
3. Adults are happy with you because you were polite.
4. You are proud of yourself for "doing the right thing."

Steps	*Remarks*
Knowing if someone has done something to deserve a "thank-you"	When someone gives you a compliment, gift, or favor
Knowing the right time and place to say "thank you"	Usually right after someone gives you a compliment, gift, or favor
Knowing the right way to say "thank you" to someone	Use words and, maybe, give them a compliment, gift, or favor later, and/or write them a thank-you note
Knowing how to say "thank you" to someone	Sound friendly, smile, use words that indicate you are sincere, and tell them why you appreciate what they did for you

Role-Play Situations
1. At school when a classmate likes your drawings.
2. On the playground when a friend helps you carry the equipment.
3. At home when a neighbor comes to visit you (because you are ill or just to play).
4 At home when a family member gives you a gift.

Homework Assignments
1. Say "thank you" to your neighbourhood friends and family members.
2. Notice what people do when you say "thank you" to them.

CONCLUSIONS

Central to the rationale for this chapter is the belief that acquisition of social skills is an important component of social-emotional development as well as a significant factor in academic performance of children. When social skills are deficient, children often miss out on rewarding interpersonal opportunities and are more likely to experience negative consequences, such as rejection. Therefore, the major goal of this chapter has been to examine the various empirically proven intervention methods that educators can use to remediate social-skills problems. To accomplish this goal, we reviewed briefly methods for assessing social skills and outlined a four-category scheme for classifying and planning treatments for social-skills deficits.

It was concluded that a multimethod approach to assessment whereby various raters (e.g., teachers, parents, self) use different methods (e.g., direct observation, rating scales, interviews) was desirable for selecting children with skill difficulties, for identifying specific skill deficits, and for evaluating treatment outcomes. The treatment options available for use with children who show social-skills deficits are numerous. However, the majority of effective interventions combine the manipulation of antecedents or consequences with modeling/coaching procedures. When a child's social difficulty results from lack of knowledge of a particular skill, it is usually necessary to use a direct intervention that involves modeling, coaching, as well as role-playing techniques. When a child fails to perform a social behavior he or she is capable of, it is likely that interventions involving the manipulation of antecedents and/or consequences will be successful. Regardless of which interventions are considered, however, the social validity of their specific intervention goals, procedures, and effects is seminal to the maintenance and generalization of appropriate social behaviors.

ANNOTATED BIBLIOGRAPHY

Cartledge, G., & Milburn, J. (Eds.). (1980). *Teaching social skills to children: Innovative approaches*. Elmsford, NY: Pergamon Press.
    Oriented toward social-skills training as a part of school curriculum. Part I sets out general assessment and teaching procedures. Part II focuses on specific populations: behavior-disordered young children, and adolescents.
Goldstein, A. P., Sprafkin, R. P., Gershaw, N. J., & Klein, P. (1980). *Skillstreaming the adolescent*. Champaign, IL: Research Press.
    Packaged structured-learning program for use with adolescents. Outlines the development of procedures and their basic principles, including assessment. Details target skills and gives sample dialogues between trainers and trainees.
Michelson, L., Sugai, D. P., Wood, R. P., & Kazdin, A. (1983). *Social skills assessment and training with children: An empirically based handbook*. New York: Plenum Press.
    Emphasis is on assessment and program-implementation details for social-skills training with aggressive or withdrawn children. Reviews relevant findings on social development and of empirical studies of intervention. Details in two hundred pages 16 different training modules and assessment materials.

REFERENCES

Allen, K. E., Hart, B. M., Buell, S., Harris, F. R., & Wolf, M. M. (1964). Effects of social reinforcement on isolate behavior of a nursery school child. *Child Development, 35*, 7–9.

Asher, S. R., & Hymel, S. (1981). Children's social competence in peer relations: Sociometric and behavioral assessment. In J. D. Wine & M. D. Smye (Eds.), *Social competence* (pp. 125–157). New York: Guilford Press.

Asher, S., Oden, S., & Gottman, J. (1977). Children's friendships in school settings. In L. G. Katz (Ed.), *Current topics in early childhood education* (Vol. 1, pp. 130–151). Hillsdale, NJ: Erlbaum.

Bandura, A. (1977). *Social learning theory*, Englewood Cliffs, NJ: Prentice-Hall.

Berler, E. S., Gross, A. M., & Drabman, R. S. (1982). Social skills training with children: Proceed with caution. *Journal of Applied Behavior Analysis, 15*, 41–53.

Black, F. (1985). *Social skills assessment for mainstreamed handicapped students: The discriminative efficiency of the Teacher Ratings of Social Skills*. Unpublished doctoral dissertation, Louisiana State University.

Bolstad, O. D., & Johnson, S. M. (1977). The relationship between teacher's assessment of students and students' actual behavior in the classroom. *Child Development, 48*, 570–578.

Clark, L., Gresham, F. M., & Elliott, S. N. (1985). Development and validation of a social skills assessment measure: The TROSS-C. *Journal of Psychoeducational Assessment, 4*, 347–356.

Coie, J. D. (1985). Fitting social skills intervention to the target group. In B. H. Schneider, K. H. Rubin, & J. E. Ledingham (Eds.), *Children's peer relations: Issues in assessment and interventions*. (pp. 141–156). New York: Springer-Verlag.

Crouch, P. L., Gresham, F. M., & Wright, W. R. (1985). Interdependent and independent group contingencies with immediate and delayed reinforcement for controlling classroom behavior. *Journal of School Psychology, 23*, 177–188.

Dietz, S., & Repp, A. (1973). Decreasing classroom misbehavior through the use of DRL schedules of reinforcement. *Journal of Applied Behavior Analysis, 6*, 457–463.

Dodge, K. A., & Murphy, R. R. (1984). The assessment of social competence in adolescents. In P. Karoly & J. J. Steffen (Eds.), *Adolescent behavior disorders: Foundations and contemporary concerns*, (pp. 61–96). Lexington, MA: Lexington Books.

Edlebrock, C. (1983). Problems in using rating scales to assess child personality and psychopathology. *School Psychology Review, 12*, 293–299.

Feldhusen, J. F., Thurston, J. R., & Benning, J. J. (1970). A longitudinal analyses of classroom behavior and school achievement. *Journal of Experimental Education, 38*, 4–10.

Foster, S. L., & Ritchey, W. L. (1979). Issues in the assessment of social competence in children. *Journal of Applied Behavior Analysis, 12*, 625–638.

Gamble, R. & Strain, P. S. (1979). The effects of dependent and interdependent group contingencies on socially appropriate responses in classes for emotionally handicapped children. *Psychology in the Schools, 16*, 253–260.

Good, T. L., & Brophy, J. E. (1978). *Looking in classrooms*. New York: Harper & Row.

Gottman, J. M., Gonso, J., & Rasmussen, B. (1975). Social interaction, social competence, and friendship in children. *Child Development, 46*, 708–718.

Gottman, J. M., Gonso, J., & Schuler, P. (1976). Teaching social skills to isolated children. *Journal of Abnormal Child Psychology, 4*, 179–197.

Gresham, F. M. (1981). Assessment of children's social skills. *Journal of School Psychology, 17*, 120–133.

Gresham, F. M. (1982). *Social skills: Principles, practices, and procedures*. Des Moines, IA: Iowa Department of Public Instruction.

Gresham, F. M. (1983a). Behavioral interviews in school psychology: Issues in psychometric adequacy and training. *School Psychology Review, 12*, 17–25.

Gresham, F. M. (1983b). Social validity in the assessment of children's social skills: Establishing standards for social competency. *Journal of Psychoeducation Assessment, 1*, 299–307.

Gresham, F. M. (1985a). Conceptual issues in the assessment of social competence in children. In P. Strain, M. Gurolnick, & H. Walker (Eds.), *Children's social behavior:*

Development, assessment, and modification (pp. 143–179). New York: Academic Press.

Gresham, F. M. (1985b). Utility of cognitive-behavioral procedures for social skills training with children: A review. *Journal of Abnormal Child Psychology*, *13*, 411–423.

Gresham, F. M. & Cavell, T. (1987). Assessment of adolescent social skills. In R. G. Harrington (Ed.), *Testing adolescents* (pp. 93–123). Kansas City, MO: Test Corporation of America.

Gresham, F. M., & Elliott, S. N. (1984). Assessment and classification of children's social skills: A review of methods and issues. *School Psychology Review*, *13*, 292–301.

Gresham, F. M., Elliott, S. N., & Black, F. (1985). *Factor structure replication and bias investigation of the Teacher Rating of Social Skills*. Unpublished manuscript, Louisiana State University.

Gresham, F. M., & Gresham, G. N. (1982). Interdependent, dependent, and independent group contingencies for controlling disruptive behavior. *Journal of Special Education*, *16*, 101–110.

Gresham, F. M., & Nagle, R. J. (1980). Social skills training with children: Responsiveness to modeling and coaching as a function of peer orientation. *Journal of Consulting and Clinical Psychology*, *48*, 718–729.

Gresham, F. M., & Reschly, D. J. (1985). Social skills and peer acceptance differences between learning disabled and nonhandicapped students. *Learning Disability Quarterly*, *9*, 23–32.

Hops, H., & Greenwood, C. R. (1981). Social skills deficits. In E. J. Mash & L. G. Terdal (Eds.), *Behavioral assessment of childhood disorders* (pp. 347–394). New York: Guildford Press.

Kazdin, A. E. (1977). Assessing the clinical or applied importance of behavior change through social validation. *Behavior Modification*, *1*, 427–451.

Kendall, P. C., & Braswell, L. (1985). *Cognitive-behavioral therapy for impulsive children*. New York: Guildford Press.

Kratochwill, T. R., & French, D. C. (1984). Social skills training for withdrawn children. *School Psychology Review*, *13*, 331–338.

Ladd, G. W. (1981). Effectiveness of a social learning method for enhancing children's social interaction and peer acceptance. *Child Development*, *52*, 171–178.

LaGreca, A. M. (1981). Peer acceptance: The correspondence between children's sociometric scores and teacher ratings of peer interactions. *Journal of Abnormal Child Psychology*, *9*, 167–178.

LaGreca, A. M., & Santogrossi, D. A. (1980). Social skills training with elementary school students: A behavioral group approach. *Journal of Consulting and Clinical Psychology*, *48*, 220–227.

Litow, L., & Pumroy, D. K. (1975). A brief review of classroom group-oriented contingencies. *Journal of Applied Behavior Analysis*, *8*, 341–347.

Madden, N. M., & Slavin, R. E. (1983). Mainstreaming students with mild handicaps: Academic and social outcomes. *Review of Educational Research*, *53*, 519–569.

Matson, J., Esveldt-Dawson, K., & Kazdin, A. E. (1983). Validation of methods for assessing social skills in children. *Journal of Clinical Child Psychology*. *12*, 174–180.

Mayhew, G., Enyart, P., & Anderson, J. (1978). Social reinforcement and the naturally occurring social responses of severely and profoundly retarded adolescents. *American Journal of Mental Deficiency*, *83*, 164–170.

Meichenbaum, D. (1977). *Cognitive behavior modification*. New York: Plenum Press.

Michelson, L., Sugai, D. P., Wood, R. P., & Kazdin, A. E. (1983). *Social skills assessment and training with children: An empirically based approach*. New York: Plenum Press.

Oden, S. L., & Asher, S. R. (1977). Coaching children in social skills for friendship making, *Child Development*, *48*, 495–506.

Page, P., & Edwards, R. (1978). Behavior change strategies for reducing disruptive classroom behavior. *Psychology in the Schools*, *15*, 413–418.

Phillips, E. L. (1978). *The social skills basis of psychopathology*. New York: Grune & Stratton.

Pinkston, E. M., Reese, N. M., Le Blanc, J. M., & Baer, D. M. (1973). Independent control of a preschool child's aggression and peer interaction by contingent teacher attention. *Journal of Applied Behavior Analysis*, *6*, 223–224.

Rinn, R., & Markle, A. (1979). Modification of social skills deficits in children. In A. Bellack & M. Hersen (Eds.). *Research and practice in social skills training* (pp. 61–83). New York: Plenum Press.

Rosenbaum, M. S., & Drabman, R. S. (1979). Self-control training in the classroom: A review and critique. *Journal of Applied Behavior Analysis, 12,* 467–485.

Stokes, T. F., & Baer, D. M. (1977). An implicit technology of generalization. *Journal of Applied Behavior Analysis, 10,* 349–367.

Stephens, T. M. (1978). *Social skills in the classroom.* Columbus, OH: Cedars Press.

Stephens, T. M. (1980). *Technical manual for the Social Behavior Assessment.* Columbus, OH: Cedars Press.

Strain, P. S. (1977). An experimental analysis of peer social initiations on the behavior of withdrawn preschool children: Some training and generalization effects. *Journal of Abnormal Child Psychology, 5,* 445–455.

Strain, P. S., & Fox, J. (1981). Peers as behavior change agents for withdrawn classmates. In B. B. lahey & A. E. Kazdin (Eds.), *Advances in clinical child psychology* (Vol. 4, pp. 167–198). New York: Plenum Press.

Strain, P. S., Shores, R. E., & Timm, M. A. (1977). Effects of peer social initiations on the behavior of withdrawn preschool children. *Journal of Applied Behavior Analysis, 10,* 289–298.

Strain, P. S. & Timm, M. A. (1974). An experimental analysis of social interaction between a behaviorally disordered preschool child and her classroom peers. *Journal of Applied Behavior Analysis, 7,* 583–590.

Stumme, V. A., Gresham, F. M., & Scott, N. A. (1982). Validity of Social Behavior Assessment in discriminating emotionally disabled from nonhandicapped students. *Journal of Behavioral Assessment, 4,* 327–342.

Stumme, V. A., Gresham, F. M., & Scott, N. A. (1983). Dimensions of children's classroom social behavior: A factor analytic investigation. *Journal of Behavioral Assessment, 5,* 161–177.

Tofte-Tipps, S., Mendonica, P., & Peach, R. V. (1982). Training and generalization of social skills: A study of two developmentally handicapped, socially isolated children. *Behavior Modification, 6,* 45–71.

Wandless, R. L., & Prinz, R. J. (1982). Methodological issues in conceptualizing and treating childhood social isolation. *Psychological Bulletin, 92,* 39–55.

Weinrott, M., Carson, J., & Wilchesky, M. (1979). Teacher-mediated treatment of social withdrawal. *Behavior Therapy, 10,* 281–294.

Weissberg, R. P. (1985). Designing effective social problem-solving programs for the classroom. In B. H. Schneider, K. H. Rubin, & J. E. Ledingham (Eds.), *Children's peer relations: Issues in assessment and intervention* (pp. 225–242). New York: Springer-Verlag.

Witt, J. C., & Elliott, S. N. (1985). Acceptability of classroom management strategies. In T. R. Kratochwill (Ed.), *Advances in school psychology* (Vol. 4, pp. 251–288). Hillsdale, NJ: Erlbaum.

Wolf, M. M. (1978). Social validity: the case for subjective measurement or how applied behavior analysis is finding its heart. *Journal of Applied Behavior Analysis, 11,* 203–214.

Zwald, L., & Gresham, F. M. (1982). Behavioral consultation in a secondary class: Using DRL to decrease negative verbal interactions. *School Psychology Review, 11,* 428–432.

10 Behavioral Self-Management in Education

F. CHARLES MACE, D. KIRBY BROWN, and BARBARA J. WEST

A significant trend in applied behavioral psychology has been the development of behavior-change techniques to alter one's own behavior toward the direction of personal and societal standards. Several terms have been used to represent the processes and procedures associated with an individual's management of their own behavior. These include but are not limited to *self-control* (Skinner, 1953), *self-regulation* (Kanfer & Gaelick, 1986), and *self-directed behavior change* (Watson & Tharp, 1972). The term *self-management* will be used in this chapter because it subsumes most of the processes and procedures identified in the literature, yet it avoids the designation of behavior's locus of control, which has been a key point of controversy among behavioral self-management theorists. Consistent with this view, self-management may be defined as the range of activities, both public and private, in which an individual may engage that increase or decrease the likelihood of the occurrence of certain behaviors. These techniques differ from other psychoeducational interventions discussed in this volume in that they represent treatments that are, to one degree or another, self-administered rather than implemented largely by educational resource or instructional personnel. Alternatively, many of the psychoeducational programs described in other chapters of this book can be translated into self-management interventions by participation of student clients in the administration of the programs.

Self-management techniques are especially suited for use in educational settings for several reasons. First, the self-management literature includes a broad range of applications to education. Empirical studies have shown self-management interventions to be effective in (a) improving academic skills such as spelling, handwriting, and mathematics; (b) decreasing maladaptive behaviors such as aggression, disruption, tardiness and anxiety disorders; (c) increasing pro-social behavior; and (d) improving the performance of teachers and school administrators (see Roberts & Dick, 1982). Second, the low ratio of resource personnel (i.e., school psychologists, counselors, educational specialists) to students has contributed greatly to the emergence of a consultation model of service delivery. Self-management strategies offer viable means for consultants to serve greater numbers of students by transferring some of the responsibility of intervention administration from the consultant to the client. Third, the classroom ecology lends itself to self-management approaches to assessment and intervention. Routine demands on teacher time typically compete with the requirements of behaviorial techniques for individualized and direct assessment and intervention. Self-management strategies alleviate this problem somewhat by involving the student in direct behavioral self-observation and by the delivery of immediate consequences for behavior. Finally, concern for the social validity of behavioral interventions has led researchers to examine the acceptability of various treatments by parents and school personnel. The results of these investigations indicate a preference for positive reinforcement procedures administered on an individual basis (Witt & Elliott, 1985), both of which are hallmarks of most self-management programs. Clearly, the compatible features of self-management and educational settings bode well for continued development of this technology for psychoeducational intervention.

Our objective is to acquaint the reader with recent developments in the behavioral self-management literature. We define and illustrate the major components of self-management: (a) self-monitoring (SM), (b) self-evaluation (SE), (c) self-reinforcement (SR), and (d) self-instruction (SI). Readers are referred to in-depth coverage of each topic. In addition, competing viewpoints regarding the mechanisms underlying the effectiveness of various self-management components are presented with the hope of stimulating further applied research. Finally, we offer suggestions to practitioners for designing and implementing self-management programs based on recent empirical research. This distinction between self-management and other management of behavior has important implications for school-based practitioners and researchers.

APPROACHES TO SELF-MANAGEMENT
Theoretical Models of Behavioral Self-Management

Many of the developments in behavioral self-management, both conceptual and procedural, have been driven by two major theoretical models. The *cognitive-behavioral* model considers self-managed behavior to be largely the product of evaluation of one's own behavior. Bandura (1977) and Kanfer and Gaelick (1986) have formulated multistage, cognitive-behavioral models of self-control comprised of various components (i.e., SM, SE, SR, SI). These components are believed to be part of a process in which individuals observe their own behavior, evaluate their performance against some standard, and provide consequences for their behavior in accord with their performance. Much of the process is thought to occur covertly, resulting in a model of self-directed behavior change that is not bound by environmental contingenies. By contrast, the *operant* model

(Nelson & Hayes, 1981) views self-managed behavior as resulting from individuals' arrangement of their environment to improve their discrimination of, and response to, the environmental contingencies that ultimately control their behavior. Although operant theorists consider behavior to be dependent on environmental contingencies, the relationship between behavior and environment is interactive. That is, individuals may behave to change the environment, which in turn may influence the behavior via reinforcement consequences.

Both of these theoretical models have shaped the development of self-management procedures and the course of applied research. For each of the self-management components discussed below (except SE), we will summarize briefly each model's perspective on the mechanisms underlying the effects of the various procedures.

Self-Monitoring

The initial step in any account of behavioral self-management is self-monitoring (SM). Self-monitoring is a two-step process of self-observation and self-recording (Nelson, 1977). First, individuals must become aware of or discriminate the presence or absence of their own target behavior. As with any behavioral assessment procedure, accurate discriminations are enhanced by definitions of target responses. Second, specific dimensions of behavior (e.g., frequency, duration, latency) are self-recorded. These recordings may be physically tangible, using data sheets, mechanical transducers, or archival recordings. Alternately, from the cognitive-behavioral perspective, records may take the form of mental notes that permit individuals to keep track of what they have done.

A particularly interesting and therapeutically useful feature of SM is its tendency to produce *reactive* effects. Reactivity of SM refers to changes that take place in the self-monitored response as a result of observing and recording one's own behavior. Research has shown that behavior change is usually in the direction of the behavior's valence; SM increases positive behavior and decreases undesirable actions (Nelson, 1977). This reactive property of SM has made the procedure especially attractive both to practitioners and to applied researchers interested in designing behavioral programs with maximum therapeutic effects. For this reason SM is a component of most self-management programs.

There is considerable evidence for reactive effects of SM in psychoeducational intervention across a broad range of subjects, settings, and disorders (Shapiro, 1984). Hallahan, Lloyd, Kosiewicz, Kauffman, and Graves, (1979) illustrated the therapeutic potential of SM independent of other self-management procedures. A 7-year-old with attentional problems was instructed to self-monitor his on- and off-task behavior, using an audiotape to occasion self-recording responses. The student was provided with a self-recording form that included an illustration of a boy reading a book with the caption, "Was I paying attention?" The child was instructed to self-record whether he was "paying attention" or not each time the tape-recorded tone sounded (on a variable interval schedule). Application of SM during math and handwriting periods resulted in substantial increases in on-task behavior relative to baseline. SM effects were evaluated using a reversal design and were found to maintain as SM was faded out and replaced with a covert self-praise procedure.

Piersel and Kratochwill (1979) illustrated the reactive benefits of SM in a program aimed at improving a 15-year-old hyperactive student's completion of assignments. At referral, the youth was described as truant, disruptive, failing academically, and remiss in assignment completion. A simple SM procedure was recommended by the school psychologist after counseling, various behavior management programs, and parent conferences had all proven ineffective. The student was taught to self-record on notebook paper the number of SRA reading units completed each day. Two weeks later, in multiple baseline fashion, he was taught to self- monitor accurate completion (75% correct) of math assignments. Reactive SM effects were apparent immediately, raising assignment completion in reading and math from zero levels in baseline to an average of approximately one assignment completed per day. Piersel and Kratochwill employed similar SM interventions with 3 other students and reported therapeutic effects on disruptive verbalizations and on worksheet completion. Readers are referred to Table 10.1 for summaries of selected studies illustrating the application of SM in psychoeducational intervention, and to comprehensive reviews by Nelson (1977), Shapiro (1984) and Mace and Kratochwill (in press).

Although several studies report reactive effects attendant to SM, others have found self-monitoring alone ineffective in altering target behaviors. Inconsistent findings have stimulated a wave of research aimed at identifying variables that affect the technique's reactivity. Nelson (1977), Shapiro (1984), and Mace and Kratochwill (in press), among others, have summarized the results of this research and its implications for practice. The following variables have been implicated in the reactive process:

1. *Motivation.* Persons motivated to change their behavior appear to be more susceptible to reactive effects.
2. *Valence.* SM tends to increase the strength of desirable behaviors, and to decrease the strength of undesirable behaviors.
3. *Target behaviors.* Effects may be more pronounced for conspicuous, nonverbal behaviors and for reliable antecedents to undesirable behavior.
4. *Goals, reinforcement and feedback.* Performance goals, performance feedback, and reinforcement for the self-monitored response tend to enhance reactivity.

TABLE 10.1: Selected Self-Management Studies

Authors	Self-management component(s)	Subjects	Setting	Target Behavior(s)	Findings
Jones, Trap, & Cooper (1977)	Self-Monitoring	22 regular education 1st graders	Inner-city classroom	Lower case manuscript letter strokes	Students were taught to record-evaluate their letter writing accurately. No reactive effects were reported.
Christie, Hiss, & Lozanoff (1984)	Self-Monitoring	3 hyperactive, regular education 3rd–4th graders	Classroom	Inattentive, disruptive, off-task behaviors	Self-Monitoring, increased on-task and decreased inappropriate behavior.
Herbert & Baer (1972)	Self-Monitoring	2 mothers of 5-year-old children with behavior problems	Home living room and kitchen	Maternal attention to appropriate and inappropriate child behaviors	Mothers' use of counters increased both maternal attention to appropriate behaviors and appropriate child behaviors.
Glynn & Thomas (1974)	Self-Monitoring plus Self-Reinforcement	9 regular education 3rd graders with attention problems	Language class	On-task during teacher instruction and seat work	SM plus SR combined with frequent cues for appropriate behaviors increased appropriate child behaviors.
Humphrey, Karoly, & Kirschenbaum (1978)	Self-Reinforcement vs. Self-Imposed Response Cost	18 regular education 2nd graders with behavior problems	Reading class	Number of reading papers attempted, percentage of intervals of disruptive behavior	Both SR and self-imposed response cost improved reading and reduced disruptive behavior. SR was more effective for reading.
Wall (1982)	Self-Monitoring plus Self-Reinforcement	85 regular education 4th graders	Classroom	Number of correct test items on history, Spanish language, and reading-comprehension tests	SM alone or in combination with SR had no effect. SR significantly increased test scores.
Bornstein & Quevillon (1976)	Self-Instruction plus Self-Reinforcement	3 hyperactive preschool boys	Headstart preschool classroom	On-task during work periods	The SI plus SR package produced large and stable improvements in on-task behavior.
Billings & Wasik (1985)	Self-Instruction	4 disruptive preschool boys	Headstart preschool classroom	Percentage intervals of attentive behavior	SI alone produced no gains in attentive behavior.
Albion & Salzberg (1982)	Self-Instruction plus External Reinforcement	4 moderately retarded preadolescents	Special education classroom	Rate per minute of correct math problems	3 of 4 students improved math performance.

5. *Timing.* Prior to the occurrence of the target response, SM can promote reactivity.
6. *Concurrent monitoring of multiple behaviors.* Reactive effects diminish as the number of monitored responses increases.
7. *Schedule of SM.* Continuous rather than intermittent monitoring appears to enhance reactivity.
8. *Nature of the SM device.* Obtrusive recording devices may increase reactive effects.

Interested readers are encouraged to consult the above references for detailed reviews of this research and for strategies to design SM programs for maximum reactive effects.

Two major theories have emerged to account for the mechanisms underlying the reactive effects of SM. Kanfer and Gaelick (1986) explain reactive SM in the context of a multistage model of self-regulation. Effective control of one's behavior is seen as a product of SM, SE, and SR. In this view, SM triggers a reactive chain, beginning with the evaluation of one's performance against personal standards. This in turn evokes automatically the self-delivery of covert consequences (i.e., thoughts, feelings) contingent on meeting or exceeding personal goals. Thus, the covert processes of SE and SR are considered responsible for the reactivity of SM.

By contrast, Nelson and Hayes (1981) proposed an operant theory of SM reactivity. Changes in the self-monitored response are believed to be occasioned by a range of contextual cues or discriminative stimuli, related to the observation and recording of one's own behavior. Stimuli implicated in the reactive process include the self-recording act, teacher or therapist instructions, training in SM, the obtrusiveness of the SM device, and feedback from others. The function of these stimuli is to strengthen the relationship between behavior and the controlling environmental consequences. Thus, external contingencies, rather than covert internal processes, are considered ultimately responsible for the reactivity of SM. Neither theory yet has substantial empirical support. However, recent research reviewed by Nelson and Hayes (1981) and Mace and West (1986) increases the plausibility of some of the tenets of the operant model.

Self-Evaluation

Self-evaluation (SE) has been generally presented as one component of self-management. Within the self-management literature there is general agreement that self-managing individuals compare dimensions of their behavior against criteria in order to determine adequacy of performance. Kanfer and Gaelick (1986) have offered the most extensive definition of SE. Self-evaluation is described as the second phase of a three-phase model in which the individual's behaviors function as cues that are assessed to determine adequacy of performance. That is, SE involves a comparison between self-monitoring information and the individual's standard for the behavior. In essence, the individual is looking for a match between what is done and what should be done.

O'Brien, Riner and Budd (1983) illustrated the effectiveness of an SE program implemented by parents in the home. The child was a kindergarten pupil referred to an outpatient clinic for abusive verbal comments and noncompliance. Following several baseline sessions in which the mother interacted normally and issued six planned instructions, the child was prompted to self-evaluate by his mother once every 5 minutes by asking him if he had followed instructions without responding with verbal abuse. The boy was allowed to take a token for each positive evaluation, regardless of whether the child's evaluation matched his mother's. To encourage more accurate self-evaluations, a subsequent phase required the student's self-evaluations to be both positive and to match his mother's evaluation in order for him to receive a token. The results of this investigation showed increases in compliance and decrements in inappropriate verbalizations during the independent SE phase. However, treatment gains began to deteriorate after a few days. Performance improved again with the addition of the mother's evaluations. Subsequent phases indicated that appropriate behavior could be maintained during the independent SE condition, as long as SE accuracy checks by the mother were implemented periodically.

SE has also been shown to be effective in promoting generalization and maintenance of treatment gains. Rhode, Morgan and Young (1983) achieved increased appropriate behavior in 6 behaviorally handicapped elementary school students through the use of a standard token-reinforcement program that included regular teacher feedback regarding students' rule-following behavior. Generalization of gains attained by the students in the resource room were generalized to their regular classroom, facilitated by the use of structured SE programs. SE consisted of teaching the students to rate their own classroom behavior on a 6-point scale during 15-minute intervals. If student ratings were within 1 point of teacher ratings of student behavior during the same interval, students were permitted to award themselves points, which were exchangeable for toys and snacks. The matching procedure was gradually faded from 100% of the intervals to 16%. Following maintenance of appropriate behavior in the resource room, the SE strategy was implemented in each student's regular classroom. SE was effective in facilitating generalized appropriate classroom behavior, requiring infrequent surprise checks to maintain accurate student self-evaluation.

Self-Reinforcement

The most intensely studied and discussed component of self-management has been self-reinforcement (SR). Mace and West (1986) described SR as "the process by which an individual, usually under conditions of satisfying a performance standard, comes into contact with a stimulus that is freely available following emission of a response, which in turn increases the probability of the occurrence of the response subject to the performance standard" (p. 151). This definition avoids some of the controversy surrounding designation of stimuli as reinforcers, the relationship between response and stimulus as contingent, and the spatial locus of the stimulus (i.e., inside or outside the skin).

In psychoeducational interventions, SR typically involves transfer of the administration of reinforcers from school personnel to the student. Thus, students award themselves points, privileges, material goods or, possibly, positive cognitions following satisfactory performance relative to some criterion or goal. In a classic illustration of SR intervention in schools, Ballard and Glynn (1975) taught third graders to self-monitor the number of sentences written and the number of action words and describing words used during 25-minute writing periods. After 12 days, SM alone effected no change in student writing skills. A SR component was added to the intervention. Students awarded themselves points for each sentence, for each verb, and for each adjective written during three separate and successive experimental phases. Points were exchangeable for any of several different privileges and activities to be engaged in during a special earned-time period. For 9 of the 14 students participating in the project, SR effects were immediate and substantial for all target behaviors. The remaining 5 children showed delayed and variable responses to the intervention.

SR procedures have been demonstrated to be effective in remediating a broad range of social and academic problems. Table 10.1 provides an overview of select SR studies. For in-depth reviews see Gross and Woljnilower (1984) and Jones, Nelson and Kazdin (1977).

Although the efficacy of SR is generally accepted, there is considerable debate regarding the nature or mechanism underlying the process. Bandura (1977) and Kanfer and Gaelick (1986) have expressed the view that the SR process is one of true reinforcement, in which individuals self-administer a reinforcer contingent upon their behavior meeting or exceeding a performance criterion. Kanfer and Gaelick consider the SR stage as an operation consequent to SE. During this stage, individuals react with feelings of satisfaction or dissatisfaction with their behavior. These feelings then alter the probability of the occurrence of a self-regulatory sequence, that is, self-monitoring and self-evaluation (Kanfer & Gaelick, 1986).

In contrast, there are three distinctive features of the operant view of

SR. First, the stimulus to which a person responds in order to gain access is not considered to be *a* reinforcer or *the* reinforcer that controls the target behavior. Rather, the self-administered consequence is seen as a discriminative stimulus for the person to respond to another environmental contingency, or for the person to mediate delayed consequences that ultimately control the target behavior (Catania, 1975; Nelson, Hayes, Spong, Jarrett, & McKnight, 1983). Second, the relationship between the target behavior and the reinforcing stimulus is considered to be temporal rather than contingent, thus not satisfying the conditions for true reinforcement. Third, the operant view acknowledges that private as well as public events may influence behavior (Skinner, 1953); however, the former are currently considered as being outside the realm of acceptable methodology in experimental analysis (see Upson & Ray, 1984 for an alternative view) and the latter are generally believed to exert greater control on behavior (Baer, 1984; Malott, 1984). Readers are referred to Jones, Nelson and Kazdin (1977), Gross and Woljnilower (1984) and Mace and West (1986) for reviews of empirical literature supporting these differing viewpoints.

Self-Instruction

The self-management procedure commonly called self-instruction (SI) has been an important tool in the kits of behaviorally oriented practitioners since the early 1970s. SI techniques have been taught to students as a means of increasing academic and social independence in the classroom. Without reference to a theoretical view of the process of SI, the procedure of SI may be described as follows: A student is presented with an academic or social problem. He or she applies certain instructions, rules or strategies in order to solve the problem either overtly or covertly.

Self-instruction has been used, with varying degrees of success, to improve academic performance. Specific subject areas such as mathematics (Burgio, Whitman, & Johnson, 1980), reading (Friedling & O'Leary, 1979), written language (Schumaker, Deshler, Alley, & Warner, 1983) and handwriting (Kosiewicz, Hallahan, Lloyd, & Graves, 1982) have been targeted for intervention through SI alone, or with SI as a component in a treatment package (see also chapter 5). In the handwriting study by Kosiewicz et al. (1982), a boy in a self-contained, learning disabilities classroom was taught to guide overtly his copying of words and passages with self-verbalized instructions. The sequence of SI, listed on a card on the student's desk, was as follows: (a) say aloud the word to be written; (b) say the first syllable; (c) name each of the letters in that syllable three times; (d) repeat each letter as it is written down; and (e) repeat steps b through d for each succeeding syllable. This procedure, used alone, substantially increased his percentage of correct letter formation. Even higher percentages of correct letter formation were obtained when the SI procedure was combined with a self-correction procedure (e.g., when the student circled errors made on the previous day's work immediately prior to copying the current day's assignment.

SI has also been incorporated into various packages designed to help students study content material (e.g., Schumaker, Deshler, Alley, Warner, & Denton, 1982). At the University of Kansas, Schumaker and his colleagues developed a number of strategies to improve learning-disabled adolescents' content learning. These strategies focused on identifying the main idea of a reading passage, notetaking, test preparation, and assignment completion. These SI strategies were improvements upon the earlier, and largely unproven SQ3R method (survey, question, read, recite and review). Interested readers should consult Fox and Kendall (1983) and A. Sheinker, J. M. Sheinker, and Stevens (1984) for excellent reviews of academic applications of SI.

Students also have been taught SI techniques to manage their nonacademic behavior in the classroom. Although SI has been used in the classroom to increase desirable behaviors such as assertiveness and other social skills (Kazdin & Mascitelli, 1982), most of the literature in this area focuses on the use of SI to reduce undesirable behaviors such as aggression, off-task, and disruptive behaviors (see Roberts & Dick, 1982, for a review of this area). Table 10.1 contains summaries of additional SI studies.

Although SI has been applied to a wide variety of classroom academic and social problems, outcomes have not been consistently successful. A review of the aftermath of the publication of a study by Bornstein and Quevillon (1976) illustrates the problem of inconsistent outcomes. Bornstein and Quevillon exposed 3 overactive preschool boys to 2 hours of massed SI training. All 3 boys were taken out of the classroom on three successive days. One boy each day received the SI training, while the other 2 boys were given attention and interacted with the training materials. When the boys were returned to the classroom, the teacher was not told who had received the training. Dramatic improvement in on-task behavior was reported. However, Friedling and O'Leary's (1979) attempt to replicate the results of the Bornstein and Quevillon (1976) study that targeted on-task behavior with older children (seven to eight years old) was not successful. Similarly, Billings and Wasik (1985) attempted an exact replication with Head Start preschoolers. Like Friedling and O'Leary they found no socially significant or durable changes in classroom behavior after SI training.

Bornstein (1985) and others wondered why the strong effects obtained in the Bornstein and Quevillon (1976) study were not replicated by Friedling and O'Leary (1979) and Billings and Wasik (1985), even though other researchers (e.g. Burgio et al., 1980) reported improved on-task behavior following SI training. Billings and Wasik (1985) proposed that a change in the nature of teacher attention may have been an important, although unintended, variable. It is possible that the teacher in the Bornstein and Quevillon (1976) study attended to the boys' inappropriate disruptive and off-task behavior before the SI training and to the boys' appropriate on-task behavior after the training because it was such a contrast to their preinstruction behavior. That is, changes in the boys' behavior may have produced changes in teacher behavior that reinforced student on-task behavior. Bornstein (1985), in his reply to Billings and Wasik (1985), concluded that the effectiveness of SI programs may depend on other variables, such as reinforcement of appropriate behavior, kinds of children, history, cognitive style, and therapist differences, that may augment or detract from therapeutic effects.

Most of the literature on SI reflects a cognitive-behavioral orientation. The cornerstone of this theoretical position is that overt behavior can be modified by the manipulation of covert thought processes or cognitions (Sheinker et al., 1984). This basic premise that thought causes behavior may explain the rationale for the elaborate SI training model that was first developed by Meichenbaum and Goodman (1971) and has been followed by most researchers and practitioners, with minor variations. A typical training procedure might resemble the following: (a) the teacher performs a task while talking aloud to the student observer; (b) the student performs the same task while the teacher instructs aloud; (c) the student performs the task again while self-instructing aloud; (d) the student performs the task while whispering instructions aloud; and (e) the student performs the task while self-instructing covertly. The purpose of this procedure is to change the student's thoughts about solving specific problems, by means of modeling and fading control of verbalizations from teacher to student. When the student's problem-solving thought processes have been modified, then overt problem-solving behavior will necessarily be changed. This premise also explains why there is such an emphasis on self-instructing aloud or on obtaining self-report measures that SI took place. Researchers need overt evidence that the "active ingredient," self-instructing statements, is being implemented by the student. Also, the role of these verbalizations can be clearly understood in the context of cognitive-behavioral self-management, as detailed earlier in this chapter. Self-instructional statements lead to changes in cognitions, which lead to changes in overt behavior, which lead to self-evaluation, and ultimately lead to self-reinforcement or punishment, which strengthens or weakens the target behavior.

In the larger context of rule-governed behavior, SI may be conceptualized alternatively from the operant perspective. Self-instruction may be defined as the formulation of self-rules by individuals by which they govern their own behavior (Zettle & Hayes, 1982). Skinner (1969) defines a *rule* as a set of discriminative stimuli constructed to describe a contingency. In the context of rule-governed behavior, SI statements may be conceptualized as one of two sets of stimuli that control a target academic or social behavior. One set, which could be verbal or nonverbal, relates directly to the target behavior and functions according to the usual operant paradigm: (a) discriminative stimulus, (b) response, and (c) reinforcing or punishing stimulus. The other set, the rule or self-instruction, functions as a discriminative stimulus that describes the contingencies for emitting the target behavior. For example, in the homework-completion study by Fish and Mendola (1986), the primary discriminative stimuli are the time of day and the presence of a homework assignment sheet. The target response is completion of the homework assignment, and the reinforcing stimuli are a completed worksheet and, possibly, praise for completion. The students' SI statements are a second set of discriminative stimuli that make clear the contingent relationship between correct responding and its consequences (completion of the homework assignment and the possibility of more remote consequences, such as praise or good grades). In this operant conceptualization, the verbalizations are not the mediators that are the active ingredients in behavior change. Rather, when students have been taught to self-instruct, they have been taught not only the contingencies between responses and consequences, but also to make statements covertly or overtly about that relationship. Thus, SI may be a more efficient way to learn academic tasks and classroom social behaviors than the application of direct consequences.

In most SI training programs, the source of reinforcement for complying with the self-instructions is assumed to be the self-reinforcing statements that are learned by the student. In the operant conceptualization, rule stating and following is maintained by coming into contact with direct consequences for the target behavior at least occasionally or, possibly by seeing others come into contact with these consequences. The failure to see the necessity for at least a very thin schedule of external reinforcement is a possible explanation why many SI studies report failure to maintain effects across time.

GUIDELINES FOR PLANNING AND EVALUATION

The following suggestions for the use of self-management procedures in psychoeducational intervention are offered on the basis of empirical findings, suggested practices, and our experiences while implementing self-management programs.

1. Target behaviors potentially amenable to self-management intervention may be identified in a variety of ways. Behavior checklists and rating scales are useful in identifying and prioritizing target behaviors from among several social and academic behavior problems common to

school-age populations. Structured behavioral interviews, such as those used in behavioral consultation, serve similar functions and also facilitate operational definitions of target behaviors and the assessment of the acceptability of various self-management procedures from the perspectives of teachers, students, and parents. The breadth of target behaviors that have been improved by self-management suggests that most problem behaviors may be responsive to this form of psychoeducational intervention.

2. Keep individual student differences in mind when using self-management techniques. Young mentally retarded or socially deprived children may have difficulty with complex SM procedures or elaborate SR contingencies, and in bringing their behavior under the control of SI rules. Such children may need carefully planned and executed training experiences, prior to self-management implementation. For older, more able children, less structured preintervention training may be acceptable.

3. The reactive and therapeutic effects of SM may be maximized by including procedures or variables that enhance the student's discrimination of the occurrence of and consequences for self-monitored behavior. Conversely, when SM is used to obtain data for program evaluation, variables known to enhance reactivity should be eliminated as much as possible.

4. The design of SM procedures should be simple yet salient, especially for young and handicapped populations, in order to facilitate response discrimination and to avoid interference with adaptive, academic, and social behavior.

5. The effectiveness of self-management programs may be enhanced by instructing students to set their own performance goals, to self-evaluate, to deliver private consequences, and by linking these procedures to external contingencies for the students' behavior.

6. SR procedures appear to be most effective when they are used in conjunction with and subsequent to externally managed contingency programs.

7. Encouraging students to set stringent performance criteria and discouraging consumption of unearned reinforcers may improve the effectiveness of SR procedures.

8. Self-instruction is more effective for helping students put together component skills already in their repertoires so that they can perform more complex tasks than it is for acquiring new skills.

9. Planned follow-up is important if SI is used. Booster sessions are often necessary to maintain independent use by students of rules, strategies, or instructions. Also, the use of SI may, at least initially, lower the rate of task completion. The teacher should plan subsequent interventions to build student fluency.

10. Self-management procedures may be used by school personnel with special and regular education students to facilitate remediation,

maintenance and generalization of a broad range of academic and social behaviors.

11. As is true of all behavioral interventions, the effectiveness of self-management programs should be empirically evaluated. In general, this entails collection of data at regular intervals (i.e., time-series data) on the target behaviors to be affected by self-management. Confident conclusions regarding the effects of these procedures may be achieved by the use of time-series research or of other program evaluation designs in which the student's performance is measured during various arrangements of the presence and absence of self-management procedures.

12. All psychoeducational interventions, including self-manangement, should be implemented in a manner consistent with the highest ethical standards. Some considerations in this regard include: (a) minimizing the intrusiveness of self-management procedures by reducing conspicuous paraphernalia; (b) involving both students and teachers in the design of self-management programs, including specification of reinforcement contingencies and selection of reinforcers and the schedules on which they are obtained; and (c) designing programs that emphasize positive reinforcement of desirable target behavior and that minimize, to the extent possible, the self-administration of aversive consequences for maladaptive behavior.

SUMMARY AND FUTURE DIRECTIONS

The purpose of this chapter has been to acquaint the reader with the major behavioral self-management techniques used in the classroom. The approaches to self-management discussed were self-monitoring, self-evaluation, self-reinforcement, and self-instruction. Two theoretical models of behavioral self-management were discussed, cognitive-behavioral and operant. Behavioral self-management is an area that the reader might wish to investigate more fully. First, it has a wide range of applications in education. Second, it is ideally suited to the consultative model of service delivery. Third, because the students are involved in the management of their own behavior, it may be a means of reducing demands on teacher time. Finally, self-management programs, because they stress positive reinforcement procedures administered on an individual basis, may be highly acceptable to students, parents, and school personnel.

Future directions for self-management practice and research include: (a) continued research aimed at discovering the mechanisms underlying the effects of various self-management components, (b) utilization of the research suggested above in the design of maximally effective self-management programs, (c) continued extension of the range of school-related problems to which self-management principles are applied (e.g., Maher, 1985), (d) further development of class-wide self-management programs for regular and special education populations, and (e) greater involvement of practitioners in the design and empirical evaluation of self-management programs in applied settings.

ANNOTATED BIBLIOGRAPHY

Karoly, P., & Kanfer, F. H. (Eds.). (1982). *Self-management and behavior change*. Elmsford, NY: Pergamon Press.
 Designed for a wide range of readers and represents the entire range of the self-management field. Includes an overview of divergent theoretical concepts in self-management. Offers discussion of applied issues of assessment, treatment, and training in the use of self-management techniques with developmentally delayed as well as with normal children and adults.
Maher, C. A. (Ed.). (1985). *Professional self-management: Techniques for special services providers*. Baltimore: Brookes.
 Guide for practitioners working in applied educational settings. Provides chapters detailing methods for managing a wide range of work-related issues (e.g., time, stress, interpersonal conflicts, work relations, and pupil cases).
Stuart, R. B. (Ed.). (1977). *Behavioral self-management: Strategies, techniques, and outcomes*. New York: Brunner/Mazel.
 Represents the initial compilation of information regarding the use of self-manangement for clinical problems. Focus is largely clinical, but the principles and applications detailed are useful to the educational practitioner. Publication sponsored by the Banff International Conference on Behavior Modification.
Thoresen, C. E., & Mahoney, M. J. (1974). *Behavorial self-control*. New York: Holt, Rinehart & Winston.
 Represents an early examination of self-control techniques. Conceptual, methodological, and clinical issues in the major areas of self-management (e.g., self-observation, self-reward, and self-punishment) are presented and analyzed. The methodological considerations presented are particularly valuable to the practitioner or scientist who has an interest in formal evaluation of the effects of self-management procedures in the classroom.
Yates, B. T. (1985). *Self-management: The science and art of helping yourself*. Belmont, CA: Wadsworth.
 This is a handbook of techniques. Offers a brief introduction to basic self-management theory, then details the procedures for implementing a self-study. The final section presents a series of self-management applications. Of particular interest to educational practitioners is a section on professional self-management in education.

REFERENCES

Baer, D. M. (1984) Does research on self-control need more control? *Analysis and Intervention in Developmental Disabilities, 4,* 211–218.
Ballard, K.D., & Glynn, T. (1975). Behavioral self-management in story writing with elementary school children. *Journal of Applied Behavior Analysis, 8,* 387–398.
Bandura, A. (1977). *Social learning theory*. Englewood Cliffs, NJ: Prentice-Hall.
Billings, P. C., & Wasik, B. H. (1985). Self-instructional training with preschoolers: An attempt to replicate. *Journal of Applied Behavior Analysis, 18,* 61–68.
Bornstein, P. H. (1985). Self-instructional training: A commentary and state-of-the-art. *Journal of Applied Behavior Analysis, 18,* 69–72.
Bornstein, P. H., & Quevillon, R. P. (1976). The effects of a self-instructional package on overactive preschool boys. *Journal of Applied Behavior Analysis, 9,* 177–188.
Burgio, L. D., Whitman, T. L., & Johnson, M. R. (1980). A self-instructional package for increasing attending behaviors in educable mentally retarded children. *Journal of Applied Behavior Analysis, 13,* 443–459.
Catania, A. C. (1975). The myth of self-reinforcement. *Behaviorism, 3,* 192–199.

Christie, D. J., Hiss, M., & Lozanoff, B. (1984). Modification of inattentive classroom behavior: Hyperactive children's use of self-reading with teacher guidance. *Behavior Modification, 8*, 391–406.

Fish, M. C., & Mendola, L. R. (1986). The effects of self-instruction training in homework completion in an elementary special education class. *School Psychology Review, 15*, 268–276.

Fox, D. E., & Kendall, P. C. (1983). Thinking through academic problems: Applications of cognitive behavior therapy to learning. In T. R. Kratochwill (Ed.), *Advances in school psychology*, (Vol. 3, pp. 269–301). Hillsdale, NJ: Erlbaum.

Friedling, C., & O'Leary, S. G. (1979). Effects of self-instructional training on second and third grade hyperactive children: A failure to replicate. *Journal of Applied Behavior Analysis, 12*, 211–220.

Glynn, E. L., & Thomas, J. D. (1974). Effect of cueing on self-control of classroom behavior. *Journal of Applied Behavior Analysis, 7*, 299–306.

Gross, A. M., & Woljnilower, D. A. (1984). Self-directed behavior change in children: Is it self-directed? *Behavior Therapy, 15*, 501–514.

Hallahan, D. P., Lloyd, J., Kosiewicz, M. M., Kauffman, J. M., & Graves, A. W. (1979). Self-monitoring of attention as a treatment for learning disabled boy's off-task behavior. *Learning Disability Quarterly, 2*, 24–32.

Herbert, E. W., & Baer, D. M. (1975). Training parents as behavior modifiers: Self-recording of contingent attention. *Journal of Applied Behavior Analysis, 5*, 139–149.

Humphrey, L. L., Karoly, P., & Kirschenbaum, D. S. (1978). Self-management in the classroom: Self-imposed response versus self-reward. *Behavior Therapy, 9*, 592–601.

Jones, R. T., Nelson, R. E., & Kazdin, A. E. (1977). The role of external variables in self-reinforcement. *Behavior Modification, 1*, 147–178.

Jones, J. C., Trap, J., & Cooper, J. O. (1977). Technical report: Students' self-recording of manuscript letter strokes. *Journal of Applied Behavior Analysis, 10*, 509–514.

Kanfer, F. H., & Gaelick, L. (1986). Self-management methods. In Kanfer F. H. & Goldstein, A. P. (Eds.), *Helping people change: A textbook of methods* (3rd ed., pp. 283–345). Elmsford, NY: Pergamon Press.

Kazdin, A. E., & Mascitelli, S. (1982). Behavioral rehearsal, self-instructions, and homework practice in developing assertiveness. *Behavior Theraphy, 13*, 346–360.

Kosiewicz, M. M., Hallahan, D. P., Lloyd, J., & Graves, A. W. (1982). Effects of self-instruction and self-correction procedures on handwriting performance. *Learning Disability Quarterly, 5*(1), 71–78.

Mace, F. C., & Kratochwill, T. R. (in press). Self-monitoring: Applications and issues. In J. Witt, S. Elliott, & F. Gresham (Eds.), *Handbook of behavior therapy in education*. Elmsford, NY: Pergamon Press.

Mace, F. C., & West, B. J. (1986). Unresolved theoretical issues in self-management: Implications for research and practice. *Professional School Psychology, 1*, 149–163.

Maher, C. A. (Ed.). (1985). *Professional self-management: Techniques for special services provides*. Baltimore: Brookes.

Malott, R. W. (1984). Rule-governed behavior, self-management, and the developmentally disabled: A theoretical analysis. *Analysis and Intervention in Developmental Disabilities, 4*, 199–209.

Meichenbaum, D., & Goodman, J. (1971). Training children to talk to themselves: A means of developing self-control. *Journal of Abnormal Psychology, 77*, 115–126.

Nelson, R. O. (1977). Methodological issues in assessment via self-monitoring. In M. Hersen, R. M. Eisler, & P. M. Miller (Eds.), *Progress in behavior modification* (Vol. 5, pp. 263–308). New York: Academic Press.

Nelson, R. O., & Hayes, S. C. (1981). Theoretical explanations for reactivity in self-monitoring. *Behavior Modification, 5*, 3–14.

Nelson, R. O., Hayes, S. C., Spong, R. T., Jarrett, R. B., & McKnight, D. L. (1983). Self-reinforcement: Appealing misnomer or effective mechanism? *Behavior Research and Therapy, 21*, 557–566.

O'Brien, T. P., Riner, L. S., and Budd, K. S. (1983). The effect of a child's self-evaluation program on compliance with parental instructions in the home. *Journal of Applied Behavior Analysis, 16, 69–80*.

Piersel, W. C., & Kratochwill, T. R. (1979). Self-observation and behavior change: Applications to academic and adjustment problems through behavioral consultation. *Journal of School Psychology, 17*, 151–161.

Rhode, G., Morgan, D. P., & Young, K. R. (1983). Generalization and maintenance of treatment gains of behaviorally handicapped students from resource rooms to regular classrooms using self-evaluation procedures. *Journal of Applied Behavior Analysis, 16*, 171–188.

Roberts, R., & Dick, L. (1982). Self-control strategies with children. In T. R. Kratochwill (Ed.), *Advances in school psychology*, (Vol. 2, pp. 275–314). Hillsdale, NJ: Erlbaum.

Schumaker, J. B., Deshler, D. D., Alley, G. R., & Warner, M. M. (1983). Toward the development of an intervention model for learning disabled adolescents: The University of Kansas Institute. *Exceptional Education Quarterly, 4*(1), 45–74.

Schumaker, J. B., Deshler, D. D., Alley, G. R., Warner, M. M., & Denton, P. H. (1982). Multi-pass: A learning strategy for improving reading comprehension. *Learning Disability Quarterly, 5*(3), 295–304.

Shapiro, E. S. (1984). Self-monitoring procedures. In T. H. Ollendick & M. Hersen (Eds.), *Child behavioral assessment: Principles and procedures* (pp. 148–165). Elmsford, NY: Pergamon Press.

Sheinker, A., Sheinker, J. M., & Stevens, L. J. (1984). Cognitive strategies for teaching the mildly handicapped. *Focus on Exceptional Children, 17*, 1–15.

Skinner, B. F. (1953). *Science and human behavior*. New York: Macmillan.

Skinner, B. F. (1969). *Contingencies of reinforcement: A theoretical analysis*. New York: Appleton-Century-Crofts.

Upson, J. D., & Ray, R. D. (1984). An interbehavioral systems model for empirical investigation in psychology. *The Psychological Record, 34*, 497–524.

Wall, S. M. (1982). Effects of systematic self-monitoring and self-reinforcement in children's management of text performance. *The Journal of Psychology, 111*, 129–136.

Watson, D. L., & Tharp, R. G. (1972). *Self-directed behavior: Self-modification for personal adjustment*. Monterey, CA: Brooks/Cole.

Witt, J. C., & Elliott, S. N. (1985). Acceptability of classroom intervention strategies. In T. R. Kratochwill (Ed.), *Advances in school psychology*, (Vol. 4, pp. 251–288). Hillsdale, NJ: Erlbaum.

Zettle, R. D., & Hayes, S. C. (1982). Rule-governed behavior: A potential theoretical framework for cognitive-behavioral therapy. In K. R. Harris & S. Graham (Eds.), *Advances in cognitive-behavioral research and therapy* (Vol. 1, pp. 73–118). New York: Academic Press.

11 Crisis Intervention

JONATHAN SANDOVAL

Teachers and school administrators are never happier to see pupil personnel workers than when a crisis is developing, whether it concerns a particular child or a group of children. Especially at these times, it is recognized that special services personnel have skills that are different from those of teachers and administrators and that are needed for helping with difficult, sensitive pupil problems. Other forms of counseling or intervention with children are important, school people acknowledge, but it takes a crisis for them to recognize their own limitations and to request help from counselors, psychologists, social workers, and nurses.

The feature of a crisis that is most dramatic is that the individuals involved frequently begin functioning with greatly diminished capacity to everyday demands. Individuals whom others have seen only as behaving competently and efficiently suddenly become disorganized, depressed, hyperactive, confused, or hysterical. Customary problem-solving activities and resources seem to evaporate. Individuals who are in what Caplan (1964) terms a state of "psychological disequilibrium" often behave irrationally and withdraw from normal contacts. They cannot be helped using usual counseling or teaching techniques.

Another characteristic of crisis is its unpredictability. Similar circumstances may create a crisis situation in one child but not in another. To explain the variability, Klein and Lindemann (1961) made a distinction between emotional hazards and crises. An emotionally hazardous situation is one in which the individual is suddenly deprived of expected relationships with others or loses the confidence to act effectively. These situations may be brought about by losses in significant relationships, by the addition of new individuals to the social environment, or by changes in status or roles. These sudden changes are considered hazards because many individuals are able to adapt to the changes with minimum difficulty and a normal amount of stress. Others, however, find themselves immobilized and potentially unalterably damaged by the occurrence that for these individuals becomes a crisis.

This book is devoted to exploring a number of interventions that may be made in children's lives to help them to resolve different situations or to make up deficits. Most of these interventions may be used with children who experience crises because they are not successfully negotiating common, emotionally hazardous situations. But the implementation of these interventions assumes that the child or adolescent is at a point of some stability. The focus of this chapter is on helping children reach this state of stability so that the interventions listed in other chapters may be attempted. For those children experiencing the shock of a crisis, special interventions must precede those described elsewhere in the book. Different kinds of crises will need to be distinguished and discussed, because each has features that should be addressed uniquely. For the balance of the chapter, the term counselor will be used, recognizing that in many instances the school-based helper will be a school psychologist, a school guidance counselor, a nurse, a social worker, teacher or related professional.

Differentiating Crisis Counseling from Other Forms of Counseling

Crisis counseling differs from other forms of counseling along a number of dimensions. To begin with, the goal of crisis counseling is to restore the pupil to equilibrium. As a result, it is more limited in its scope and is briefer in duration than traditional school counseling. The counselor has an objective in mind and proceeds to achieve it, not waiting for the client to identify the goal. Because the goal is set, the process may proceed quickly. Encounters ranging from one meeting to eight sessions are the norm, and meetings may occur as often as twice a day (Golan, 1978).

A second goal is that of taking action rather than listening and then allowing pupils to take responsibility and control of their own decision making and understanding. Accordingly, crisis counseling is far more directive than usual methods of counseling. One aspect of this directiveness is the increased amount of verbal production on the part of the counselor. Whereas in typical counseling the counselor listens, reflects, and summarizes, but talks relatively infrequently, in crisis counseling the counselor takes a much more active role: providing information and offering strategies to the counselee, as well as giving advice and suggestions. (Of course, the crisis counselor does use active listening techniques.) A principal objective in traditional counseling is to avoid dependency on the counselor. In crisis counseling there may be times when temporary dependency is encouraged and necessary, in order to help a person survive extreme disequilibrium.

Other techniques common to traditional counseling, having to do with confronting a counselee and the use of self-disclosure (Egan, 1986), probably have little place in crisis counseling. These techniques are more relevant to personality change-oriented therapy and are thus not applicable to crisis counseling. The goal in crisis counseling is, rather, to restore equilibrium and to free the individual from troubling symptomatic behavior.

Many similarities exist between crisis counseling and traditional counseling. Certainly the active listening skills that characterize most counseling are important in crisis counseling. It is also important to establish empathy and trust in the client, and the counselor has no better tools than reflecting feelings, restating the client's ideas, and summarizing (Benjamin, 1981). Carl Rogers' (1957) basic ideas of empathetic understanding, genuineness, and warmth all have their place in crisis counseling.

Crises in the Student Population

Later I will outline a taxonomy of crises that occur in the public school student population. Hazardous situations that may develop into crises include such disparate events as the birth of a sibling or the occurrence of child abuse. Hazards range from the relatively common to the relatively rare. All children make school transitions from one level of schooling to another, for example. Around 50% of all children experience a geographical move, the death of a significant other, or the birth of siblings. A large number of children experience the divorce of parents, school failure, or, during adolescence, significant conflicts with their parents. Less common are adolescent pregnancy, child maltreatment, chronic illness, and suicide attempts. Nevertheless, when taken together, these hazardous situations confront almost the total pupil population at one time or another. The probability of avoiding all of these hazards is essentially zero. School personnel might anticipate encountering at least one child in crisis in almost every week of the school year.

The purpose of this chapter is first to introduce the reader to a set of generic crisis-counseling principles and then to discuss a taxonomy of crises, each element of which suggests different approaches. In addition to discussion of counseling approaches to children who experience crises, prevention programs will also be covered, as well as will techniques for facilitating referrals to other counselors as necessary. The chapter will conclude with comments on the ethical and legal issues of crisis intervention in the schools and will conclude with a discussion of the research needs for furthering our strategies to assist children in facing normal emotionally hazardous situations.

GENERIC COUNSELING PRINCIPLES

Crisis counseling is different from the usual process of counseling; therefore, it is useful to indicate a general strategy for helping people in a crisis situation. What follows is a general model derived from the work of Lindemann (1944), Caplan (1964), Rusk (1971), and others (see Golan,

1978, for an exhaustive model). An individual counselor will change and adapt these techniques depending on the type of crisis, the age of the counselee, and the specifics of the type of crisis. Although I have outlined the principles in the order in which they are generally applied in a crisis, they are not necessarily sequential in practice.

In working with a pupil in crisis:

1. *Intervene immediately.* By definition, a crisis is a time when a child is in danger of becoming extremely impaired emotionally. The longer the pupil remains in a hazardous situation and is unable to take action, the more difficult it will be for the counselor to facilitate the child's ability to cope and return to equilibrium. When a person remains in a situation of confusion without any kind of human support, anxiety and pain are sure to result.

2. *Be concerned and competent.* The pupil will need a certain amount of reassurance during a crisis situation. The more the counselor can represent a model of competent problem solving and can demonstrate the process of taking in information, choosing between alternatives, and taking action, the more the counselee will be able to begin to function adequately. Higher functioning will result from both a sense of safety and from the security of observing a clear model. The focus is not on the competence of the counselor but rather on the client—the counselor's self-assuredness should be natural and integrated into an interest in the child.

3. *Listen to the facts of the situation.* Before proceeding, the counselor must gather carefully information about the events leading up to the crisis, eliciting as many details as possible. Not only will solutions come from these facts, but also concrete knowledge of the situation will shed light on whether the pupil is behaving rationally or irrationally, allowing the counselor to judge the severity of crisis and to proceed accordingly.

4. *Reflect the individual's feelings.* The counselor should explicitly focus the discussion on the pupil's affect and should encourage its expression. The objective here is not only to create empathetic understanding, but also to legitimize affect and to communicate that feelings can be discussed and are an important part of problem solving. By reflecting feelings, the counselor also primes the pump, giving the counselee a way to begin and to continue exploration of the crisis occurrence.

5. *Help the child accept that the crisis situation has occurred.* Do not accept the child's defensiveness and do not let the mechanisms of denial or other primitive defenses operate and prolong the crisis situation. Encourage the pupil to explore the crisis events without becoming overwhelmed. By asking appropriate and well-timed questions, the counselor can control the pace of exploration.

6. *Do not encourage or support blaming.* This action, too, is a way of avoiding the pupil's defensiveness. If one can leave blame aside, and focus on what has occurred, the child may more quickly move on, because

dwelling on being a victim leaves one in a passive position rather than in an active role. Shifting the focus to self and internal strengths, rather than remaining oriented toward external causation or guilt, leaves the way open to eventual coping with the crisis, and to restoring healthy defenses.

7. *Do not give false reassurance.* The counselor should always remain truthful and realistic. The individual in crisis will always suffer anxiety, depression or tension, and the counselor must acknowledge that the discomfort will probably continue for some time. At the same time, it is possible to provide some sense of hope and expectation that the person will ultimately overcome the crisis. The counselor is clear to acknowledge that there will always be scars and tenderness resulting from a crisis. Nevertheless, a person will be able to proceed with life eventually, and may even develop new strengths.

8. *Recognize the primacy of taking action.* The individual will need real assistance in accomplishing everyday tasks during the time of crisis. Every crisis counseling interview should have as an ultimate outcome some action that the client is able to take. Restoring the client to the position of actor rather than of victim is critical to success, because taking effective action helps to restore a sense of self.

9. *Facilitate the reestablishment of a social-support network.* If possible, get the child to accept some help from others. It is usually possible to find either a group of peers or family members who can provide both support and temporary assistance during the crisis time, so that the pupil's energies may be devoted to resolving the crisis situation. If family is not available, there are often community resources that may be helpful, and the counselor should be knowledgeable about them (Sandoval, 1985a).

10. *Engage in focused problem solving.* Once the counselor has been able to formulate a comprehensive statement about the counselee's problem, identifying all of the sources of concern, and once the couselee agrees on the statement of the problem, it will be possible to begin the process of exploring potential strategies to improve or to resolve the emotionally hazardous situation. Jointly, the counselor and pupil review the strategies explored and select one for trial. This is much like the problem solving that occurs in other kinds of counseling, but must be preceded by the steps mentioned above. Moving too quickly to problem solving is a common mistake of novices (Egan, 1986). However effective the problem-solving process is, the very fact that the counselee's attention has turned to the future, away from the past, has a beneficial effect in and of itself.

11. *Focus on self-concept.* Any strategies and any solutions to problems must be implemented in the context of what the client thinks is possible to accomplish. The crisis situation often leads to a diminution in self-esteem and to the acceptance of blame for the crisis. With an emphasis on how the person has coped well, considering the situation so far, and how the person has arrived at a strategy for moving forward, there can be a restoration of

the now-damaged view of the self. Emphasize what is positive in the situation, even if only that the pupil has survived intact.

12. *Encourage self-reliance.* During the process of crisis counseling, the counselee will have become temporarily dependent on the counselor for direct advice, to stimulate action, and for hope. This is a temporary situation and before the crisis intervention interviews are over the counselor must spend time planning ways to restore the individual to self-reliance and self-confidence. In typical counseling, this is done by the counselor's moving consciously into a position of equality with the counselee, sharing the responsibility and authority. Although earlier the counselor has taken charge, eventually there must be a return to a more democratic stance. Techniques such as *onedownsmanship*, in which the counselor acknowledges the pupil's contribution to problem solving while minimizing her or his own contribution (Caplan, 1970), permit the counselee to leave the crisis intervention with a sense of self-responsibility.

Although these principles may apply generally to all crisis counseling, it is important to realize that there are specific techniques appropriate to a given kind of crisis. Recently, books and articles that offer chapters on how to work with pupils in particular hazardous states (e.g., Sandoval, 1985b) have begun to appear. Therefore, it is worthwhile to look at classifications of crises and counseling techniques applicable to particular types of crisis situations.

TYPES OF CRISES

Although there are a number of ways that crises may be defined and outlined, perhaps the most comprehensive taxonomy has been developed by Baldwin (1978). Baldwin, drawing on his work in a mental health clinic at the student health service at the University of North Carolina, noted six major types of emotional crises.

His first class is that of *dispositional crises*. These crises are "distress resulting from a problematic situation in which the therapist responds to the client in ways peripheral to a therapeutic role; the intervention is not primarily directed at the emotional level" (Baldwin, 1978, p. 540). In a dispositional crisis, an individual typically lacks both information and the general permission to go about solving a problem in an unusual way. The school psychologist who helps a pupil learn about a local program for overweight teenagers might be dealing with such a crisis.

In general the major counseling strategy with these pupils is to provide information, particularly information that would be difficult for the children or adolescents to obtain on their own. If the clients are capable of doing most of the research by themselves, the counselor merely points the way. The act of obtaining the information on one's own builds self-confidence and increases the chance that the information will be believed and assimilated, because it comes from a source more "objective" than the counselor.

Another specific strategy is to rule out hidden, serious emotional implications of the student's ostensible request. The counselor must make sure that the contact has been initiated because of the problem mentioned. Be sure the current problem is not a symptom of another, more serious crisis.

The counselor should also consider whether to refer the individual to another expert. The expert may provide information that is more comprehensive or more authorative than that the counselor has. And in the case that the real reason for the request is a more serious problem, outside of the scope of the school, this expert may provide long-term therapeutic intervention.

Baldwin's second category are crises of *anticipated life transitions*. He defines these crises as the type "that reflect anticipated but usually normative, life transitions over which the client may or may not have substantial control" (Baldwin, 1978, p. 542). Common transitions for children are entering school, moving from grade to grade, moving to another school, or moving from a self-contained special education classroom to a mainstreamed one. Chronic childhood illness and the birth of a sibling also fit this category, inasmuch as they are transitions from one status (well child or only child) to another (sick child or sibling).

One approach to dealing with crises related to life transitions is to provide anticipatory guidance or information about what is going to occur in the person's life. I will discuss anticipatory guidance as a preventive technique, in another section, however, a child in the middle of a transition also needs to know what will occur next and what the normal experiences and emotions are for others who go through the transition. This kind of normative information can be provided by the counselor.

An alternative is to let peers supply the information, possibly by establishing support groups that consist of a number of children facing the same transition. If the group functions well, it may facilitate the expression of feeling and the acquisition of productive coping mechanisms, as members share experiences and join in mutual problem solving. Even young children, through devices such as a Magic Circle, can engage in productive group problem solving.

A third class of crises results from *traumatic stress*. These are "emotional crises precipitated by externally imposed stressors or situations that are unexpected and uncontrolled, and that are emotionally overwhelming" (Baldwin, 1978, p. 543). Traumatic events for children in school include the sudden death of a family member, catastrophic illness, hospitalization, parental disablement, parental divorce, physical abuse, pregnancy, sexual assault, or sometimes, academic failure. Often these kinds of crises are precipitated by a single traumatic event or by a series of events occurring together rapidly. In this situation, the pupil is emotionally overwhelmed and unable to bring a previously learned coping strategy into play.

The counselor's first goal is to help the child understand the impact of what has occurred. Because of the suddenness of occurrence, the counselee probably has not had time to think through all of the implications of what has happened. Exploration of the event and of the attendant feelings will give the child needed perspective to overcome defensive reactions. Traditional nondirective helping interviews (Benjamin, 1981) can accomplish this task.

Another goal in this kind of crisis is to mobilize the child's existing coping mechanisms. If the individual has characteristic ways of dealing with stress in other situations, the counselor can remind the child of these and help the client transfer the coping strategy to the new crisis (Brenner, 1984).

If the counselee is not coping at all, it may be possible to provide the pupil with new coping mechanisms. Brenner (1984) refers to the process as teaching new coping strategies, and believes that the new technique will be more easily learned if it is similar to the child's initial reaction.

For example, Joshua's teacher helped him substitute sublimation for impulsive acting out as a coping technique after his mother deserted him. Josh's first impulse was to express his anger by running around the classroom, pushing furniture and people out of his way. His teacher helped him to think of several vigorous physical activities which would not be destructive but which would still serve to release his pent-up emotions. (Brenner, 1984, p. 173).

Another way of helping victims of traumatic crisis is to relieve them of other, unrelated stressors (Brenner, 1984). A child whose parents are in the process of divorce may be relieved of certain expectations at school if those expectations contribute to the child's sense of being overwhelmed. If, however, the child is using schoolwork as a sublimation strategy, it might be wiser to search for other potential sources of stress to eliminate.

Regardless of whether schoolwork is a major source of stress, it is likely to be neglected by pupils undergoing crisis. Academic support will most likely be needed to keep the child functioning effectively. Coupled with other specific short-term projects generated in counseling, continued success in school will help to maintain the child's self-esteem and sense of well-being.

Baldwin's fourth category is *maturational/developmental crises*. These are crises "resulting from attempts to deal with an interpersonal situation reflecting a struggle with a deeper (but usually circumscribed) issue that has not been resolved adaptively in the past and that represents an attempt to gain emotional maturity" (Baldwin, 1978, p. 544). Baldwin gives examples of crises with focal issues involving dependency, value conflicts, sexual identity, capacity for emotional intimacy, responses to authority, or attaining reasonable self-discipline. All these difficulties may erupt in school children and are different from others in that they usually occur as another episode in a pattern of relationship problems that have similar dynamics. Struggles with parents and teachers during adolescence often have the quality of a crisis of this class. In secondary schools, the attainment of sexual maturity by young people precipitates a number of these crises, as does adolescence in general. A special case is the discovery in adolescence of a homosexual orientation (Ross-Reynolds & Hardy, 1985).

Once again the counselor can be of help with students in this kind of crisis by facilitating the exploration of thoughts and feelings. In this instance, however, the hope is to identify issues underlying the crisis. This strategy will be particularly attractive to dynamically oriented counselors. What thoughts and feelings does the client have about significant others and the self? What value conflicts are being experienced and what are their origins? What themes and conflicts appear to be unresolved? Are there issues related to trust, acceptance and control of aggression, attitudes toward learning, separation, accepting limits from others, and so on?

Next the counselor acts to support the pupil in redefining relationships and in developing adaptive interpersonal responses. Since most of these crises involve creating new ways of interacting with other people in the student's social environment, helping them learn new prosocial strategies is effective. Strategies for making friends may be taught directly (Stocking, Arezzo, & Leavitt, 1980), but providing models to observe (or even to read about, e.g., Fassler, 1978) is also beneficial.

A fifth category of crises according to Baldwin is *crises reflecting psychopathology.* "These are emotional crises in which a preexisting psychopathology has been instrumental in precipitating the crisis or in which psychopathology significantly impairs or complicates adaptive resolution" (Baldwin, 1978, p. 546). A child who hallucinates while in school might be in great distress, for example. These kinds of crises, although present in the school, are often not the kind that special services practitioners are able to cope with or to treat, and thus are usually referred to outside community resources. School personnel have a role in preventing deterioration of the child's adjustment by maintaining academic functioning as much as possible. In addition, the special services personnel may assist teachers and administrators to appreciate that the child has problems that cannot be resolved in school, but can be managed in a reasonable way in the classroom.

With children experiencing this kind of crisis, it is usually wise not to respond to the underlying problem. This in-depth treatment is a task for professionals who have more expertise or more time and resources than do those who are usually available in public schools.

What can be done is to support the child's attempts to respond to the stressful situation as adaptively as possible. Whatever the child is doing in school that is appropriate and productive can be acknowledged and encouraged. At the same time, the counselor and the student search for ways to reduce stress, especially by eliminating any stressors that may be pushing the child beyond the capacity to cope. As soon as possible, the counselor must attend to the process of making a referral to an outside expert. In addition, the counselor must look for ways to support other school staff, and even parents, who will also undergo trauma in dealing with a psychopathological child. Consultation skills and techniques are particularly valuable in this respect.

A sixth category of crises consists of *psychiatric emergencies*. These are "crisis situations in which general functioning has been severely impaired and the individual rendered incompetent or unable to assume personal responsibility" (Baldwin, 1978, p. 547). Examples include acutely suicidal children, alcohol intoxication, drug overdoses, reactions to hallucinogenic drugs, acute psychoses, and uncontrollable anger. These are all classic crises, of the type in which the individual is often dangerous to himself or herself or to others.

The counselor's efforts in this type of crisis are directed at assessing the danger by attempting to learn what the physical or psychiatric condition of the pupil is. Facts must be gathered to clarify the situation so that action may be taken quickly and appropriately. Much of this information may need to be obtained from persons other than the child.

The first principle in psychiatric crises is to intervene quickly in order to reduce danger. The counselor must be willing to mobilize all necessary medical or psychiatric resources and thus must be familiar with state law and with local community agencies. Prior to the need for such information, school practitioners should familiarize themselves with community resources and agencies. Not only must they know about which agencies exist, but they must also learn in detail what services are offered and know the key personnel to contact (Sandoval, 1985a).

Learning which pupils to refer to outside experts takes a novice a long time because of the need to follow up on referred cases, and the difficulty in evaluating one's own competence. School practitioners must routinely review their cases with supervisors and peers. The review needs to examine not only counselor knowledge and skill, but also counselor objectivity.

FACILITATING REFERRALS

Some of the types of crises encountered in the school can be handled with little difficulty by sensitive guidance workers, teachers, and parents. Others, particularly Baldwin's type 5 and 6, need to be referred to other professionals. How does one effect a useful referral?

First, it becomes important to know when one's own competence is exceeded by the demands of the situation. Effective helpers, however, will err on the side of referring too frequently, rather than waiting too long.

Second, it is important that both the child and the involved family are aware that you will, if necessary, be taking steps to make a referral. The referral must be made with the consent of parents in most instances, and it may be necessary to obtain written permission to release school information to other professionals. The focus of explaining the need for referral to parents is on the importance of getting the appropriate help for their children. Parents must realize that the main concern on the part of school personnel is that children are helped appropriately, not that the school is unwilling or is uninterested in the situation and wishes to abdicate responsibility in the matter.

Parents should exercise some choice in the matter of referral insofar as this is possible. It is important to offer more than one alternative treatment source, assuming they are available, and to list the advantages and disadvantages and characteristics of each. It is also important to communicate what the choices are openly and without bias.

During discussion of referral with parents or adolescents, it is valuable to give them time to digest the information they receive. Of course, time is often severely limited in a crisis situation. Nevertheless, both the student and the parents will need time to react to the news, to ask questions, and to become accustomed to the idea of referral. They will probably also need to be assisted in anticipating what will occur when dealing with the new treatment agency and professional. Other institutions do not work like schools, yet that will be the institution with which parents will have had the most contact.

When the referral is made, the special services worker must be prepared to present the situation as perceived to the referral agency. This means a willingness to write down or to communicate what has occured to date, and to spend time with the receiving professional or agency in reviewing the circumstances that led to the referral. In communicating with the new agency, the school professional may need to adapt to the vocabulary of the new institution and to recognize that, conversely, much of what occurs in schools and much educational jargon will be unfamiliar to them. In short, the counselor must be prepared to act as liaison (Zins & Hopkins, 1981) because, among school professionals, special services personnel command the best understanding of mental health jargon and procedures and can move matters along in both settings. With patience and care, the counselor may facilitate the provision of help to children in crisis.

PREVENTION PROGRAMS

Many of the early pioneers in crisis intervention (e.g., Caplan, 1961; Klein & Lindemann, 1961) came from a background in public health and stressed the prevention of crises. At least five general strategies have been used in the schools to prevent the occurrence of various kinds of crises.

They are educational workshops, anticipatory guidance, screening, consultation, and research (Sandoval, 1982).

An *educational workshop* is a short intensive course of study emphasizing student participation and discussion. It is preventive to the extent that the topic of the workshop is intended to forestall future educational problems. A number of programs exist for children under the general heading of psychological education. Programs such as classroom meetings, Magic Circle, and others (Miller, 1976) help children to express their feelings about what is occurring in the social environment of the classroom, and they attempt to free students from the anxiety that may occur from crisis situations. Others have pointed out the value of a psychologist's role in all curriculum design (Jones, 1968).

The second technique, known as *anticipatory guidance*, also has a variant called emotional inoculation. In offering participatory guidance, the counselor is orienting a person to events likely to occur in the future and helping the client to prepare effective coping strategies. Emotional inoculation puts the emphasis on future feelings, rather than on the cognitive level. Events in question are ones that are usually difficult for individuals to cope with and may influence educational performance. Examples of anticipatory guidance are courses in death and dying, orientation programs designed to help children adjust to new institutional settings, and letting students know what to expect when they are about to go to a hospital for a medical procedure.

A third preventive technique is the implementation of *screening programs*. Screening programs consist of designing techniques (usually by means of questionnaires, rating scales, or group tests) to determine who is at high risk of encountering a particular type of crisis, and then assigning to an appropriate intervention any individuals so identified. Intervention may be anticipatory guidance, a workshop, or a special remediation program. Screening has been particularly effective in identifying children who are at risk of educational failure, but it is conceivable that screening could be designed to identify children who are also at risk for other kinds of crises. An example would be an effort to learn which families, in the near future, will enlarge their numbers so that children might be identified for assignments to workshops designed to facilitate the adjustment to a new sibling.

Serving as a *consultant* is another important way that special services personnel can act preventively in crises. Consultation is defined as one professional helping a second professional be more effective in his or her job. For the purposes of this chapter, a consultant is defined as a special services worker who collaborates with teachers, administrators, or parents to help them deal more effectively with the child or teacher in crisis. By working with teachers, and with parents when possible, a psychologist can help these key adults to support children who are involved in a crisis situation and to be sensitive to the various emotional needs of a child in crisis.

Research is not usually conceived of as a preventive activity. Nevertheless, the more that is known about a phenomenon through research, the better we are able to predict and to control that phenomenon. The more we understand about crises, the more effective we are in creating workshops, educational curriculum, anticipatory guidance programs, screening programs, and consultation interventions. Evaluative and case-study research on crises are within the realm of the school practitioner and should be thought of as important preventive activites.

ETHICAL AND LEGAL ISSUES IN CRISIS COUNSELING AND INTERVENTION

Another aspect of crisis counseling is the application of ethical principles. Concerns for the counselee's welfare should cause concern for and heightened awareness of ethical principles that are not normally invoked in traditional counseling. There are times when counselors must breach confidentiality, as when the pupil is a danger to self and to others (K. M. Denkowski & G. C. Denkowski, 1982); when counselors must carefully evaluate their own competence to continue working with the child, as in dealing with possible psychotic conditions; and when counselors must carefully consider and weigh parental permission and informed consent, as in dealing with substance abuse and abortion—situations in which the child may hold the confidence, depending on state law. Litigation in the *Tarassoff* (*Tarasoff v. Regents of the University of California*, 1973) case has suggested that there are a number of legal ramifications of holding strict limits on confidentiality in life-threatening situations (Bersoff, 1976). The ethical challenges to the school special services worker are magnified by the nature of the crisis situation, as well as by its potential impact on a child's lifetime adjustment. Since time is of the essence, resolving ethical dilemmas may place the counselor under considerable stress.

In addition to ethical concerns of confidentiality, responsibility, and client welfare, there exists a subtler set of issues that have to do with any efforts directed at the general population or to clients at risk. Preventive activities proceed on the basis of the probability of an occurrence. As a result, there will be a number of false positives (those we believe to be in crisis but who are not) and false negatives (those we do not believe to be in crisis but who are) in any population. By erroneously involving in prevention programs pupils who will not encounter the hazards, or who will not experience the crisis a program is directed at, we may be wasting their time. Weighing the cost of programs, against the probability of helping someone, or contemplating the magnitude of the negative impact of the crisis on even a single individual, there may not be a justifiable trade-off for the small number of people helped. Making such a determination, of course, is very difficult and perhaps politically sensitive exercise.

A legal difficulty yet to be tested is whether participants in a prevention activity who later *do* develop a crisis have indeed been injured by the prevention activity. When prevention is seemingly unsuccessful, has there been a breach of contract? For example, can the originators of a suicide-prevention program be sued if one of the participants later commits suicide? In California, such a threat of litigation has recently held up a program on suicide prevention (Sandoval, Davis, & Wilson, in press). Tort actions have not yet taken place in situations in which crisis counseling and intervention have not proved successful.

RESEARCH ON CRISIS INTERVENTION

Crisis counseling and intervention is by nature difficult to evaluate. Crises occur spontaneously, and must be dealt with immediately; thus it is difficult to study in vivo either the process of crisis counseling or the subtleties or relative effectiveness of each of the generic principles listed earlier. As previously mentioned, the generic principles were derived from a review of clinical descriptions of case studies. To date they have not been evaluated for their effectiveness.

A fruitful line of research might explore the specific strategies indicated for the crisis categories to determine their validity for any or all of the crises listed in the category and the possible employment of additional strategies. Perhaps, however, the type of crisis is less important for predicting outcome and intervention strategy than is the severity of the disorganization that accompanies the crisis. It would be difficult, however, to design experiments in which people in crisis are given an alternative placebo treatment, because their need is so great. One should proceed on the basis of best practice and should not experiment with individuals in crisis. Perhaps simulation studies could be attempted, but it may prove difficult to simulate the critical features of crises.

Although there is not a substantial literature in the field, programs designed to prevent crisis situations, ones aimed either at primary prevention or at secondary prevention, are being evaluated with increasing frequency. Evaluations may focus on one or on both of two factors: (a) changes in behavior on the part of children receiving the program, or (b) changes in attitude that will reduce hazards. Successful programs presumably decrease the incidence of crises. Because many crisis events are rare and there is a tendency to focus on occurrence of problems rather than on the absence of them, efforts at program evaluation have not received a great deal of support from funding agencies or investigators. We can only hope that the decades to come will bring more support for evaluation of crisis-prevention programs.

CONCLUSION

Intervention in crisis situations requires very special skills. Successful resolutions depend on the speed of action, on the sensitivity of the counselor, and on the counselor's ability to select applicable counseling strategies that may be either more or less directive than those usually employed by school personnel. Although individual crises are rare, one would anticipate that all children in school encounter a number of them in the course of their lives. School personnel must recognize their own important role in dealing with children in crisis and the special opportunities it provides. Successful intervention at the time of crisis is an important factor for improving the overall mental health of our school-age population.

ANNOTATED BIBLIOGRAPHY

Brenner, A. (1984). *Helping children cope with stress*. Lexington, MA: D. C. Heath.

For both mental health and non-mental health professionals. The topic of stress and stress reduction is more general than is that of crisis, but this volume explores a number of relevant topics, such as stress in different family constellations, neglect, and other childhood crises such as death, adoption, divorce, sexual abuse, and parental alcoholism.

Fassler, J. (1978). *Helping children cope: Mastering stress through books and stories*. New York: Macmillan.

Prepared for mental-health professionals and librarians. Provides the basis for conducting bibliotherapy with children who experience crises of various sorts. Outlines basic concepts of bibliotherapy and presents a detailed listing of children's literature. Listed are books on topics such as divorce, death, hospitalization, and illness, annotated with reading difficulty levels and plot summaries.

Golan, N. (1978). *Treatment in crisis situations*. New York: Free Press.

A classic work on crisis intervention written from a social work perspective. In addition to discussion of theories of crisis and of crisis intervention, this book features a detailed best-practice model of proceeding with the victims of crisis. Differentiates three types of crises: (a) natural and man-made disasters, (b) developmental and transitional life crises, and (c) situational crises.

Janosik, E. H. (ed.). (1984). *Crisis counseling: A contemporary approach*. Belmont, CA: Wadsworth.

Oriented toward nursing, this book presents basic crisis-intervention techniques and features a comprehensive approach. Clinical case studies supplement best-practice guidelines. Topics include rape, incest, child and spouse abuse, multiple trauma, and delayed stress reactions.

Sandoval, J. (Ed.). (1985). Mini-series on crisis counseling in the schools [Special issue]. *School Psychology Review, 14*.

This special issue of the journal contains a number of articles detailing how school special services personnel, particularly school psychologists, can intervene in and prevent a number of common crises in children's lives. Separate articles address learning problems, divorce, maltreatment, pregnancy and homosexuality, and suicide.

REFERENCES

Baldwin, B. A. (1978). A paradigm for the classification of emotional crises: Implications for crisis intervention. *American Journal of Orthopsychiatry, 48*, 538–551.

Benjamin, A. (1981). *The helping interview* (3rd ed.). Boston: Houghton Mifflin.

Bersoff, D. N. (1976). Therapists as protectors and policemen: New Roles as a result of Tarasoff? *Professional Psychology, 7*, 267–273.

Brenner, A. (1984). *Helping children cope with stress.* Lexington, MA: D. C. Heath.

Caplan, G. (1961). *An approach to community mental health.* New York: Grune & Stratton.

Caplan, G. (1964). *Principles of preventative psychiatry.* New York: Basic Books.

Caplan, G. (1970). *Theory and practice of mental health consultation.* New York: Basic Books.

Denkowski, K. M., & Denkowski, G. C. (1982). Client–counselor confidentiality: An update of rationale, legal status, and implications. *Personnel and Guidance Journal, 60,* 371–375.

Egan, G. (1986). *The skilled helper* (3rd ed.). Monterey, CA: Brooks/Cole.

Fassler, J. (1978). *Helping children cope: Mastering stress through books and stories.* New York: Macmillan.

Golan, N. (1978). *Treatment in crisis situations.* New York: Free Press.

Jones, R. M. (1968). *Fantasy and feeling in education.* New York: New York University Press.

Klein, D. C., & Lindemann, E. (1961). Preventive intervention in individual and family crisis situations. In G. Caplan, (Ed.), *Prevention of mental disorders in children* (pp. 283–306). New York: Basic Books.

Lindemann, E. (1944). Symptomatology and management of acute grief. *American Journal of Psychiatry, 101,* 141–148.

Miller, J. P. (1976). *Humanizing the classroom,* New York: Praeger.

Rogers, C. R. (1957). The necessary and sufficient conditions of therapeutic personality change. *Journal of Consulting Psychology, 21,* 95–103.

Ross-Reynolds, G., & Hardy, B. S. Crisis Counseling for disparate adolescent sexual dilemmas: Pregnancy and homosexuality. *School Psychology Review, 14,* 300–312.

Rusk, T. N. (1971). Opportunity and technique in crisis psychiatry. *Comprehensive Psychiatry, 12,* 249–263.

Sandoval, J. (1982). El psicólogo y la prevención del fracaso educación. *Psicologia* (Venezuela), *9,* 3–13.

Sandoval, J. (1985a). Notes on teaching school psychologists about community resources and agencies. *Trainers' Forum, 5* (2), 1–4.

Sandoval, J. (Ed.). (1985b). Mini-series on crisis counseling in the schools [Special issue]. *School Psychology Review, 14.*

Sandoval, J., Davis, J. M., & Wilson, M. P. (in press). The prevention of adolescent suicide in the schools. *Special Services in the Schools.*

Stocking, S. H., Arezzo, D., & Leavitt, S. (1980). *Helping kids make friends.* Niles, IL: Argus Communications.

Tarasoff v. Regents of the University of California, 33 Cal. App. 3d 275 (1973).

Zins, J. E., & Hopkins, R. A. (1981). Referral out: Increasing the number of kept appointments. *School Psychology Review, 10,* 107–111.

Author Index

Subject Index

About the Editors and Contributors

Charles A. Maher received his PsyD in professional psychology from Rutgers, The State University of New Jersey, where he is currently Professor and Chairperson of the Department of School Psychology, Graduate School of Applied and Professional Psychology, as well as Director of the Rutgers School Planning and Evaluation Center. Additionally, he possesses over 15 years experience as a teacher of the handicapped; director of a residential school for emotionally disturbed adolescents; school psychologist; coordinator of special services; and assistant superintendent of schools. Dr. Maher consults worldwide to educational systems, business, and industry on matters of service delivery, personnel and organizational development, program planning and evaluation. He is the author and editor of 15 books, and author or coauthor of over 300 journal articles. He is also the editor of *Special Services in the Schools* and a member of 12 journal editorial boards.

Joseph E. Zins received his EdD in School Psychology from the University of Cincinnati in 1977, where he is currently Associate Professor of School Psychology. He also is a consulting psychologist with the Beechwood (KY) Public Schools. Dr. Zins has conducted research and published numerous articles and chapters on consultation, prevention, and the delivery of psychological services in educational settings. He also coedited *The Theory and Practice of School Consultation*, *Organizational Psychology in the Schools*, and *Health Promotion in the Schools*, and is Consulting Editor (with Charles A. Maher) of the book series, *Psychoeducational Interventions: Guidebooks for School Practitioners*. Furthermore, Professor Zins is a member of five editorial boards, and secretary of the National Association of School Psychologists.

***

Patricia L. Amish is a doctoral student in clinical psychology at the University of South Florida. She received her BS at Cornell University and worked subsequently at the Mt. Hope Family Center in Rochester, New

York for the treatment of abused children. Her current interests are child abuse and social skills training with children.

Gilbert J. Botvin received his PhD from Columbia University in 1977. He is currently an Associate Professor of Psychology at Cornell University Medical College in the Departments of Public Health and Psychiatry. He is also Director of Cornell's Laboratory of Health Behavior Research, and is an Associate Attending Psychologist at the New York Hospital-Cornell Medical Center. The author or coauthor of numerous articles and chapters concerning cognitive development, chronic disease risk reduction, and substance abuse prevention, Dr. Botvin has been the Principal Investigator and Project Director on eight federally-funded research grants in the area of tobacco, alcohol, and drug abuse prevention. He has served as a consultant to several state, federal, and local agencies, and is currently a member of NIDA's editorial advisory committee.

D. Kirby Brown received his PhD in Educational Psychology from the University of Arizona in 1980. He is a Research Scientist for the Lehigh University Project on Developmental Disabilities and an adjunct faculty member in the Department of Counseling Psychology, School Psychology, and Special Education at Lehigh University.

Mary B. Byrley is a doctoral student in Counselor Education at Ohio State University, where she is a graduate research associate after having received her MA in counseling in 1985.

Michael J. Curtis received his PhD from the University of Texas at Austin in 1974, and is currently Professor and Coordinator of School Psychology at the University of Cincinnati. His teaching, writing, and research have emphasized consultation, problem solving and organization development. He is coauthor of a book on prereferral intervention programs and coeditor of books on alternative educational service delivery systems and school consultation.

Linda Dusenbury received her PhD from the University of Vermont in 1984. She is currently a senior research associate in the Department of Public Health at Cornell Medical College. She is also a Project Manager of a smoking prevention project as part of Cornell's Laboratory of Health Behavior Research. She is the author or coauthor of articles and chapters concerning the primary prevention of psychopathology and health promotion.

Stephen N. Elliott received his PhD in Educational Psychology from Arizona State University in 1980. He is currently Associate Professor of

Psychology at Louisiana State University and Editor of *School Psychology Review*, the official journal of the National Association of School Psychologists. Dr. Elliott has coauthored several books on school psychology, including *School Psychology: Essentials of Theory and Practice* and *The Delivery of Psychological Services in Schools*, and is currently working with Frank M. Gresham on standardizing the *Social Skills Rating Scales*, a multirater, normative rating scale for children 3 through 18 years of age.

Judy L. Genshaft received her BA from the University of Wisconsin-Madison, and her MA and PhD from Kent State University. She is Professor of School Psychology and Acting Associate Provost at Ohio State University. Her research and clinical interests include mathematical anxiety in adolescent women, child psychopathology, and the assessment of cognitive development in children.

Ellis L. Gesten received his PhD in clinical psychology from the University of Rochester in 1975. After serving as Research Coordinator of the school-based Primary Mental Health Project for six years, he moved to the University of South Florida, where he is currently Professor of Psychology. He is interested in the development and dissemination of preventive interventions, social problem-solving and skills training with children, family interaction and therapy. He serves on the editorial board for the *American Journal of Community Psychology*, and contributed a chapter to the 1987 *Annual Review of Psychology*.

Janet L. Graden received her PhD from the University of Minnesota in 1984 and is currently Assistant Professor of School Psychology at the University of Cincinnati. Dr. Graden's research and writing have focused on special education decision-making and service delivery; she is coauthor of a book on prereferral intervention programs, and coeditor of *Alternative Educational Delivery Systems: Enhancing Instructional Options for all Students*.

Frank M. Gresham received his PhD in Psychology from the University of South Carolina in 1979. Currently, he is Professor of Psychology at Louisiana State University. Dr. Gresham serves on numerous editorial boards, and has published over 30 articles in professional journals on the topics of social skills assessment and intervention. He is a coauthor with Stephen N. Elliott of the *Social Skills Rating Scales*, a normative multirater screening test to be published by American Guidance Service.

Robert W. Heffer received his MA from Louisiana State University in 1985 and is currently a doctoral candidate at Louisiana State University. Mr. Heffer's area of specialization is pediatric psychology.

Howard M. Knoff received his PhD in School Psychology from Syracuse University in 1980. Currently, he is an Assistant Professor of School Psychology in the Department of Psychological Foundations at the University of South Florida, where he specializes in consultation and intervention processes, personality assessment, and professional issues in school psychology. He is the author of over 35 journal articles and book chapters, as well as two recent books: *The Assessment of Child and Adolescent Personality* and *The Kinetic Drawing System for Family and School.*

F. Charles Mace received his PhD in educational psychology from the University of Arizona. He is currently an assistant professor of school psychology at Lehigh University and director of the Lehigh Project on Developmental Disabilities. Dr. Mace has been an associate editor for *Professional School Psychology* since 1984.

Janice A. Miller received her PhD from the University of Illinois at Chicago in Public Policy Analysis in 1986. Currently, she is an administrator with the LaGrange, IL, Area Department of Special Education. Her interests center on the education and integration within the regular classroom of the mildy handicapped student.

David W. Peterson is an administrator with the LaGrange, IL, Area Department of Special Education, who received his masters in school psychology from Western Illinois University and is a doctoral candidate in educational psychology at Northern Illinois University. His interests include behavioral consultation and performance-based assessment.

Jonathan Sandoval received his PhD in School Psychology from the University of California, Berkeley, and is now Professor of Education and director of the School Psychology Program at the University of California, Davis. His research and writing has spanned a number of areas in school psychology, including: hyperactive children, school-based consultation, the practice of nonpromotion in schools, cultural bias in tests, learning disabilities, and most recently, the childhood crisis of geographic mobility.

Janet K. Smith is a doctoral student in Clinical Psychology at the University of South Florida. She received her BA at New College in Sarasota, Florida. Her current interests are assessment and psychotherapy with children and the use of language, particularly metaphors, in therapy.

Judith Springer, MEd is a school psychologist working as a high school behavioral counselor. She is currently enrolled in the School Psychology doctoral program at the Graduate School of Applied and Professional Psychology at Rutgers University. Previous professional experiences include teaching, and working as the managing editor of a small educational publishing company. Her research and service interests include enhancing the school functioning of mainstreamed emotionally disturbed students, and facilitating cooperative relationships between parents and school professionals.

Roger P. Weissberg received his PhD in Psychology from the University of Rochester in 1980. Currently, he is an Assistant Professor of Psychology at Yale University. He recently received a five-year Faculty Scholars Award from the William T. Grant Foundation in support of his efforts to design and evaluate school-based, social competence-promotion programs for children and adolescents.

Barbara J. West received her MEd from Lehigh University in 1985. Currently, she is completing a doctoral program in School Psychology at Lehigh University, where she is the Research Scientist for two model group homes for mentally retarded adults.

Pamela S. Wise received her PhD in Counseling Psychology from the State University of New York at Buffalo, in 1984, and possesses a Masters' degree in School Counseling from the same university. Currently, Dr. Wise is an assistant Professor in the Human Services Education Department at Ohio State University. She teaches courses in clinical counseling, and her research interests include counseling treatments for children and the study of empathy.

Pergamon General Psychology Series

Editors: Arnold P. Goldstein, Syracuse University
Leonard Krasner, Stanford University &
SUNY at Stony Brook

*Out of print in original format. Available in custom reprint edition.